Mission to Kilimanjaro

Mission to Kilimanjaro

The Founding History of a Catholic Mission in East Africa

Mgr. Alexandre Le Roy, C.S.Sp.

TRANSLATED BY Adrian Edwards, C.S.Sp.
EDITED BY James Chukwuma Okoye, C.S.Sp.
FOREWORD BY John Fogarty, C.S.Sp.

WIPF & STOCK · Eugene, Oregon

MISSION TO KILIMANJARO
The Founding History of a Catholic Mission in East Africa

Copyright © 2019 James Chukwuma Okoye. All rights reserved. Except for brief quotations in critical publications or reviews, no part of this book may be reproduced in any manner without prior written permission from the publisher. Write: Permissions, Wipf and Stock Publishers, 199 W. 8th Ave., Suite 3, Eugene, OR 97401.

Wipf & Stock
An Imprint of Wipf and Stock Publishers
199 W. 8th Ave., Suite 3
Eugene, OR 97401

www.wipfandstock.com

PAPERBACK ISBN: 978-1-5326-9352-6
HARDCOVER ISBN: 978-1-5326-9353-3
EBOOK ISBN: 978-1-5326-9354-0

Originally printed as *Au Kilima-Ndjaro. Histoire de la fondation d'une mission Catholique en Afrique Orientale*, Maison-Mère des PP. du Saint-Esprit, 30 Rue Lhomond, Paris V^e 1914.

Manufactured in the U.S.A.   10/11/19

Bishop Raoul de Courmont, C.S.Sp.
Founder of the Kilimanjaro Mission
Died in Paris, 1925, aged 83 years

Dedicated to the Memory of
Fr. Adrian Edwards, C.S.Sp.

Contents

Foreword by John Fogarty, C.S.Sp. | ix
Author's Preface (1914 Edition) | xi
Editor's Preface | xiii

PART ONE
From Zanzibar to Kilimanjaro

Chapter 1: Etymology, Discovery, Exploration | 3
Chapter 2: Arrival at Mombasa | 10
Chapter 3: Delayed | 14
Chapter 4: In Digo Country | 20
Chapter 5: At Gasi | 27
Chapter 6: Further On | 31
Chapter 7: At Vanga | 39
Chapter 8: The First Mountains on Our Route | 45
Chapter 9: Travelling through the Desert | 54
Chapter 10: The Valley of the Umba | 62
Chapter 11: At the Mbaramo Pass | 74
Chapter 12: At Gonja | 78
Chapter 13: Pare | 83
Chapter 14: At Lake Jipe | 91
Chapter 15: Taveta | 106

PART TWO
To Kilimanjaro

Chapter 16: On the Mountain—Kilema | 117
Chapter 17: On the Mountain—Moshi | 130
Chapter 18: On the Mountain—Machame | 139
Chapter 19: On the Mountain—Kibosho | 148
Chapter 20: The Ascent | 156
Chapter 21: The Kilimanjaro Mountain Range | 169
Chapter 22: The Population of Kilimanjaro | 178

PART THREE
From Kilimanjaro to Zanzibar

Chapter 23: Kahe | 195
Chapter 24: Lower Arusha | 200
Chapter 25: In Maasai Land | 206
Chapter 26: The Maasai | 215
Chapter 27: The Sambara | 225
Chapter 28: Zigua | 231

Postscript: Twenty-Four Years Later (1890–1914) | 238

Biography of Fr. Adrian Edwards, C.S.Sp. | 255
Bibliography | 257

Foreword

The late Fr. Adrian Edwards, C.S.Sp., renowned author and anthropologist, has provided a wonderful service in carefully translating into English the classic missionary ouvrage of Mgr. Alexandre Le Roy, C.S.Sp., *Au Kilima-Ndjaro*, first published in French in 1914, thus making the publication available to a wider contemporary audience. As an experienced missionary and academic, Fr. Edwards clearly saw the importance of this work in the history of missiology, and its translation, completed shortly before his unexpected death in 2017, effectively serves as his final legacy to the mission of evangelization to which he dedicated his life and talents.

Mgr. Le Roy, an intrepid missionary, accomplished ethnologist, and artist, had a profound interest in, and a deep love of and respect for, the people he encountered on his extensive travels, as well as their culture, customs, values, and artwork, an approach which shaped his vision and strategy for evangelization at a time when many of his contemporaries shared a significantly narrower worldview. His classic work, *Au Kilima-Ndjaro*, is a fascinating account of the arduous journey into the East African interior undertaken in July 1890 by the author and two other members of the Congregation of the Holy Spirit, Fr. Auguste Gommenginger and Bishop Jean-Marie de Courmont, together with their entourage of almost 300 men, from the initial base at Bagamoyo on the coast, founded in 1868. With his unique insights and perspective, Le Roy describes in graphic detail the various stages of the almost six-week journey, the internal organization of the group for maximum efficiency, his impressions of the region, and the people along the way, together with the difficulties encountered which included inadequate water, illness, and threats from wild animals in the unchartered territory of the semi-arid Maasai steppe. His memoirs culminate in the striking description of their final destination, the majestic snow-capped peak of Kilimanjaro, which clearly evoked awe and amazement in Le Roy and his companions:

> The spectacle we have before our eyes is something that will remain unforgettable. Underneath a completely blue sky, there in front of us, we see the immense profile of the marvelous mountain. The two peaks [Kibo and Mawenzi] appear to be supported by this enormous pedestal... as a candelabra lit in the course of centuries to the glory of the Creator.[1]

As noted by the African historian, Matthew V. Bender,[2] the subsequent sixty years of Spiritan missionary activity on the slopes of Mount Kilimanjaro saw the establishment of one of the largest and most prosperous Catholic communities on the continent of Africa. In addition to the founding of dozens of mission stations among the Chagga people, the economic and social landscapes of the mountain were transformed through the establishment of schools and hospitals and the cultivation of Arabica coffee, which became a lucrative business for the population, to the extent that the region had the highest ratio of schools to students, the highest school enrollment figures, and the most medical facilities per capita in any part of rural Eastern Africa.

I have no doubt that this publication, available in English for the first time, will be of considerable interest to historians and missiologists alike, as well as to the general public at a time of increasing research into African history and culture.

John Fogarty, C.S.Sp.
Superior General

---

1. Bender, "Holy Ghost in the Highlands," 69.
2. Bender, "Holy Ghost in the Highlands," 69-89.

Author's Preface (1914 Edition)

The pages you are about to read contain the report of a voyage of exploration to Kilimanjaro (East Africa). The voyage was undertaken in 1890 in order to study then-unknown nations so as to found new centers of evangelization.

Written for the Catholic Missions of Lyon, these pages first appeared as serial articles in that journal; they were then put together into one volume (Mame, Tours). That edition quickly ran out, but demand continued.

Truth to tell, Africa, still a closed continent only yesterday, is quickly transforming itself through European action. It thus serves some purpose to recall, albeit in ramble souvenirs, the way this great continent became open. This simple story of the founding of a Catholic mission was written for benefactors, associates, and friends; it appears today just as then published. The only change is in the last chapter, where the author, surprised to be still alive when so many of his confreres and friends have gone to the Master, indicates what became of the Catholic attempt at penetration into the interior, specifically into Kilimanjaro. And this would be for the serious reader—that is, for you all—the principal interest of this report, a report that never thought of becoming a book, and having become one, did not hope to again see the light of day.

One can see colleges, sponsors, seminaries, apostolic schools, boarding schools, and parish libraries finding readings of this genre as interesting as many others equally instructive and wholesome. In the past, such readings even inspired missionary vocations. They still can do so. May God be praised! May this prove to be so!

Alex. L. R.

Editor's Preface

The original title, *Au Kilima-Ndjaro*, means "To Kilima-Ndjaro." The editor has rendered all names of places and persons in their current Swahili form, hence Kilimanjaro. The editor adjusted the title to *Mission to Kilimanjaro*. French phonetics was easily recognizable in Voumba for Vumba. But the nonnative may not know that Lake Dyipe is currently Lake Jipe. The editor is beholden to Fr. Dr. Florentine Mallya, C.S.Sp., who meticulously reviewed for us the thousand or so Swahili names of people and places.

The French original was published in several editions and formats from the 1890s to 1942. Translated here is the edition of 1914; this edition exists in at least two recensions. We stuck to the recension used by the translator, except for the engravings by Mgr. Le Roy and corrections noted in later editions (see, for example, note 1 on page 91).

The late Fr. Dr. Adrian Edwards, C.S.Sp. lamented the lack of social anthropology in the formation of today's Spiritan missionaries. We began a discussion that eventually led to his translating this book. Mgr. Alexandre Le Roy was a Spiritan missionary whom Fr. Adrian greatly admired and saw as modelling the well-formed Spiritan missionary. At first, he wanted to translate a few chapters he regarded as most relevant for Spiritans in formation. Under gentle prodding, he happily and with accustomed grit translated the entire work. Fr. Edwards, lecturer and social anthropologist, died in Chester on October 31, 2017, while this work was being prepared for publication. As far as I know, this is the first and only English translation of this primal source.

Fr. Kenneth Oguzie, C.S.Sp., graduate assistant at the Center for Spiritan Studies, carefully photographed the engravings. Mary Beth Calorie, the then-administrative assistant, diligently inserted the photos. Fr. William Cleary, C.S.Sp. came on board as Associate Director late in the editing process. The book is dedicated to the memory of Fr. Adrian Edwards, C.S.Sp.

James Chukwuma Okoye, C.S.Sp.
Director, Center for Spiritan Studies

PART ONE

From Zanzibar to Kilimanjaro

Chapter 1: Etymology, Discovery, Exploration

Its Scientific, Political, and Religious Importance. Taking the Road.

The Arabs and the Swahili of the east coast of Africa, followed by European travelers and geographers, have given the name *Kilima-Ndjaro* to an isolated massif of volcanic origin which is situated a little below the third degree of south latitude, about 280 kilometers in a straight line from the coast. For a long time, people have been asking, and in fact they are still asking, the meaning of these two words, or rather of the second word, since the first, *Kilima*, means "mountain" in Swahili and in several languages of the East African hinterland. But nobody seems to know the meaning of the second word, *Ndaro* or *Njaro*. However, in order not to seem ill-informed, which would have been a pity, the recognized travelers have quickly produced a meaning. Here is what Mr. Joseph Thomson, who passed by the mountain in 1883 had to say:

> The name, Kilimanjaro, means, it is generally said, "the Great Mountain"; but it seems to me that its meaning really is "the White Mountain," the term *Njaro* having been formerly used to indicate whiteness. This meaning has become out of date on the coast, but it can still be found among some tribes in the hinterland.

In fact, on the coast, this usage is so out of date that nobody recalls it, not even among the bearded elders. And as regards the hinterland tribes, who are supposed to know it still, let me be blunt and say that Mr. Thomson would have his work cut out to find them. Mr. H. H. Johnston stated his view in 1886: "This word comes from *Kilima*, 'mountain' and *Njaro*, the name of a demon, who is thought to cause the cold weather." With all due respect, this is surely a case of etymology by auto-suggestion.

In reality, the name Kilimanjaro is absolutely unknown to the Wachagga or the Chagga who live upon the mountain. For them there is no general name for the mountain as a whole. Each inhabited area has its own special name. The vast forest that forms a ring round the mountain is called *Msitu*, "dark wood." The highest peak is called *Kibo*, "the white," and the other peak is called *Mawenzi*, "the companion mountain." The Maasai say in their own language, *Oi Doinyo Oebor*, "The White Mountain." As to this word *Njaro*, which Thomson thinks means "something white," and which Johnston takes for "a demon," we had it in mind to make a serious study of its meaning when, it so happened, at Taveta, that we were taking a walk with some local children. One of them asked us if we had to stay a long time at Kilimanjaro. I replied, "What are you saying? *Kilima-Njaro*?" He answered, "Yes." "But what does that mean, *Njaro*?" "*Njaro, Njaro*, in the Maasai language, and for that matter in our own, it is 'water.' And that big mountain over there is called 'the mountain of water' because all the rivers here and everywhere come from there." We concluded that this must be the real meaning. At Taveta, which one can say is at the foot of the famous mountain, traders up from the coast would have heard *Kilima-Njaro* (in the Mombasa dialect of Swahili) and *Kilima-Ngaro* (in the Pangani dialect). British travelers have written *Njaro*, using "j" for "dj." The Germans, not wishing to have to say "*Ngaro*," find themselves obliged to write "*Ndscharo*." In our opinion, French geographers, who wish to follow the correct coastal pronunciation, should not follow the Germans.

The Portuguese, established at Mombasa from 1507, seem to have had some idea of the existence of this massif, and H. H. Johnston cites a navigator of that period, Enciso, who wrote:

> To the west of the harbor of Mombasa, there is Ethiopia's Mount Olympus, which is very high and beyond which there rise the Mountains of the Moon, where the sources of the Nile are. In all this country, there is a lot of gold and a great number of wild beasts. The population eats locusts.

The old sailor has got a lot of things right in this short passage. Certainly, till now, nobody has seen a lot of gold come from this country; but also, if Kilimanjaro is the African Olympus, it is quite correct to say that, moving westward from the coast further inland one would find these high mountains from which the Nile flows, and which were rediscovered by Stanley. Everywhere in the hinterland, there are fierce animals. As to the locusts, the missionaries who have recently settled on Kilimanjaro know they exist since they have eaten all their corn.

But it was Mr. Rebmann, a German, who worked for the Church Missionary Society of London, who had the honor of having rediscovered Olympus in this century. His compatriot, the Rev. Dr. Krapf, working for the Church Missionary Society, had established a mission in the neighborhood of Mombasa. In 1847–48, Rebmann undertook a journey to the interior, accompanied by only eight porters and an umbrella. The direction he took was at first toward the Taita Mountains, then, on 11th May, he saw across a desert the superb summit of Kibo, covered with snow and shining, under the powerful equatorial sun, like a massive block of silver.

His discovery, subsequently reported to European savants, was very ill-received by them. The President of the Royal Geographical Society of London, Mr. Desborough Cooley, had just invented a very ingenious system for filling up the blank spaces in the map of Africa. Unfortunately, his system did not make any allowance for mountains, particularly snow-covered mountains, in the precise place where poor Mr. Rebmann had seen, and indeed climbed up, them. Mr. Cooley produced a seemingly convincing argument that the missionary had had an apocalyptic vision—very interesting from a psychiatrist's point of view, but utterly unacceptable in a geographical handbook. Dr. Krapf attempted to come to the support of his friend by going to see the mountain himself, only to be treated in the same manner. And so these missionaries did not dare to raise their voices again to assert the existence of Kilimanjaro.

It was more than a decade later, in 1861, when a German traveler, Baron von der Decken, later killed by the Somalis at Bordera on the Juba River, had the idea of going to look for himself. He saw the mountain, unshaken by the anathemas of the men of science. He then came back the next year and went up it to a height of 3,500 meters. He and his fellow traveler, Kersten, carried out a detailed survey of the Kilimanjaro area, and produced a map which subsequent travelers have accepted as largely correct.

Finally, quite recently, another German traveler, Dr. Hans Meyer, and Mr. Putscheller, an Austrian mountaineer, have been able, with the necessary climbing apparatus, to reach the highest summit, namely, Kibo, whose height they estimate at 6,100 meters, the Mawenzi would have been 5,300 meters, and the plateau between them 4,400 meters.

It is easy to understand how, as soon as this astonishing massif was recognized as existing in reality and not as a missionary daydream, the scientific world was very interested, and the same London societies which had denied its existence wanted to cover up their error in sending a distinguished traveler, Mr. H. H. Johnston, to make an on-the-spot study. Mr. Cooley was unfortunately dead; it would have been a great joke to send him. Johnston, in a very interesting account of his expedition (not translated into French), indicates its significance from a scientific point of view. He writes:

> Although the Kilimanjaro massif rises rather sharply from a wide-spreading plain, it would be difficult to describe it as isolated. In fact, it would be more correct to say that an almost unbroken succession of mountain chains and independent peaks link Kilimanjaro with Ethiopia to the north, Natal to the south, and perhaps even Cameroon to the west. Judging by the flora which cover its upper slopes, Kilimanjaro may be seen as a meeting place for a number of botanical species which characterize these three mountain zones, despite very great distances between them.
>
> In the great height of Kilimanjaro and in the equatorial location of this snow-capped mountain—which factors result in an extraordinary variety of climatic factors active on its slopes—there seem to be sufficient causes to explain the birth or development of many surprising features of its fauna and flora. Similar conditions have only been found in Central and South America, for nowhere else do tropical mountains reach the level of permanent snow.
>
> Moreover, the long mountain chains reported from little-known regions are extremely interesting for naturalists. The high mountains isolated from other peaks are rather like islands in a mighty ocean: they serve as last-resort homes to primitive types or local variations which, in larger more crowded spaces, would

be caught up in a conflict for resources, and would disappear in the struggle for life. Alternatively, some zoological species or botanical variety, which was formerly present in a large area, finds itself, as the result of varying circumstances, confined to a particular mountain chain or a desert island. There it has shelter and protection in its own development against the dangers coming from the presence of competing species. This can enable it, free from threatening competition, to develop an exuberant range of individual members.

Another interesting aspect of the fauna and flora of these high mountains is that they often still possess elements of an earlier natural system which has been replaced in the lowlands by more recent arrivals for a long period. Thus the Kinabalu, the highest mountain in Borneo, still has on its highest slopes a range of plants related to those of Australia, while on the surrounding plain the vegetation is of Indian origin. In the Alps, one finds butterflies from the arctic fringe of Europe. In the mountains of Ethiopia, there are families and species of animals and plants which belong to countries with temperate climates to the north and south, from Europe to the Cape of Good Hope. The question of how the fauna and flora of Kilimanjaro relate to those of other geographical regions is a very interesting one, and, when it has been solved, it will help us to resolve a number of puzzles concerning the geographical distribution of living organisms.[1]

Kilimanjaro has therefore considerable scientific interest, but it is still more a cause of interest from the political aspect. As soon as the question of the partition of East Africa was raised, contenders lined up as though it were a competition for climbing the greasy pole. The winner would be whoever laid their hands on the icy mountain. Those who were simply spectators of the changing fortunes of the countries and peoples of this part of the world have seen some curious scenes appear, one after another.

For a period of three or four years, agents of the Sultan of Zanzibar, of the German Empire, and of the United Kingdom, have been leading caravans loaded with presents, accompanied by interpreters whose mouths were full of the most beautiful phrases. When they got to Kilimanjaro, each one of the twenty independent chiefs was ready to claim to be the paramount chief over all the others. The agent was welcomed and his presents were accepted, with promises of unshakable friendship. When the next agent arrived, a month later, the chief had no difficulty in changing his flag. It was a jolly time.

1. Johnston, *Kilima-Ndjaro Expedition*, 3–5.

However, everything has to come to an end, even questions of the transfer of power. By the treaty of London, a line, now found on all the maps, was drawn from Vanga to the Kavirondo Bay in Lake Victoria Nyanza, which specifically assigned Kilimanjaro to Germany. But where does this massif begin and where does it end? Two delegates, one British and one German, tried unsuccessfully to settle this question, one of them considering that the lowlands extended into the mountain area, the other considering that the mountain included a good deal of the supposed lowlands. It has always been said that human perception varies from individual to individual, and this episode provides an interesting proof of this assertion. Finally, two new commissioners, Dr. Karl Peters for Germany, and Lieutenant C. A. Smith for Britain, were appointed and, at the moment of writing, are still at work.[2]

Looking at it from yet another aspect, Kilimanjaro has also awakened missionary interest. Following Sir H. H. Johnston's journey, the Anglican Church Society (The Church Missionary Society) sent one of its members from Mombasa to start a mission (1885). On his side, Mgr. R. de Courmont, Vicar Apostolic of Zanzibar, was very eager to go up this mountain, plant there the cross which the Redeemer has left as his sign to the world, and set up an altar for the sacrifice of the mass, the heritage of the Catholic Church. Every year, however, there were difficulties about attempting such a journey. Soon we seemed to feel that, though Kilimanjaro was not so far away, the Arab saying about it—"an enchanted mountain which moves, which one tries to reach, but one can never get there"—was only too true.

This time, however, we seemed to have a good chance of getting there. From Bagamoyo on the coast, we at Zanzibar had been sent thirty-five porters, chosen from among the best of the barefooted carriers of that place. We had taken care to house them immediately at the mission, just as in countries with parliamentary elections voters who will vote correctly are kept under observation and are only let out in a cart at the right moment. But despite everything, ten were misled by a Belgian company which took them from us to send them to the Congo, and seven by a British company which recruited them for the Kavirondo. Nevertheless, we were determined to go forward all the same! Everybody needs to live. Our freight was ready. We took passage on a British steamer going to Mombasa and we disembarked there, hoping to recruit the extra porters we would need. We prayed that the guardian angel of Kilimanjaro should help us and lead us to the mountain.

---

2. It is now known that Germany's claim to the Kilimanjaro massif was accepted.

CHAPTER 1: ETYMOLOGY, DISCOVERY, EXPLORATION

Cycas Circinalis (Bagamoyo)

Chapter 2: Arrival at Mombasa

How we Broke the Law. New Recruits. Let's Go. Our Route.

July 10, 1890

Since Mombasa became the capital of the British Protectorate of Zanzibar, the residence of the Administrator General of the Imperial British East African Company, and the point of departure for the railway line, this old and unpretentious town has known a new lease of life. The railway line linked the Indian Ocean to Lake Victoria Nyanza and was intended as tradesmen's entry to Upper Egypt. There are, facing the dark and solid Portuguese fortress inherited from the distant past, small new buildings scattered beneath the green coconut palms of English Point, whose style tells us that the Europeans have returned. This was brought home to us in a straightforward, down-to-earth manner. We did not want to burden the town with our baggage and porters, nor did we have the intention, the time, or the opportunity to find a house. We went straight to a place outside the edge of the city, where nobody was living, and where big mango trees offered their branches as protection. And so we made our camp. But, in the evening shadows, when the flames

CHAPTER 2: ARRIVAL AT MOMBASA

had just begun to flicker around the cooking pots, we saw a Sudanese soldier, a member of the Imperial British East African Company police, running up with a letter from the Administrator General. We began to wonder if we had been taken for a gang of pirates and if we would have to go and sleep at the post. I squatted down and read the letter by the light of the cooking fires. The message was simply this: our caravan had piston rifles, hunting rifles, military rifles of good quality, and revolvers, and that if we took these dangerous inventions into the interior without their being marked with the Company's special (and profitable) sign, we would have to pay a fine, big enough to frighten explorers richer than us.

The next day, I went to see the Secretary General of the Imperial British Company who had been so kind as to send me this warning. I assured him on my conscience and my soul that we did not wish to engage in arms smuggling nor slave raiding, nor violate the laws of civilized conduct. Finally, our guns were marked with the sacramental stamp, which made them harmless in the future. We were given a document as proof. But while the guns were being stamped, I could not stop myself pointing out that we had the honor of being given the number one and to be the first to have our guns stamped, although before us, plenty of guns had been taken into the interior, perhaps for purposes less peaceful than our own.

During the day, Mgr. de Courmont paid a visit to Sir Francis de Winton, who received him very well. He invited us to dinner. While he had the chance to see that our intentions were entirely honorable, we, on our side, concluded that there are some people who are much less frightening at table than when in their office. The next day, Mgr. de Courmont celebrated mass in a new house which he had been asked to bless. It had been put at our disposition by Mr. A. Pereira and Mr. D. Pereira, natives of Goa. Thirty people—the whole Catholic community—came to the mass.

The next step was to recruit porters to replace those who had left us at Zanzibar. We had hopes of recruiting from among the 200 slaves whom the British Navy had captured, set free, and settled at Mombasa over the previous two years. Alas! The only signs of them were their wives and their houses, both equally shabby. The freed slaves themselves have been recruited by the company for large-scale expeditions in the interior. We were obliged to choose from among the innumerable crowd of runaway slaves, thieves, liars, drunkards, deserters, vagabonds, do-nothings, rogues, and caravan pirates, whose game is to get themselves taken on by newly arrived European travelers, ask for and get an advance, and then disappear. Messengers were sent into the suburbs and they came back with people they had found who looked useful. I had them put in line and started speaking to the man who had the most honest-looking face and with clear-cut features. However, he did not look as though he merited very high wages.

I asked, "What is your name?"

He replied, "Haroun-al-Rashid."

I said, "Excellent, but you look as though you have drunk a little too much."

"Oh, that's not possible. I was released from prison less than an hour ago."

I have to say that for a Muslim who has simply been lacking politeness to a European by pinching his watch or emptying some of his bottles, or losing his wallet, a spell in prison does not damage his reputation. In fact it enhances it. However, it is from among such dodgy characters one has to choose. After some had been chosen, each was given a small advance payment—impossible not to do this—and the hour of departure was fixed, 2 p.m. on 14th July. And when two o'clock came, we found that five porters had disappeared. All the same, we had to get out of there. If we only considered the shelter given by the mango trees, we had a marvelous campsite. But, getting down to earth, we had to admit that this rural retreat had so strong a smell of rotting flesh and sewage as to reduce much of its charm. Moreover, the longer we stayed on the edges of the town, the more problems would we have: there is always something wrong with suburbs.

And so the caravan set off. Striking southwards, we moved along the narrow pathways of the Isle of Mombasa without any great enthusiasm.

These pathways run across modest rows of sweet potatoes, patches of peas, and cassava plants. On the burning sand, fat dung beetles were vigorously rolling the balls, an activity which for them is a career. There was no shelter, save here and there, near thick undergrowth, where the wild jasmine grew, whose white flowers cover the rubber creeper, and where also the swinging plume of the coconut tree and the majestic head of the mango trees spread out to attract our attention. At the Likoni ford, the boats were ready, and in less than an hour, everybody had crossed.

But the first thing to do was to decide on the route to follow. Our target was Kilimanjaro. From Mombasa, the shortest route, and the one which most travelers had taken, was that through Taita. But water was very scarce at that time of year. Moreover, the area has already been explored, and, with the possible exception of one particular point, it does not seem to offer opportunities for missionary work. To the south we have the Digo country, which has been very little studied. If we passed through it, we could finish that part of the journey at Vanga, and, from there, go on to Sambara and Pare country, Lake Jipe, and Taveta. Such a journey would be twice as long as the other route; but, in making it, we would have water and food for the caravan, and we would be able to see the different areas where, sooner or later, missions must be started.

Chapter 3: Delayed

The First Difficulties.
Likoni and the Country Outside Mombasa.
The Caravan, its Members, and Equipment.

When we had made the crossing, we set up our camp under the trees, near to an old well, and facing the blue sea. We were obliged to lose three, almost four days, and these extracts from the expedition diary show what happened.

14 July	Camp set up at Likoni. We looked for the porters who had deserted us or for possible substitutes; nothing found.
15 July	We are still looking for porters, and we do not have sufficient food for those who are with us. We had to go to town to buy rice. None here.
16 July	Rain all day; a fine, depressing sort of rain. We dined on a poor turtledove; for supper, we had crayfish. By evening, we had found five men; we shall leave tomorrow.
17 July	In the night, six porters ran away.

We spent our time like that. This part of the coast, like Mombasa Island, and like almost all the East African coast, rests on a bed of coral. For centuries, the wind and the waves have beaten against it, sometimes cutting it into sharp-pointed needles, sometimes hollowing out deep caves.

The soil suitable for growing fruit trees is less thick than it is to the south, toward Bagamoyo. Nevertheless, it is put to good use. Coconut trees thrive, and they surround Mombasa Island with a half-crown of tropical greenery. Mango trees (*Mangifera indica*) do equally well. There are custard-apple trees (*anona sqamosa*) to be seen, as well as orange trees (*citrus aurantium*), lemon trees (*citrus limonum*), and milk-trees (*Artocarpus integrifolia*); the cashew tree (*anacardium occidentale*) is used for its wood, its fruit, and its nuts. Where fruit trees can no longer grow in the harsh and stony plain, the doum palms (*hyphaene Thebaica*) take their place.

Here and there, small oblong houses are scattered under the green branches. Their occupants—a mixture of Swahili, Digo, and ex-slaves from all over, all more or less Islamized—seem to have little interest in world affairs. The children look after a certain number of cows, bringing them out into the unenclosed land, close to the sea; the women cultivate, apart from the ground around the coconut trees, little fields of cassava, sweet potatoes, beans, pistachio trees (*harachys hypogoea*), maize, guinea corn, and so on; the men are mainly interested in palm wine. It is generally known that this "wine," which is produced by every variety of the palm tree, is simply the sap of the tree. With coconut trees, it is obtained by cutting the base of the branch which can produce flowers and fruit, and putting something there to receive the sap. The doum palm is less valuable; the branches are trimmed, leaving only one or two leaves on each, and afterwards abandoning it to its fate. Some die straightaway, others survive, though enfeebled. The sap is gathered three times in twenty-four hours, and each time approximately a glass of liquid is obtained. When it is fresh, it is whitish, sugary, and a bit cloying; after it has been left to ferment for a day, it acquires a sharp tang and can intoxicate. When it is left for a long time in the open air, it becomes really good vinegar.

Some of the local people are fishermen. Some of them go out to the open sea to fish with a line; others use a fishing basket or a net; others, finally, profit from the changes of the tides to build barrages with narrow rods, where the fish can enter when the tide comes in. When the tide goes out, the fish remain; all that is needed is to take them by hand.

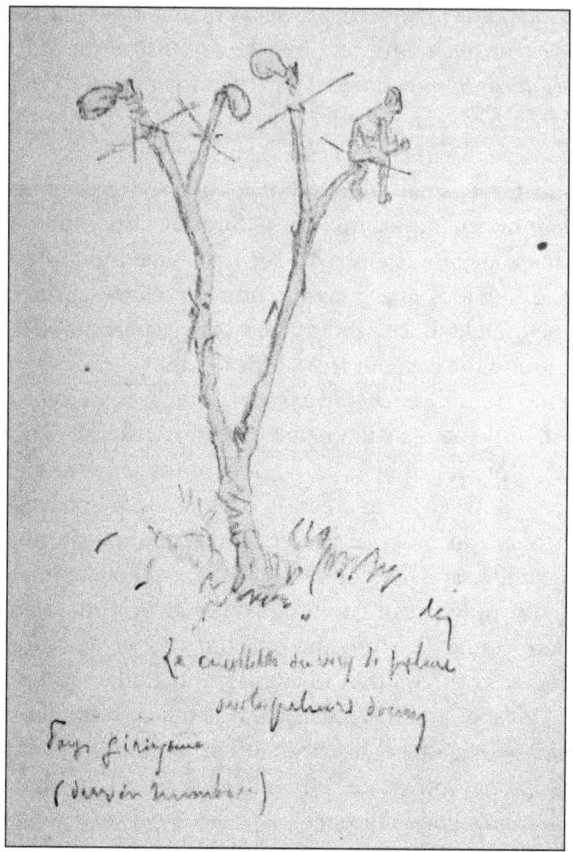

Extracting wine from the doum

Strolling about the neighborhood, we were able to note that these rather simple people were not at all hostile. The children flocked around us, and when they had noticed that Father Auguste Gommenginger and I were looking for insects as a hobby, they brought us dung beetles, weevils and scarabs—everything was acceptable. But, among all these, there was one, found in great numbers, under the dried grass of a newly cleared field, which was of interest both to the children and ourselves. It was a little beetle of 0.015 to 0.020 meters in size, not brightly colored, whose outer wings showed part of the body. Zoologists call it brachine (*brachinas crepitans*) and ordinary mortals refer to it as "the bombardier." This is because, when someone tries to get hold of it, it vigorously discharges through its anus some drops of a caustic liquid which immediately vaporizes, making a crackling sound which is enough to frighten a fly and astonish a man.

CHAPTER 3: DELAYED

But we must come back to our caravan. On the morning of the 17th, the six porters who had disappeared during the night returned, with very red eyes, but walking normally. They claimed that their sense of duty had led them to say goodbye to their beloved families. This was a very suitable attitude; we said nothing, but insisted on starting as soon as possible.

Apart from Mgr. de Courmont, we were two missionaries, Le Roy and Gommenginger, and two young Christians. Old Selemani (this name, written Séliman in the course of this work, is read Selemani), our devoted and trustworthy servant, was with us. He did the cooking, and, whenever our watches stopped, it was he who decided what the time was. He had an extraordinary skill for that, and he was never as flattered as when you asked him where the sun was. As for the moon, he has a really personal knowledge of it. The poor old man was not in good health, but he had overcome all problems to follow us. What was his illness? He suffered, he explained in his kitchen French, from "a cold in his ham" ("*un rhume à son jambon*"). Informed people will realize that it was a case of rheumatism in his thigh [he had confused *jambe*, leg, and *jambon*, ham—translator].

Mombasa-fish barrages

The rest of the caravan was composed of forty porters, each in a section with its leader. If you want to find out how much these thirty men can carry, you have to understand that each man has not merely his cooking utensils, his personal luggage, and his rifle, but thirty kilos of luggage to be carried on his head or his shoulders according to his choice. There were three kinds of unbleached linen; two sorts of red linen, differing in quality; big and small sizes of calico; then printed calico and various cotton fabrics; linen clothes for whose shape and coloring I cannot find the correct words in any European language. There were also blankets, rolls of iron wire, both large and small, as well as rolls of copper wire, both red and yellow. Then there were glass pearls of varying colors, shape, and size—some like peas, some like a grain of hempseed, some like the head of a pin, some red, some yellow, some white, some blue, some rose-colored, and some green.

We must add pickaxes, axes, knives, soap, flutes, files (tools), small chains in gold and silver. Then there are household items, mirrors, thread, needles, small bells, necklaces, fishing hooks, paraffin, candles, and armchair nails which ladies use as ornaments on their noses. Finally, I have not included our provisions, medicines for different diseases, some pots of jam, coffee, oil, vinegar, tea, sugar, rice, beans, three tents, a portable altar, a hammock, three barrels of gunpowder, a hundred Gras cartridges, four bottles of rum, and a jug for water. This jug could be filled up at any river, stream, swift-flowing torrent, spring, lake, pond, or pool. We had materials for an excellent shop of which we were the shopkeepers.

From Zanzibar onwards, we had given ourselves different responsibilities. Mgr. de Courmont was to decide on the route, and where we should camp. Fr. Gommenginger was to look after the cooking, buy food, and work out with Selemani the important question of the daily menu. Fr. Le Roy was to keep the caravan in good order and to see that we moved together as a group.

Everything was ready. At nine o'clock, we took breakfast, the baggage was packed, and off we went.

Banana tree

Chapter 4: In Digo Country

*From Mombasa to Vanga. The Layout of the Land.
The Digo People. With Chief Kubo.
Weapons and Poisons.*

The country between Mombasa and Vanga is inhabited by the Wadigo, or, as one would say in English or French, the Digo. They are scattered more or less everywhere, but there is a Swahili colony established at Gasi, and the remaining groups of the earlier population who have been pushed into an area of the coast called Vumba. Our route was to pass through these three regions rarely visited by Europeans, incompletely explored, and yet rather interesting. From a geological point of view, the region consists of three levels, which can be clearly recognized from the sea: a low level, a medium level, and an upper level.

The first, the coastline, is composed of a bed of old coral covered by sand and humus, at many points too shallow to be fertile. It is then occupied by undergrowth, filaos (*casuarina equisetifolia*), deon palms, and pandanus trees (*pandanus odoratissimus*). A little behind this uncultivated ground, we get signs of human habitation in the form of coconut trees. There are a few small harbors on this coast, but they are only fit to be used by dhows and local boats. The names of these harbors are Tiwi, Gasi, Funzi, Pongwe, Chugu, Wasini, Vanga, and Mwoa. Going south along the coast, the sea cuts into the land and creates wide lagoons flanked by mangroves. Boats can come and leave on the high tide, carrying wood for fires to make lime and for beams and rafters. Except for Gasi, Pongwe, Wasini and Vanga, the coastline is thinly populated.

The medium level is higher up and also more fertile, more farmed, and more populated. This is Digo country in the strict sense, with the districts of Matooga, Tiwi, Ndiani, Ukunda, Mafisi, Mwa Doonda, etc. The upper level, as a whole, reaches a height of about 300 meters. It consists of Shimba, which one can see from Mombasa, looking like a table; Longo, which is next

CHAPTER 4: IN DIGO COUNTRY

to it; Mwabila, which today is almost a wilderness, but which is watered and fertile; and Mwele, where Mbaruku, the ruler of Gasi, has a slave settlement. Finally, to the south, there is a small, well-shaped mountain which is uninhabited because there are no sources of water; this is Jombo.

Behind this range of hills, there is an immense area, between the territories of the Sambara, the Pare, the Taveta, and the Kamba, which when viewed from a high vantage point looks like an endless forest, dull and gloomy, only broken by the heights of Kilibasi, Kasigeo, and Mwangoo, and, further away, the picturesque mountains of Ndara and Boora. It is a desert, not the sandy desert of the Sahara, but a plateau where everything—the soil, the grass, the trees, the insects, the birds, the mammals, human beings included—has this dry, sad way of existing which can be summed up in one word: desert-ified. There is little or no water; this explains everything else.

However, some rivers rise from within this plateau and create, parallel to the coast, a pleasantly green zone. The main ones are: the river Pemba, which runs out into Mombasa Bay, and the Mkwakwa, which enters the sea at Tiwi and which flows down from Mwabila. We must add to these the Mkooroomodyi, which comes from Mwele, the Ramisi, which emerges from Ada (Doorooma) and whose water is slightly brackish. There are also, in the middle level of this country, a certain number of pools and springs which are very useful to the local people. Villages get built near them.

The Digo belong, by their physical type, customs, and language, to the great African family called Bantu. In general, they are short rather than tall, lean, relaxed, and not too bad-looking. We stayed a whole week with them, and everywhere we were received with evident friendliness. The chiefs brought us little gifts, the sick came in crowds to get treatment, and some children, who seem close to death, were there and then baptized. Some day we shall meet them again in heaven, where they form part of the vision described by St. John, a great crowd which nobody could count from every nation, race, tribe, and language (Rev 7:9).

However, there are Digo and Digo. The main difference is brought about by the spread of Islam. To the north of Gasi, Islam hardly exists; to the south, it has a very definite influence.

Let us take the case of a traditionalist village, or, if you prefer the phrase, a pagan village. It is usually to be found in a place with abundant undergrowth, which can serve as a hiding place for women and children, and even the men in time of war: this is certainly not, let me say straightaway, a purely imaginary situation. You enter the village by a long corridor which has been cut into the forest and which has two or three doorways, in succession, which provide a way into the village. Near the entry, there is an earthen bowl held in place by three sticks which is the rain bowl. One has to keep some water in this earthenware vessel, make an occasional offering of a piece of cloth which is hung above it, and burn some oil there and so on. This is the way in this dry land to avoid shortages of water. All the same, water is often scarce. But when one says this to the magician, he will reply that without the marvelous bowl, water would be much scarcer.

Rain gourd

Near at hand, in the thickets, is the little house of the Mwanza. From it, on certain days, there comes a sound so frightening that everyone who hears it shuts himself up in his house. The noise marks the passing of the Mwanza.

What is the Mwanza? Nobody is quite sure, but when he asks for something, he must have it without delay. It is hardly necessary to say that this kind of werewolf has as spokesman the local magician or the chief—two roles which are often combined in the same person. Sometimes, sacrifices are made to him. It may be to drive away war or an epidemic or famine, to rid oneself of some problem, to free oneself from the pressure of disturbing dreams; but also to make something succeed.

But how does this Mwanza speak? Reader, it is a big secret. However, if you promise me not to tell anybody, I can take you into my confidence. You take a tree trunk, which can be cut easily, you make of it a block of wood one-meter-long, you hollow out the inside, you close one end with a fully stretched skin, as you would do for a drum. Across the middle of this skin, a piece of gut, acting as a cord, passes through a hole. It is fixed to the interior of the cylinder and, on the outside, it is held in place by a stick which can be moved about. In the depths of the forest, and in the hands of a skilled operator, the instrument can produce sounds which freeze simple people with fear and bring them to the magician's feet, to ask, "What does the Mwanza want?"

CHAPTER 4: IN DIGO COUNTRY

The wise soothsayer takes pity on them and commits himself to appease the angry creature, provided one does what he wants or makes an appropriate sacrifice. There is a rather surprising feature, which shows that this institution must go back to the distant past. It is found in one form or another in all the neighboring Nyika around, in the valley of the Tana, and as far away as the Congo and the Ogowe (Gabon). But what a pity that European Heads of State do not have at their disposal something similar to frighten their parliamentarians into voting for the measures submitted to them.

Digo villages do not occupy large stretches of ground. Along the coastline, one often sees isolated houses or a few houses close together. Further up, one can find villages of twenty, thirty, or forty houses, thrown together without any systematic plan, sometimes very close to each other, built in an unusual shape, neither round nor square. The door, the roof, and the walls are all made of interwoven coconut tree branches. One can wonder, if there should be a fire in such a community, what would be left. I posed this question to a member of one of the village councils. He smiled at my Western naivety, and, without saying a word, he pointed to the coconut trees, whose multi-colored leaves provided a covering for the village.

Side of a village on the coast.

Then I understood; when houses have become little heaps of ashes, the materials for rebuilding are always at hand.

The Digo do not do very much work. The coconut tree is such a help to them. It gives them food, it gives them drink. Often coconut trees are quite high, but the Digo learn to climb at the same time as they learn to walk. Moreover, they have developed techniques. People living near the coast make cuts in the trunk of a tree as it grows; this produces a kind of stairway. Other Digo, further inland, tie two long poles to the coconut tree, and attach them to different points on the tree with pieces of creepers, making them a kind of permanent ladder.

Palm wine tapping is for them a major occupation. However, they also plant cassava, guinea corn, maize, beans, pistachio trees, ambrevades (*leganus indicos*), various marrows, and a little sesame. When they can, they keep cattle, but they generally keep chickens, goats, sheep, and small dogs, which they keep for hunting.

As warriors, they are not remarkable. They get on reasonably well with each other, although they have a reputation of being quibblers. They are keen drinkers. They love wearing ornaments and music and dancing. They are very good at both these arts, and bring them into very many of their ceremonies, such as those for births, marriages, burials, anniversaries of a funeral, in fact any kind of social occasion. I once saw, as the closing ceremony at the annual remembrance service for the chief of Matonga—quite a minor figure—more than 2,000 dancers who had come from all over for this "anniversary service." For these occasions, a special costume is worn, whose picturesque quality varies according to taste and resources. Hair oil is available in the form of red ochre mixed with the oil of the castor oil plant, which, poured on the heads of participants, produces a bright red coloring which is much admired. But for ordinary days, men dress in a simple loincloth with a piece of linen hanging from the shoulders. Women wear a sort of double short skirt and ornaments such as pendant earrings, pearl necklaces, copper bracelets, etc.

Many children and young people have, hanging from their necks, an eyebrow tweezer with which to remove hair from their eyebrows.

Digo country is divided into a large number of small chiefdoms, each with its own chief. However, all these chiefs accept, as at least honorary president, Kubo, who lived at Kikone in southern Digo country, and whom we wanted to visit.

When, however, we arrived at Kikone, brave old Kubo was not there. All the same, we settled down on the town square, which was actually outside the village, around a tamarind tree whose kindly head normally sheltered the local unemployed. We waited for a good hour or more; then we saw a large body, lean and elderly, clad in a slightly worn red overcoat, with, on top, a head severely marked by smallpox, accompanied by quite a lot of people, with, in front, a musician playing a trumpet. The body and the head were Kubo's.

We found him a good conversationalist, welcoming, and well intentioned in his attitudes. He readily shared with us his loves and hates: he took a favorable view of the Arab governor of Vanga, but detested Mbaruku, the Swahili chief of Gasi, who had killed his uncle and three of his brothers and had ravaged the whole of Digo country. Kubo had understandably bitter feelings toward him.

We quickly noticed differences between the people at Kikone and those on the higher ground. Here people look at you in a less trustful way, they put on more clothes, and their way of acting is less straightforward; here, the influence of Islam was beginning to make itself felt.

For weapons, the Digo have rifles, spears, head-smashing clubs, big broad straight cutlasses, and bows. Here also you can find the arrow poison which is used in so many underdeveloped countries in Africa, the Americas, and Asia. It is taken from a tree. Unfortunately, I have never seen the tree which produces it, and I have never travelled in the area when the tree produces flowers at the end of the dry season. However, an old warrior who gave me some of this poison, gave me also some charming details about it. Here they are.

"You find it in a tree," said he, "created specifically to be a poison tree. The birds are well aware of it, and they and the animals know many things at which we humans can only guess. They do not speak, and perhaps it is so that they do not reveal their secrets. The birds know what a poison tree looks like. They never settle on its branches, and you will find a lot of dead insects around its roots. To make the poison you have to cut pieces of wood from the tree, take also the roots, cut them all into small pieces, and boil them slowly in an earthenware bowl filled with fresh water, stirring it all the time with a long stick. You do that deep in the forest, not wearing any clothes. Every so often you should throw into the bowl some snake poison, the skin of a toad, then leaves from the forest, grass from the meadows, dust from the path, some shadow."

"Shadow?" I exclaimed.

"Yes, and the idea is that for the man or animal hit by a poisoned arrow, everything should bring poison, death, and destruction. Surely an animal hit by an arrow will try and find relief by resting in the shadow of trees? Well, then, that shadow must strengthen the effect of the poison. What if he lies down on the grass? That grass must also become poison for him. What if the dust from the path sticks to his feet? That dust must also be poisonous for him, just as the water he drinks and the leaves he nibbles simply add to the poison. Nothing can make him better: he is lost, he has to die."

"Then," I asked, "is there no cure?"

"There is," he said. "It is a root ground into powder. We carry it on us in wartime and we swallow it with water or saliva. But often we have not the time to take it to the man who has been hit. As you have asked me for it, I am giving you some of this poison, but do not let your younger brothers and sisters keep it. You are laughing? Well, if you shoot an arrow which is carrying this poison into the bark of a tree, the next day its leaves will fall."

"And," I said, "if your arrow hits a man?"

"He is as good as dead."

I followed the advice of my old friend. I did not hand over my supply of poison to my little brothers and sisters. Instead, I handed it over to a highly competent Parisian scientist, Dr J. V. Laborde, who made a thorough study and produced a detailed report. The tests he applied show that this poison first affects the nervous system and then brings death "by suspending the influence of the heart on the breathing organs." Dr. Laborde is very skeptical about the possibility of an antidote in view of the extremely toxic nature of this substance.

Chapter 5: At Gasi

The Digo people have always found themselves trapped between two enemies: the Maasai, who carry off their cattle, and the Swahili, who take their young people, their women, and their children. The main center for Swahili raiding is at Gasi, where the notorious Mbaruku rules. Mbaruku, Embareuk, Baraka, and Baruch come from the same Semitic word meaning "blessing." It is rather ironical that this should be the name of the chief of Gasi.

Mbaruku was descended from the powerful old family of the Mazrui. This family was given power over Mombasa by the Imam of Muscat in the eighteenth century. When the Busaidi Dynasty established itself at Zanzibar, the Mazrui family refused to recognize them. Mbaruku spent his life fighting against Seyyid Said, Seyyid Majid and Seyyid Barghash. Practically all his time he concealed himself with a band of followers in the hinterland on the upper slopes of Mount Mwele, and had friendly contacts with the Arabs to whom he provided slaves and from whom he got the gunpowder and rifles necessary to raid the ill-equipped Digo villages. When the European powers began—some years ago—to look with covetous eyes on this part of Africa, Mbaruku was exactly the man for whom they were looking. He played his part, accepting in turn the various flags that were offered to him. Finally, since the place where he was living was made British territory, the British gave him Gasi as his capital, paid him a salary, and gave him enough guns and soldiers for him to regard himself as the local sultan. I do not know how he makes use of his power. But the Digo unanimously state that in the past he turned their villages into ruins, turned the magnificent countryside into lonely deserts, and sent three-quarters of the population into slavery in the island of Pemba or Arabia.

Sometimes, one asks oneself, on seeing so few of the coastal ethnic groups much influenced by Islam, how and why they have remained traditionalist. The answer is very simple. The Muslims have freely avoided propagating Islam among them, in order to be able to gain regular profits from them. They regard these neighboring tribes as simply a slave reserve kept going and also exploited in a businesslike manner, where a family is allowed to reproduce itself, by having, say, six children. At the right moment, four of these are taken and two are left to keep the family going.

Mbaruku! We were delighted to see with our own eyes this bold adventurer. A little turning toward the coast brought us to his capital. Many slaves were busy in rice farms; we went through fields of guinea corn and beyond a big lagoon which we managed to pass without wetting our feet. We soon saw two rows of houses in Swahili style, new, even unfinished. In each house four walls formed an oblong building, with a little veranda at the front and a number of separate rooms inside. Some rooms are built with stones, but the majority have trellis work with earth inside, covered with coconut palms. There is only one road, but surprisingly, it is entirely straight.

Our porters installed themselves on an unclaimed stretch of ground at the way into Gasi, and we went straight to what we were told was the sheikh's residence. We had to wait a long time in an inner room where the local big men were seated in two lines. The conversation was far from lively, rather formal, somewhat embarrassed, such as you might imagine you would have with visitors when you would prefer to be a hundred leagues away. Finally, Mbaruku arrived in Arab dress. He was a big lad of about forty, light-skinned even though his mother was entirely African. His face was calm and had nothing to remind us of Ali Baba, whose exploits he had imitated in this country, with the help of the forty thieves who had been his companions and who were still at hand.

He welcomed us as though he was very interested in us. We told him that we were only passing through, that we were going to Vanga, and from there to Kilimanjaro, and that we had not wished to travel across the country without paying him a formal visit. He heard what we said but did not believe it. In his career as a local ruler, he had already met quite a number of Europeans, and, as each of them had put forward political proposals, he expected to see us, at any moment, pull some flag or other out of our pockets. He tried to see what we wanted, asking questions and then putting them a little differently: he asked us a good many things in a rather probing way.

"Why did you take this road? What are you going to do at Kilimanjaro? Is it true that that mountain is covered with silver? Do you know where precious stones are hidden? What are Europeans looking for in this country? Are the French still in Madagascar? What is your impression of the Sultan of Zanzibar? Is he not very mean? Do you think the British will suppress slavery? Is Sir Francis (the British Company's administrator) a decent sort? Have you yourselves plans to take over some country? Are you rich? Have you nothing to say to me in private? What do you want me to do for you?"

This final question was the most practical one, and we could, at least, reply to it unambiguously. "Great Sheikh, let us rest, for we are tired (meaning, but not saying, "Of your questioning.")." With that we withdrew, we set up our tents where our men had settled and we took a stroll to know the place a bit.

With a definitive peace, the new village came into being. It has the name of Kau-Kabani, wisely taken from the Quran, and it is Mbaruku's official residence. The real Gasi faces it, on the other side of a little lagoon which is covered by the tide almost every day. We went there and found that it consists of a few fisherman's houses. Certainly a rather sad place, but it is a good shelter for slave-traders, as it is out of the way and unknown and cannot be approached by big ships.

Embarking

Moreover, when the wind blows favorably, one can sail in one night from there to the Isle of Pemba, where there is always someone in this land of abundant clove trees who will buy "the commodity that works and speaks." If need be, supposing one sees the smoke of a British warship on the horizon, nothing is simpler than to tie a stone to the slave's foot and throw him overboard. You can see, below a verandah, half-a-dozen unhappy slaves, their ankles fettered with iron shackles, sitting in a kind of dazed silence, waiting to be shipped. At one side, the slave superintendent looks out to sea, a whip in his hand.

Coming back to the camp, we found a plate of rice and another with chicken. Each one was kept hot under a kind of cone-shaped covering of plaited straw, ornamented with designs in colored wool, as used in the best

Muslim society: they had been sent by the Sheikh. His rice was excellent; but the cook had spoilt the sauce by putting in too much lemon juice.

Mbaruku himself came later on, to repay the courtesy call which we had made. He seemed to have finally realized that as we were not planning an annexation, nor wanted to present him with a flag, nor to give presents which would signify our sovereignty, we were much less important than his other European visitors.

All the same, there were those who thought that there was a chance to profit from these unbelievers. When Mbaruku had gone, we saw a dear little man with a wizened face, both sly and smiling, and a bent back, come up to us, holding a big Muslim rosary in one hand, and a long stick in the other. It was Bohero, who had been—can you guess?—the guide of Baron von der Decken in 1861 on his first expedition to Kilimanjaro. Now, he was just coming back from a journey to the interior. He told us he knew the hinterland like the palm of his hand. He spoke of a place which he called Molok, in Maasai country, where there is a mysterious cave which he had managed to enter one day, and, so he assured us, was full of marvels. For instance, big stones, neatly trimmed, and covered with inscriptions, in an unknown script. We were very thrilled to hear this; he saw our reaction and offered straightaway to be our guide—for 100,000 piasters!

Oh, really, Bohero? We had looked forward to a fascinating conversation, but it soon became burdensome and tedious, with frequent stops, as he launched pious ejaculations toward heaven, no doubt to ask pardon of the heavenly powers for spending so much time with unbelievers. Finally, he left us to pray or so he claimed, but assuring us he would come back. He did really come back, when night had fallen. The poor fellow wanted a case of rum.

I said, "But the Prophet has forbidden believers to drink stuff like that!"

He replied, "Oh yes, but I just take a little now and then, not as drink, but as medicine."

He coughed energetically.

I asked, "How much do you take at a time?"

"Oh, perhaps a half-bottle, a full bottle."

We said we would deal with his request in the morning. That morning, we felt very happy as we said farewell to Mbaruku, to Gasi, to Bohero, and to that whole place, swarming with slave-traders and crooks.

Chapter 6: Further On

A Beautiful Unpeopled Land. Attacked by Amazons. African Ants. Vumba Country and its Palm Trees. The Devil's Well.

Leaving Gasi, we went up to the high ground to avoid the lagoons and estuaries which we would have had to cross if we had kept to the coast. We were also anxious to see our Digo friends again. The country through which we passed was magnificent, composed of hills and valleys, with a fertile soil and bright green vegetation, well-watered, in places thickly wooded, but practically unpopulated. Who is responsible for this depopulation? Only Mbaruku is to blame.

Here and there, some turtledoves could be heard warbling as we went. They must have been astonished to see human beings. Surely what keeps them living in such a wilderness are the ears of maize and guinea corn still growing in the abandoned fields. Squawking he-parrots flit from tree to tree. Bands of monkeys roam, out for what they can get, but one does not see what they can take. There are many flowers on the paths and, among the flowers, many orchids. One of them, small and beautiful, provides a carpet for a big clearing in the forest; another, the lissochilos, is yellow and grows among various kinds of grass in a place where it can catch the full warmth of the sun. Yet another variety, which is really marvelous, can be seen in a stretch of forest, covering a large old tree which has fallen across the path and which provides a place for it to grow.

Yellow *Lissochilus* (ground orchid)

Further along, on the edge of the forest, one can find enormous flowers with a very strong scent, and whose calyx is more than twenty centimeters in length. They hang from a kind of creeper and form a lovely bouquet. Its name is *gardenia*, but only insects seem to appreciate it, if one can conclude from the hundreds that swarm on it with delight.

We reached Mafisi, a village whose inhabitants are all Digo. What delightful people! At least here we experienced a hospitality that comes from the heart, and really it put us at our ease. Night fell, we enjoyed the customary evening chatter, we went to bed, we closed our eyes . . . then a cry, coming from Mgr. de Courmont's tent, frightened us all. It was a surprise attack; we got ready to fight.

We started running, and by the light of the brands which had been given out to everyone, we saw the scurrying battalions of those fat black ants called Siafu. They are here, they are there, and they are everywhere; really, it was an invasion. But then the porters who had run up were themselves invaded. They were jumping about in the grass, holding their torches in their hands. They cried out, they rubbed the various parts of their bodies, they threw their clothes away, they rolled about on the ground, they twisted this way and that, they ranted and raved, they burst into laughter; it was a fascinating night-time show.

But while you watch and enjoy the scene, you suddenly feel yourself nipped, and put your hand to the place, then it happens elsewhere, and then yet again elsewhere; you yourself have been invaded and before you can sort yourself out, you find that these devilish creatures are on your legs, your chest, your arms, your beard, your hair. You feel you are going crazy.

I must tell you that these African ants outdo every living creature in ferocity. Their role in the order of things is to remove the remains of dead animals from the ground; however, if a living creature gets in the way of this work, its existence is at an end—insects, lizards, birds, even snakes are surrounded, attacked and destroyed.

As with many other similar insects, these ants exist in two forms: one, the smaller, is never larger than 0.008 of a meter. It has a regular appearance and is not really a great nuisance. The other species is twice as big, with a big head, in proportion to its size, has a dangerous pair of pincers, and can be diabolically malicious. The first is the male ant, the second the female, which, because of its warlike attitudes, naturalists call "the amazon."

Among these amazons, a community of ants chooses one who is the object of very special care, being stuffed with food, and so becoming huge, often as large as a man's little finger, and incapable of moving. Her only occupation is to produce new ants, and she fulfills this duty conscientiously, without stopping; there is always a baby ant coming out of her, to be immediately snatched up and put in its place by an old midwife ant. Really, ants are manufactured. One day, knocking down an old wall, I came across a Siafu queen-mother, and as I had scores to settle, I was bold enough to put her in a flask of alcohol. And so I can give you an exact portrait of her, of an ordinary "amazon" and of a mere male.

Often enough, in damp places, I have met a tribe of these ants, scattered here and there, moving ahead in dispersed order, looking for its everyday nourishment, busy with this and that. But also, for reasons which they themselves know—perhaps they want to start a new colony—they often gather together, organize themselves into military-style columns, and march ahead. Really, you should see them then! Their determination to march in order produces a small corridor, flanked by two ramparts of neat sand. This hollow road is only followed by the males, those inoffensive creatures: on each side the amazons crowd together, with their thick heads in the air, and their pincers set wide open, threatening and terrifying, ready to protect the others, and reminding me of the "archway of swords" which the Freemasons make with swords crossed over the heads of their dear members. Moreover, in the world of ants, perhaps they are, as it were, female freemasons, if only because they are not at all frank and they do not do any building. Whatever the case is, they follow their path, and if they enter a house because it lies on their route, or some animal remains attract them—provided that one leaves them to carry on—they will all do so, leaving no trace except their little track.

But if one should start to annoy them, to crush them, to push them about, their column will scatter straightaway, and they will attack you with the same determination that David showed against Goliath. Without delay, they put their pincers to work on your arms, your clothes, your skin, and you can see the little creature twisting around to give ever more effective pinches, clinging on for dear life, killing itself by a surfeit of rage. I have never seen one fall off; what you must do is to tear off the body first, and then the head. If there were a similar army of human amazons, they would be invincible.

We met them throughout our journeys. But repeated attacks teach the art of defense. When one of us noticed an ant army on the march, he made it known, and, straightaway, without noise, without a fuss being made, without disturbing the stretches of grass—which to the ants are what a big forest is for us—one of us would take boiling water in a kettle and pour it over the ant army as it advanced. Another tactic is to throw burning torches on to them. But in any case, do not let them get on to your legs.

The Siafu are not the only African ants; there are many others. There is a species of small red ants, whose scurrying soldiers sometimes take over roads and fields. There is also a species of black ants, even smaller than the red ones, which lives under tree trunks, under the bark of trees, and beneath stones. These often have small beetles living among them, the Clavigere (key-holder), and another, a rather fatter one, the Paussus, whom they keep well-fed, and from whom they ask the favor of an occasional lick.

Another kind of ant, a transparent red in color and middle-sized, is found on the East African coast. It likes to live in orange and mango trees, and gathers their leaves to make its home.

There is another kind of ant, whose members live alone. It is fat, long, and black. It smells so strongly of carrion, that you can smell one at two or three meters' distance. I have put some of them into flasks, which, even when opened and washed, have kept the smell for more than a year. Now, if the substance of this little creature were used in the perfumery trade, the results would be startling.

Yet another fascinating species can often be found on pathways. They are slightly longer than the ferocious Siafu, and extremely black. They also advance in army-style columns, and are about 0.02 or 0.03 meters is size. They do not protect each other; it is an individualistic society. However, the humming sound which they produce is so strong that you hear them before you see them. But for all their determination, there is a simple, albeit rather strange, way of halting their march, and we owe it to Father Gommenginger. Take a stick, and kill the ant who is leading the column and leave his body lying there. Immediately, those who were following him, will stop and cluster round, they are clearly very shaken, gradually they turn round, and go back to wherever they started. This is a tribe for which, it would seem, that a body lying across the path is an evil omen.

But where do these long columns go? Mgr. de Courmont has often decided to follow them, and he told us he has repeatedly seen them fall on a nest of termites or white ants which they literally plunder. These are then useful ants, and since no remedy has been found for termites and their ravaging, it might be a good idea to breed a tribe of these Sungu-Sungu ants near the building liable to be attacked by termites. The results might be very satisfactory.

But just look how I have got sidetracked! I wanted to talk about human beings, but the ants delayed me. Certainly, in the countries where both breeds dwell, there are marked similarities between the two species. Ants are constantly at war, and so are our men; ants are slave-owners and so are men; ants do not keep food supplies in reserve, nor do men.

From Mafisi, we had to march for three hours to get to Mwadunda, a canton whose capital is Kikone, where we found the old chief Kubo, who has been already mentioned.

From there, we came near to the sea and, crossing a low-lying and uncultivated plain, where several varieties of palm tree were growing, such as the Egyptian palm, the elegant Guinean palm, and the majestic borassus palm from Ethiopia, we came to a little village with practically no one there, and we encamped there. We had arrived at Madzoreni, that is to say "The fan at the palm trees." The enormous number of beautiful palm trees that one can see here make this a very appropriate name. But if you look closely, you find there is something wrong. The good people of this part of the world had thought that the best way to get palm wine is to cut off the heads of the palm tree and to make a little hole at the top where they could find palm wine every morning. Unhappily, neither men nor trees live long without heads, and the palm trees are dead. Only their long trunks, straight, but with a bulge toward the top, stand on the plain, and, at night, when the wind blows from the beach, the moon casts a sad light on these survivors. You would think they were the palaces and temples of an ancient town, whose columns survive as the proof of their past splendor.

Palm trunks at Vumba (drawing by author)

Here we find ourselves facing Wasini, a small inhabited island, with a good harbor, but not much drinking water. The inhabitants have farms and wells on the continent which they face, at Chuyu, at Pongwe, at Madzoreni, where we had arrived, and at Vanga, where we were going. All these places, which together are called Vumba, an area which goes up to Pangani, was formerly occupied by settlements of Persian Shirazi, so says tradition, and there are ruins to prove it. Nowadays the inhabitants have a rather poor standard of living; some farm, others fish, a few make salt. Every three days at a place near here, the coastal people and the people from the interior come here for a market and exchange commodities and news. The Digo enjoy these markets and people sometimes come from a great distance.

About half an hour after our arrival, a large group of people came to Mgr. de Courmont, who told them to come and see me. What was up?

The spokesman, after some steady coughing, the result of his being overcome by emotion, began by saying as follows.

"A long time ago, a very long time ago, people about whom we know nothing, but who must surely have been Europeans, came here. We were not born, nor were our fathers, nor even our grandfathers. It was long ago. And these Europeans built a town, of which one can see the ruins, and they dug a well and put a wall of stone around it. Why afterwards did they leave our country? We do not know; but it is still the case with Europeans that they travel around everywhere, and just when you think they have settled down, they disappear. Every tribe has its own manner of living. We stay where we are: but you are nomads. Well, to come back to these Europeans, ever since they left, the Devil has been controlling the well, and this is particularly regrettable since it seems to have clean water, something we often lack."

"Well, then?" said I.

"Well, when we saw you coming here today, you being the first Europeans to come here after those who came before our grandfathers were born, we said to each other, 'It is God, who has sent them.' Please, drive out the Devil, whom your brothers have placed there and let us draw water from your well."

"All right, we give you our permission."

"Many thanks. We were sure such kind people as you would agree, but please drive the Devil out before we start."

Straightaway, I explained the problem to the bishop and asked for authorization to perform an exorcism, for evidently the problem was a very serious one.

"I give you all necessary powers," said Mgr. de Courmont.

Then, in a great crowd—locals, porters, children, old men, and old women—we set off to find the bedeviled well. Really, it was a story to set your blood tingling. After marching for a quarter of an hour, we found ourselves caught up in a maze of creepers, undergrowth, and tall trees. Finally, we came up against ruins, probably of Persian origin, certainly not left by Europeans. On one side, there was a hole, guarded by a stone wall, about six meters deep and quite broad, with, at the bottom, a pool of greenish water covering a heap of rotten leaves. The oldest man in the crowd took my hand, and, with an air of mystery, whispered to me, "Here it is."

Fr. Gommenginger, who roared with laughter like a pagan, made it difficult for me to keep a straight face. But, finally, I pulled myself together, I asked people to bring dead trees and dry leaves. They brought me armfuls which I hurled into the frightening hole. A deep silence gripped us all. In front of us, an enormous trunk of a baobab tree lay, stretched out. A narrow path went up to it, and so I guessed that here was one of the shrines where traditional Africans make sacrifices.

"If" said I, "you want the Devil to leave, you must renounce him. Do you renounce him?"

"We renounce him," they cried.

"Then destroy the shrine you have built there and stop going there with your offerings; only God has a right to sacrifices."

People were astonished.

"Who can have shown him the shrine?" said some. "Surely he is a powerful wizard."

While one of our children, a Christian, went toward the place indicated, found the shrine, and destroyed it, I myself, a little carried away by the situation, made a big sign of the cross over the Devil's well. Then something astonishing happened. There was an extraordinary noise behind the old baobab, everybody jumped back by instinct and, lo and behold, an enormous vampire bat, flew out of the hole, and, flying in a confused manner, was lost among the trees. The crowd kept silent, as though it were a face-to-face meeting with the Devil. Without wasting time, I threw down the bottom of the hole some handfuls of lighted straw, the dead leaves caught fire, the blaze spread, great clouds of black smoke rose, and the Devil's well really looked like an ante-chamber of hell.

As you have understood, the point of doing all this is not to drive out the evil spirit, who is used to fire, but to clear out the unhealthy air; for I had been so rash as to say that I would go down into the well, and drink its water: then it would be in the public domain.

When the fire had gone out, a kind of improvised ladder, made there and then, was placed against the wall and I went down to the depths. Then, I climbed up safe and sound back to my fellow humans, carrying in a coconut cup, a little muddy water, unpleasant to look at, and smelling like rotten eggs, or, if you prefer, like hydroxide sulphuric acid. But, for local public opinion, the smell and the taste were entirely explicable by the prolonged diabolical presence. After us, those who had come with us dipped their lips eagerly in the cup. Then five or six workmen went down into the well to clean it out. I like to think that since then, the Prince of Darkness has not made a nuisance of himself to these poor human beings.

That evening, our services were rewarded by the gift of an old cock. Is there any French journalist, however prone to anticlerical diatribes, who would dare to suggest that I had not earned it?

Chapter 7: At Vanga

Where is Vanga? The Town and its Population.
A Magician's Secret. Rescuing an Innocent.
On Strike. A Prison Door.

We got to Vanga after marching for four hours across lonely lagoons, muddy marshland, and remnants of forests.[1] Vanga is a small town belonging to the old Vumba country, which is still represented here by an old and powerless chief, a Diwani, whose name is Mohammed. He said that his family came from Jeddah in Arabia and claims to be the ruler of all the people of the coastline as far as Pangani, despite the claims of the Sultan of Zanzibar, the Germans, and the British. Alas! What a lot of princes there are throughout the world who lack nothing except the actual power to rule.

In fact, who really owns Vanga? When Britain and Germany divided the country, this was a major problem for the two of them. Recourse was had to the map, as though it were a source of scientific certainty. Then it was found that the map put Vanga to the south of the river Umba, therefore in German territory, but in the actual layout of the land, Vanga was north of the river, in the British zone. The first explorer who had drawn the first map, had thought that a stretch of water was the river's estuary, but in fact it was only a lagoon! There was a very definite disagreement, but the two sides did not want to resort to war, so they agreed to seek arbitration, and the chosen arbitrator was the commander of a French warship at harbor in Zanzibar.

He asked, "Is there salt water in Vanga?"

"Plenty," replied the German representative.

"Then it is British."

---

1. Baron von der Decken, who was German, was the first to write Wanga (with a W), W being the German equivalent of the French V, and the German V being the equivalent of the French F. But after him, all the British and French mapmakers scrupulously write "Wanga." British residents in the country pronounce it with an English "w," thinking perhaps that the mapmakers are better informed than the indigenous inhabitants. This is just one example of the innumerable mistakes made with place names. What is worse is that the experts are not prepared to listen to criticisms.

However, the German did not accept this.

"Then," said the Frenchman, "let us rely on the judgment of Solomon. When the tide is in, and Vanga is surrounded by water, it will be British. When the tide is out, it will be German."

This proposal was not, however, accepted, and it was decided that River Umba, which enters the sea half an hour's walk south from the town, would be the boundary between the two spheres of interest. Vanga then belongs to the British, or to the Sultan of Zanzibar, who is under British protection. His representative there is the governor, an old Baluchi soldier, who cannot be called educated, as he does not know how to read, but who seems honest.

The town is built on a stretch of ground rather higher than the lagoons which surround it. At the season of very high tides, it is surrounded by water on all sides, and any Europeans who wanted to come there to spend their salaries would find it quite unattractive. It contains at the present time perhaps 2,000–3,000 inhabitants, namely Arabs, Swahilis, Africans, some free but many more slaves, with an Indian who is in charge of the customs office, and some Hindu traders. Small East African boats come into the harbor often. Some years ago a wall of stone, with a quadrangular shape, was built to defend the town against raids by the notorious Mbaruku, the terror of all the coastal area.

We camped in the shelter of coconut trees, at a cool, dry place where the wind from the sea played gently around us. We stayed there for two days.

Such as it is, with its unsatisfactory harbor and its malaria, Vanga has a certain relative importance. First of all, it is, as we have said, the town which marks the southernmost point of British territory, and an agent of the Imperial British East African Company lives opposite it, at Chuyu. Then, between Mombasa and Tanga, it is the coastal town which has most local boat traffic, indigenous traders, and people from the hinterland—Digo, Segeju, Pare, Taita, and Kamba—each coming with his products, his needs, his style of clothing, and his own facial appearance.

Naturally, our arrival, which was, as always announced by our men giving a volley of rifle shots, created some excitement in the place, and we were soon surrounded by a crowd of curious well-wishers, who helped us to set up camp: men, women, goats, hens, sheep, and children.

Among them, we immediately picked out a big fellow, who had a very unusual air, very definitely a rural African, and, to be fair, with something likeable about him. He came from Kamba country, up north, a long way in from the coast. From the point of view of public order, he was a vagabond. By profession, he was a magician. His dress was a real warehouse of rags, bits of skins, gourds, horns, claws, shells, bit of wood, and anthropological curiosities of every kind; his stature, his manner, his head, and his rig-out,

CHAPTER 7: AT VANGA

all gave him the respect of the local people. From childhood onwards, he has been a wanderer in the African world, and he can speak in detail about all the villages and encampments spread out between Mount Kenya and Kilimanjaro, and from Vanga to Kavirondo. Straightaway, he told us about a route for crossing from Vanga to Taita and from there to Taveta, where we had been planning to go, across the great desert plateau, which has already been mentioned. This route has not been explored; in any case, we would not take it. But with regard to the man who had come to speak to us, I thought perhaps we could take him as a guide, for we really needed one.

While I was thinking this over, he took me aside, led me behind my tent, and with a very charming manner said, "Listen, I see that you are my friend and I am yours. You are a magician for the whites. I am a magician for the blacks: we must cooperate."

"Well," I said, "let us do so."

"Often people ask me for some medicine for this or that. You understand."

"Yes, to cure people."

"Oh, no. To kill somebody."

"Oh!"

"Yes. And I should be very happy and very grateful—if you could be so kind—if you can give me some medicine which kills people quietly, without leaving any trace, and which is always effective."

This extraordinary request astonished and angered me. I felt it my duty to quickly give my "colleague" some sound moral teaching. But I had hardly begun when he slipped away. What a lot of strange professions there are in the world.

That evening, there was a rather different situation. A young man, who looked decent and straightforward came to find me.

"I am," he said, "from Pare," a mountainous country lying on our route. "I am a son of Chief Kimbute, and I would be happy if you would let me join your caravan so that I can get home. If I went by myself, I would be captured on the way; with you, I have nothing to fear."

"That is all right by me. Are you tired of Vanga?"

"Things have gone wrong."

"How, exactly?"

"Bohero, Mbaruku's man, came to us in Pare. He said to my father, 'Give me some cattle as a present for our great man, Mbaruku, and an ivory tusk. I shall give them to him as coming from you and he will send you enough cloth to fill a house.' So my father gave him the cattle and the ivory, and five men to carry the cloth. At Gasi, Mbaruku said, 'That is fine. Would you like to make a trip in a boat?' I was ill, but my mates said yes, so they set off, but did not come back."

"Where did they go?"

"I was told they had gone to Pemba, which is an island, on this side. Well, I came here and an Arab comes and wants to send me to walk about Pemba, but I want to go home to Pare."

What touching innocence and what a lucky escape! If we had not met, he also would have been sent to the unknown island where his friends had been taken by trickery and sold. Pemba is the graveyard of slaves. So we agreed that this decent country boy would stay in our camp until we left, and then would follow our caravan.

This leads me to the subject of the caravan, of which I have really said nothing. But this is not because our Mombasa recruits let the days pass without causing any problems. Just when we got started, a not very intelligent person, born at Makka (Mecca), declared, puffing and blowing, that he could not carry his load, and had to be discharged. Then there was a runaway slave, whose master caught up with him. Again, there was a porter, who had run up heavy debts, who had the misfortune to meet his creditor on the way, and so we had to leave him behind. Every day, a friendly chat turned into a quarrel, and the quarrel turned into a fight. Often, in the villages, there were cases of noisy and offensive drunkenness, accompanied by disturbances of the peace at night, boisterous buffoonery, insults, breaking of bowls, and noses pushed out of shape. Finally, on the march or in the camp, there are things said that must be hushed, things which would make gorillas or even journalists blush.

But last night, it was something rather different. All that unattractive crowd of Muslims recruited at Mombasa—our Bagamoyo men were comparatively reasonable—had decided to put us decisively to the test by going on strike, for strikes take place in Africa too. One morning, when I was distributing *posho*, the money for buying a day's food, the first porter called to collect his share. One-eyed Hamisi was planning to refuse it and to ask for double the amount. I knew what was going to happen through overheard conversations and warnings given me by "someone in the know," a member, so to say, of my secret police.

The time came for the call to be made.

"One-eyed Hamisi!"

"Present."

"Here is your food money."

Hamisi who had drunk rather too much with a view to getting more energy, took his money with a contemptuous air and threw it away across a group of coconut trees. "Only that? Then go and look for porters where you can find them."

There was a moment of silence among the porters, the silence in which one can hear a pin drop. Just as Hamisi was feeling very pleased with himself for having produced his little speech, he was thrown into confusion by a couple of vigorous slaps in the face—it seemed to me a case for obeying the biblical injunction, "Be angry and sin not." Before he could come to his senses, we were standing before the worthy governor, with the whole group of porters, who shouted, "We shall all go, we shall all go." I had not had the time to say what had happened. When the old Baluchi made a sign, his soldiers rushed for their weapons and, three minutes later all the porters found themselves in prison. Ah, dear European readers, if you find legal proceedings are slow, let me recommend the governor of Vanga for you.

But, frankly, I was the man most embarrassed by this display of energy; for if they all leave us, how could we replace them here, where there are no porters available? Mgr. de Courmont and Father Auguste were still at the camp. As there was nobody to give me advice, I tried to compose one of those speeches termed "*Conciones*," which, it seems, the generals of the classical world used to enjoy composing when faced by a mutiny of their troops. Now that I am writing the story of my adventures, I have quite forgotten the exact text of my impromptu discourse, but I do remember vaguely that, having poured out bitter reproaches on poor Hamisi who had been rather stupid, I pretended to believe that the real conspirators were more or less innocent. I claimed to have the power to keep them in fetters for the rest of their days, and to let them die on the damp straw of their unlit dungeons, but, having received a magnificent sheep from the governor, I would not deprive all of them from eating it because of one man's fault. That sheep was very influential!

Little words with individuals, friendly tellings off, jovial poking of the tummies of some leaders—these all helped to win over my rebellious listeners. There was Ali, a former sailor, who claimed to be a French citizen through having passed a fortnight at Mayotte. We had found him, completely destitute, on our way. He now swore that he was ready to follow us to the heights of heaven or the depths of hell, and everybody swore the same. But Hamisi had to pass, as was only right, a day in prison, so true it is that history repeats itself everywhere, and that, for someone who is a bit stupid, trying his hand at revolution is dangerous.

However, we did not enjoy a long peace. In the evening of this exciting day, there was, just when everyone in the camp was going to sleep and the campfires were going out, another uproar. We got up hastily and came out of the tents. This time, it was the governor in person coming to us, with all his soldiers, and a large crowd, shouting at the top of their voices. "Are they men?" shouted one voice, "They are dirty cows. I am tied up by cows! Ah! *Sakerapoute!*" And Ali, for it was our great Ali, with his hands tied behind his back, fell at our feet, crying, as though he were possessed by the devil. "A French citizen. *Sakerapoute! Sakerapoute!*" I said,

"What are you saying, Ali? Come on, calm down."

"Oh, I express my feelings in French, just as at Mayotte. *Sakerapoute!* That is what the governor said when it happened to him."

At this, the governor, that is to say of Vanga, not Mayotte, added that the aforementioned Ali is guilty of an offense, because he was found in town in a state of evident intoxication.

"But," I said, "you should have put him in prison."

"That was done."

"Well, what happened?"

"A quarter of an hour after he had been put in prison, he removed the prison door and came and banged it against my door."

The old Baluchi was extremely annoyed by this episode, which surely throws some light on what the Bible tells us about Samson. Life is certainly not all cakes and ale, surely, when one is where the action is, and has the moral responsibility for other people. Finally, a private house was found, safer than the official jail. Ali had to spend the night there, and, in the morning, when everything had settled down, we took leave of this conscientious governor and of his dangerous town.

Chapter 8: The First Mountains on Our Route

The Course of the Umba. Another Kind of Landscape. Bwiti. Segeju and Taita. Up and Down the Mountain. The African Savannah. At Daluni. An Elaborate Funeral.

Scarcely two kilometers from Vanga, the river Umba runs flanked by high banks on either side, the result of the great quantity of sand and silt which the river has brought down. When we were there, there was not much water, but in the rainy season the river drains water from a very large valley on both its right and its left and overflows its banks, which therefore become, especially near the estuary, very fertile stretches of ground that the local people are very careful to cultivate.

We had thought that, in travelling from Vanga to Pare, we would simply have to follow the unexplored course of the river, which would have had the advantage of providing us every day with water and food, without any serious detours. But do not be too ready to accept geographical guesswork, or maps, or scientific theorizing. We discovered that after the village of Gonja, inhabited by the Digo, both sides of the Umba are completely uninhabited, the Maasai having developed a regular habit of plundering villages that had tried to settle there.

Moreover, on each side of the river, the strip of ground that can be cultivated is quite narrow. If we followed the line of the river, we would then have been obliged to make a path through the forest, and to live on clean water, which would not have satisfied either ourselves or our men. And so, we took a southwestern route to reach the foothills of the Sambara Mountains, and pass beside them as far as Pare. Our caravan moved on slowly, and we took three days to reach the first foothills at Bwiti. Before that we had passed through Dooga and Mikonde, going through a dry land, not very fertile, with occasional brackish streams, with some hills, with great, uninhabited woodlands with stunted trees, which just about managed to grow in red soil. Here and there, a thick gneiss and shale came to the surface.

There was a lot of brushwood, thorn bushes, acacias, euphorbias, wild vines, and, sometimes, some rather beautiful Egyptian palm trees. In the valleys, where there was water, big trees were growing, as well as creepers and wild date trees. We managed to find villages where we could encamp and get what we needed to live. These were Digo villages, built here on high ground, surrounded by stockades, made of solid pieces of wood. Generally, a sycamore or tamarind tree grows near the village, providing a friendly shade for villagers who wanted to sleep, or to do this or that. In these lands of sunshine, the house is really only a place for sleeping at night, and perhaps that is why it is so simply constructed. What good would be these immovable houses of stone when there is so little to keep there, when there is no winter, and the open air is so pleasant.

For our part, we had made a final and unpleasant march across a forest devoid of living creatures—except for two magnificent herds of antelopes. As for the antelopes, we had chased them unsuccessfully, and in the chase, I lost a straw skullcap which I had had for seven years. We felt really happy when suddenly we saw a valley where absolutely everything was green. Here there was plenty of water, fresh, clean, and flowing; there was also an absolute forest of coconut palms, some rice, flowers which were bursting into bud, insects which buzzed, frogs which croaked, and, there, on our way, a plant which grew in abundance and attracted our attention. It was called Job's Tear (*coix lacrima*), an unusual plant of the grass family. Previously, I had only seen the seeds, a bright grey in color, threaded into rosaries or necklaces.

Facing us there was a mountain, whose higher slopes were occupied by the Taita people, and whose lower slopes by the Segeju. We camped in the middle of a Segeju village. We had reached Bwiti. These Segeju are a tribe scattered in several different areas. Their original home is said to be on the banks of the River Tana, but they were driven from there by the Galla. They then established small communities at various points on the coast, to the north of Lamu, to the south of Gasi, and, particularly, round about Tanga in the area where we were. They are usually farmers or traders, and almost all profess Islam, but are rather selective in what they choose to practice. Their names, their house, their way of dressing, and their customs have much in common with those of the Swahili and lack anything that is particularly interesting. They received us in a friendly fashion, but insisted that we speak well of them to the German authorities at Tanga, of whom they have a healthy fear. They have made Bwiti into a trading center with a market where the local Africans come every so often to sell what they have grown and buy goods from the coast. It is the last place inland where money is useful.

The Taita who have settled here did so as refugees from raids and warfare in their homeland, and they have chosen the crevices of the

CHAPTER 8: THE FIRST MOUNTAINS ON OUR ROUTE

mountain to make their nests. Yes, nests, for that is what they are, these little round huts, ill-balanced and wretched, which one can see on the upper reaches of the mountain. Their owners, however, live reasonably happy lives, free, if a bit hard. They have goats, sheep, cattle, beans, maize, and bananas, and they are free from the innumerable sets of commercial regulations, taxes, and service charges, as well as from the paternalism of the state and dynamite explosions.

That evening, we held a council to plan our advance. Daluni, where we had to go the following day, lies just behind the mountain which pushes into the plane, as an enormous buttress of Sambara country. Should we take the direct way over this rampart, or would it be better to go round it? At first, most of the porters wanted to go round it, but when they saw we were determined to follow the goat path which ran upwards before us, they gradually decided to go with us. We had left them perfectly free to choose, and that, no doubt, made them show how brave they were.

The next morning, everything was ready for our climb. Our first step was to cross the little stream, which flowed through the valley, bubbling merrily in the shadow of the tall sycamore fig trees, and striking its bright water against the rocks through which it has hollowed its way. We followed it for a long way and then left it to struggle up the steep slopes which we, the missionaries, managed to scale without too much trouble, while our porters, with loads of from thirty to thirty-five kilograms, found it a severe trial. But they were not downhearted. Was it to show themselves brave men, was it to play games with themselves, and was it simply to forget their tiredness? At any rate, they had the mountain echoing to shouts, jeers, laughter, and songs, which gave an enormous thrill to the women who at that moment were gathering beans, and the children who were looking after the goats. However, the sun, which in the early mornings in Europe brings refreshing light and warmth, can soon become oppressive here. More and more sweat poured down the ebony skins of our men, they were gasping for breath, and finally even the sturdiest fell silent.

But providence is rich in kindness. Just at the right moment, in a really green section of the mountainside, where moss and ferns are mingled with banana trees and thorns, lo and behold, a granite basin into which flows a stream of water, so clean, so fresh, so crystal-clear, that one would not dream of exchanging it for the same quantity of the finest Medoc wine, made by the most modern scientific techniques.

On Bwiti Mountain, a tree covered with creepers

Courage! We had reached the plateau. The same path which had led us along treeless slopes passed now through a magnificently rich forest, with superb creepers and trees, whose towering straightness recalled ships with tall masts. Marching in this exuberant forest, with its shade, its glimpses of landscapes, on this turf and among these flowers, was marvelously relaxing. Unhappily, every ascent is followed by a descent. The caravan arrives down at Daluni, having stumbled over the roots which on the far side of the mountain slowed down our march, and having banged our toes against sharp-edged rocks, sometimes running, sometimes gasping, sometimes groaning. But we were in reasonably good form, and proud of what we had done.

But I must tell you about the range of views which are available up there; it has a fierce greatness which is simply magnificent. On the plateau, the soil is humid, the air cool, and the trees and plants are superb. You can take it as an observation post, which spreads out like an enormous promontory, dominating everything around. Behind you, to the south and the west, there is the huge cluster of the Sambara Mountains; on your right, there is the shady valley of Bwiti where we passed; on your left, the valley of Daluni, which is parallel, and where we had to go down; beyond that and facing you, in fact everywhere else, and as far as the eye can reach under this cloudless sky on this land without mists, down there is an immense forest which has grown up in the African savannah. In color, this forest is of an unchanging grey, with occasional red patches and some isolated peaks thrown here and there, as it were to serve as landmarks to the elephants who roam in this lonely wilderness. Only the River Umba shows its silent course, by means of a greenish line without the smoke of any village, with no sign of growing crops, and where the waters are only of use to the wild animals who come by night from the depths of the savannah to slake their thirst.

In Europe, such a great stretch of country would always be linked to some historical memory, to some indicator of times past; there would be traditions, and legends, and, parallel to its position in space, it would provide a perspective on the past. Here, there is nothing like that, everything is in the same order of things, everything is new, and everything has lasted forever. Men have certainly passed here, but they have left nothing—no palaces, no ruins, no columns, and no tombs. There is scarcely even a straight path which, as the seasons change, shifts or disappears; there are villages which, from time to time, need to be rebuilt. There are fields carved out of the forest and which will be retaken by the forest that is Africa. Man is present there as a ship is present on an ocean, or a bird in the air. But thinking about life like that has a certain greatness, reminding us of our original poverty. Let us not be too attached to the earth; our stay on it is so short, we achieve so little on it and we leave it such sad remains of ourselves.

At Daluni, we came back to the valley where there was a young and magnificent forest of coconut palms. Under the palm trees, there were signs of an encampment, and we chose the site for our own tents. There were still fires under the ashes of the deserted hearths; in the ramshackle huts, the lice were waiting for new guests; we had evidently arrived at exactly the right moment.

Incidentally, I would like to make a point. It is often said that a coconut palm needs to be near the sea in order to develop properly. Perhaps; but here, we are already three days' march from the shore, and these trees are really splendid, and bring a full yield. This is the case also on the shores of Lake Tanganyika. It would seem then that the coconut palm, if planted in light cool soil, can live and flourish far from the sea; what it needs more than anything is water and watery mist.

This valley is inhabited by a small number of Digo, occupying five or six villages. Their reputation is not good, and they live up to it. They are extremely superstitious, inhospitable, exacting, and not very bright. They would seem, however, to take farming seriously. The coconut palms are really beautiful, and beside them there are big fields of sugar cane. The local people know how to extract from them by pounding the canes, the precious juice which provides Europeans with rum and sugar, and these Africans with *pombé* and syrup. Higher up on the grounds which get less water, guinea corn, maize, cassava, sweet potatoes, and various kinds of beans are all cultivated. Moreover, if the yield is not as good as one expects, this is not through lack of amulets; they are all over the place.

To give an example: at the foot of a large hollow tree there is a little hut intended for a Mzimu, the wandering ghost of some ancestor; it comes there to rest and, so that it will settle down there, an offering is made of an ear of maize, some grains of rice, and a libation of guinea corn beer. Or, to give another example, there is at a crossroads where two or three paths meet some twisted straw fixed with stakes and containing a pinch of grain to feed suffering spirits. Elsewhere, there can be a little calabash, full of palm wine, hanging from a tree trunk, intended for the mysterious guardian spirit of the coconut plantation so that through ill will he does not let the juice dry up. In the fields, there may be a piece of forked wood, decorated with odd-looking objects, in order to frighten, not the birds, but rather prowling thieves. At the beginning of a path leading to a plantation, there may be a coconut palm leaf set across the path on two stakes, with shells and pieces of carved wood, to warn that if one went down the path, one would certainly suffer terrible illnesses, or be eaten by crocodiles, or bitten by snakes.

I said above that we came to Daluni country at the right time; I should explain that we got there for a funeral. That very day, in fact, the last rites were performed for an old minor chief, who did not seem to be unduly regretted, but who, having had a certain dignity in his life on this earth, had to be sent to the land of the dead with a certain amount of ceremony. Consequently, the neighboring chief, who had to conduct the rituals, came to ask us for guns, gunpowder, and linen, all of which, he said, would make the funeral more prestigious and please the spirit of the dead man. We gave him what he asked

CHAPTER 8: THE FIRST MOUNTAINS ON OUR ROUTE 51

for, a courtesy which, we trusted, would be repaid to us. Soon, the procession was on its way, with the corpse wrapped up in a variety of cloths, tom-toms were being played in the fields, the women trilled toward heaven piercing cries which were artistically ordered, with regular intervals, and guns were fired one after the other. So the procession moved toward the tomb where the petty chief would take his rest. Our porters, always ready to make fun of the "bushmen"—for it is obvious that only they themselves can be considered "civilized"—would have been very happy to go and join in the ceremony, dancing their version of a saraband, but we strictly forbade it.

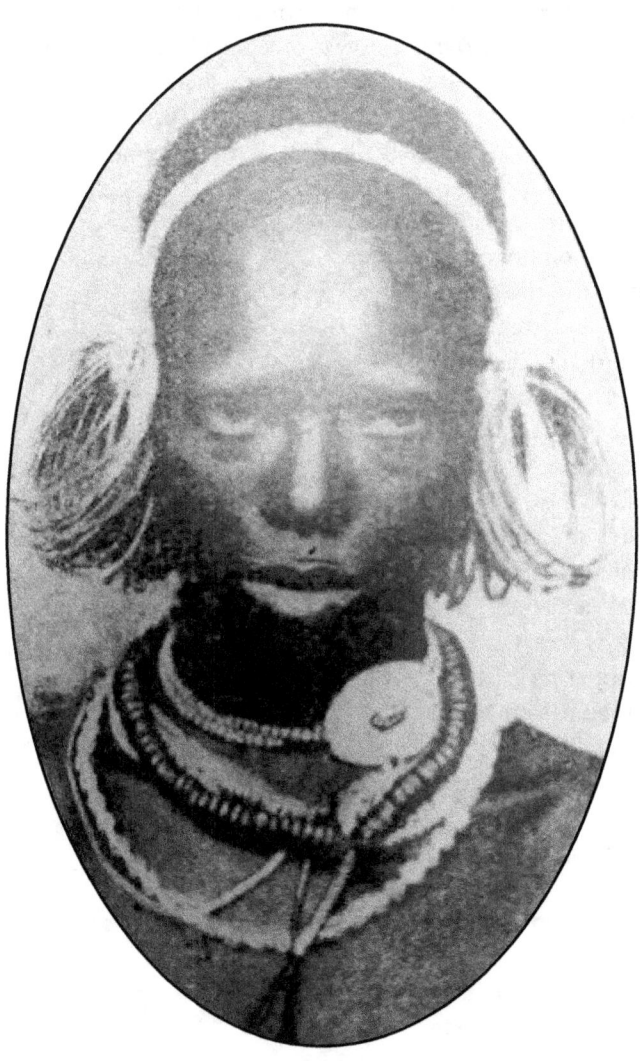

But we could not escape the final act. While the men, having filled in the grave, returned to the village, a large group of old women, wrinkled, with parchment-like skins, altogether hideous, skinny as witches, came to install themselves at a point where three paths met, in front of our camp though a certain distance away. From there they gave us a melodrama which even Shakespeare could not have better directed. They came to wash their own linen and that of the dead man. Custom demands that on such an occasion their skins are practically the only covering they wear; but, I hasten to add, given their distance from us and their age, nobody would feel offended by their state of dress. Several of them carried earthenware bowls into which they uttered the most frightful howls, others had various kinds of musical instruments. The leader was an old shrew, who held a basket full of cockleshells and directed the cries, the dancing, and their procession. Then they reached the crossroads where the last act of the ceremony must take place.

The old mistress of ceremonies gave orders, her long, hag-like arm pointing to the mountain, her bony fingers spread out and trembling, her face turned radiant, her swollen eyes staring, her harsh voice uttering strange, wave-like sounds, which are answered by the cries and the gestures of her women companions.

What are they saying? Ah, it is a very special *Libera*.[1] In various expressions, sometimes so offensive and laughable that the women themselves laugh at them, they exhort the Mzimu, that is, the shade of the dead man, to stay where he is, at the foot of his tree, and never to come and make a nuisance of himself to them as they continue to

---

1. Reference to a Catholic prayer for the dead.

live the life which he has left. They will give him maize and rice, some stalks of sugar cane, a little of the palm wine of which he was so fond.

If he wants to keep wandering about, he can go to the mountains, he can amuse himself in the wilderness, he can play around the baobabs in the forest, he can go to sleep night or day in the woodlands, but let him not disturb the men, the women, and the little children of the village. His place has been taken.

These farewell exhortations went on a long time. One can guess that in this strange monologue regularly interrupted by a kind of varying refrain, repeated by the choir of women present, place was found for delicate allusions and biting witticisms directed at the memory of the old chief who was "a kindly father and a devoted husband."

But, at the end, the mistress of ceremonies, summoning all her strength, launched a final broadside of shrill cries, which was answered by terrifying howls into the earthenware bowls. She then threw the white cockleshells from her basket, all the bowls were smashed, and the group of women dispersed, each to her own home. A very serious duty has been faithfully carried out.

Chapter 9: Travelling Through the Desert

DOCTOR AND DENTIST. AMONG THE HIGHWAY ROBBERS.
THE NIGHT MARCH. MIDDAY, ON AN IRON ROAD.
THE GURUVA DESERT.

We stayed two days at Daluni, mainly to get provisions and calabashes—calabashes for carrying water for we have before us the crossing of a fearful desert. Both provisions and calabashes were not easily obtained among these people, who were unhelpful, lacking in politeness, and inclined to begging. It was the best-tempered of our porters who felt it his duty to make respectful remonstrations to me.

"How is it," he said to me, "that these primitives do not want to sell us anything, but when they come to show us their illnesses, you cure them without asking any payment? It is really silly."

Certainly, in Digo country, free medicine was a great success. The sick, that is, those who were really sick, or who had been, or were afraid of falling sick, came in crowds to find us, and had a touching faith in the contents of our little medicine bottles. I take the example of one old leper who brought his wife to see me. She was blind. The old man told me, "She has been blind for eight years. You must give her back her sight." I was modest enough to confess that I could not do this, but I was not believed. I then said that I had left at Zanzibar the medicine he wanted. The poor fellow showed me a small bottle of carbolic acid, "Is this bottle only for monkeys?" Further arguments were useless, so I gave the old lady a little piece of cotton which I had dipped, a trifle mysteriously, in clean water, and I gave her husband three pills made up of dampened biscuit. I declared that if they were not both cured in a week's time, they probably never would be cured. Poor simple people! At any rate they will have a week of hope in their lives.

But I could not always satisfy my patients like that. A child came up to me; without saying anything, he opened his little round mouth before me, shut one eye, pulled a wry face and pointed with his tongue to a wobbly tooth. This was a less difficult case than the one I mentioned previously,

CHAPTER 9: TRAVELLING THROUGH THE DESERT

and I squeezed the tooth between my thumb and my index finger. Immediately, the news of this marvel spread, and in less than half an hour, it seemed as though every jaw in the place had been shown to me. Most of these good people had no complaints about their two rows of teeth, but all the same asked me to take out teeth that might give trouble in future. Ah! What a fine country for dentists.

But, lo and behold, at the end, there came a patient of whom I had never dared to think: it was our marvelous old cook, Selemani, in person. He declared that for about fifty years, he had had a tooth which, from time to time, pained him, and as the occasion presented itself, he had decided that this was the day to say good-bye to it. In support of his claim, he opened his really frightful mouth; I shrank back, horrified. He stepped forward. Good Lord! Did he want to take a bite out of me?

Finding that he had no such intentions, I stood and looked carefully down into this dental museum. There was just about everything there: there was an extraordinary tongue, not unlike the sole of a gendarme's shoe, wriggling about under a deformed palate; there were also huge molars, yellow, white, red, green, pointing in all directions, like carved stumps of old wood. Other teeth, whose shapes did not seem to fit into dental anatomy, were growing here and there. Then there were big gaps. Finally, all alone in its corner, was the tooth marked down for removal.

In a moment, swift as lighting, my mind went back to the far-off days when, as

Man under an acacia tree in the Guruva desert.

an adventurous little boy, I loved going to the fairs in lower Normandy and stopping before those splendid coaches, where a big man with a big helmet which had a big plume, spoke to the crowd which had gathered, with great eloquence. Inspired by an irresistible passion to put himself at the service of suffering humanity, he had roamed the world, pulling decayed teeth. And I seemed to see again that man plunging his hand into a large basket and drawing out a lot of molars, incisors, and canine teeth, proof that what he was saying was true: "Here is a tooth that belonged to Queen Victoria. This one belonged to the Sultan of Turkey. And this other one, to whom do you think it belonged? You will never guess. It is quite beyond you. It is a fossilized tooth that I found in Noah's jaw." And this big man added, shaking golden Louis coins in his fists (I now think they were very recently coined centimes and sous), "Do not think I have come here just to get money. Ladies and gentlemen, I am a philanthropist. I do good for the sake of goodness. And now, keep your sous, but give me your jaws."

While the musicians played their drums and trombones on the top of the coach, an ordinary little man climbed up, with his blue blouse stretched over a black cardigan, and his round hat resting on his stomach, with a rather unusually shaped head, and a very naive look about him. The fairground dentist made him sit down, and then made him open his mouth as wide as possible, before a very impressed audience. "Ladies and gentlemen, do you see this opening? There is a case of infection—it is just like the stable of Augias, into which Hercules, in order to clean it up, had to channel the Mississippi."

What marvels there were at that time in the country fairs and what eloquent dentists there were! For my part, at that age, I would never have dared to have the ambition to share one day in that man's glory. And yet, here I had before me a crowd similar to that which he had brought together, and Selemani, with his yawning mouth, took the part of the little man with his blue blouse. But Selemani put on such a grotesque face that Mgr. de Courmont slipped back into his tent, so as not to upset the situation by untimely laughter. Fr. Auguste, less inhibited, burst out into a prolonged gale of merriment. The porters, standing around in a circle, could not conceal the signs of gentle amusement; the people from the neighboring villages, sitting in groups under the big tamarind tree which provided us with its shade, joined in the general roars of laughter.

Finally, before the crowd, so numerous and so jolly, I solemnly rolled up my sleeves, I took a pair of pincers for dealing with insects, I pushed them into his mouth, I pulled them out, and . . . Selemani took a frightening tumble on to the ground! But I had the tooth. With the vigor of a boy, Selemani got up, seized the tooth, tied it tightly in a piece of old linen, and spitting here and there on the feet of the audience, ran to his kitchen where there was an unmistakable smell of burning. Mgr. de Courmont provided us

CHAPTER 9: TRAVELLING THROUGH THE DESERT

with a final conclusion: "Let us hope that, in this evening's goat's leg, we do not find that old molar put in as a substitute for garlic."

When we left Daluni, we first of all crossed the little river that is also called Daluni, and then, half an hour later, we crossed the Mbambara; the two rivers join and flow toward the Umba, but with the African sun and this kind of soil, they only get there during the rainy season.

This was the time for making ready for our next step. On our left, there were high mountains, piled up one upon another. On our right, a waterless plain, and along the arid path we followed, stunted trees scattered here and there, yellowish, rather scarce grass, and in places strange groves created by an incredible entanglement of creepers, euphorbias, and bushes of every kind, whose leaves have been replaced by thorns. One of these plants characterizes the group as a whole; it is a passionflower (*Adenia globosa, Engler*), whose round, tuberous, and enormous foot lies in the soil like a huge pumpkin—it is a meter in diameter—and gives birth to several creepers whose color is a bright green, like holly. These creepers sometimes cover a great deal of ground on which they creep. They twist and they climb up, they come down, they entwine with each other, forming by themselves a jungle so thick that even a bird would have difficulty in entering it. At the top of these creepers, there is an abundance of thorns, long and straight. At the base of each creeper there are two round leaves, but so small, so little developed, that the eye can hardly detect them. The flowers are white and not particularly noticeable; the fruit is of the size of a red currant. The soil which produces such an ugly crop is sandy and stony, resting on rocks which are very coarse-grained and always grey in color. Sometimes there are big red stretches of open ground, where iron oxide is present.

Toward eleven o'clock, we reached a little stream, where big sycamore trees provided shade, and where I killed some green pigeons to provide our dinner. The place was called Kikumbi, which is pass (of the Maasai). The river bed was dry, and full of enormous stones; but we were told that if we went up the bed toward the source, we would find water, which proved to be true. Up in the Mshiwi Mountain, from which the stream flows down, there were Taita, who had settled there to rob small caravans, and who could sell us provisions. So we fired a few shots to inform these helpful bandits that we were down there and to invite them to drop in on us, but they did not oblige. Finally, five or six porters set off into these remote gorges, and the rest of the caravan settled down to take a short nap, after which we would leave in the evening for a night march.

And so we spent the afternoon, not knowing what had happened to the men who had gone to see the Taita. Could it be that the mountain people had seized them, kept them prisoner, and even eaten them? It was possible, since this is their line of business. And so we were preparing to make an armed reconnaissance, when suddenly we heard shouts and songs from the stream bed. Our explorers had returned, loaded with provisions, grain, honey, chickens, pumpkins, and calabashes. The Taita had been convinced, when they heard our rifle shots that a well-armed expedition was coming to avenge the Arabs whom they had recently robbed. They had fled, shutting up the herds of goats, sheep, and cows, whom they kept on the mountains. Our men had spent their time calling on them to come back.

At six o'clock in the evening, we set out. In front of us, the sun disappeared behind a mountain which we would have to go around. Its red globe, like some huge eye, threw us a last glance over the mountain top, then suddenly disappeared, leaving ill-shaped shadows to take its place, till the moon rose to take its place in the sky to guide us in our adventurous march. Mwalimu, our guide, was very careful to give us his advice.

> Waungwana, my brothers, hear well. We are going to have a horrible night. But it is necessary, so that we have a much shorter march tomorrow and can cross the big Guruva Desert. Listen to me then, Tumbo-Rumbo. The big Guruva Desert. Let us go in single file, one after the other, calmly, without saying anything, without any noise, without sneezing or spitting. If anybody really needs to stop, he should say, 'I really must stop.' Then everyone will stop. And when he can start again, everybody will start again. For it would be a pity if he was gobbled up by a lion. Who would take over his load? Who would claim it? No noise, no sneezing, no spitting. For if the buffaloes hear us, they will say, 'Who is it passing there?' And they will come and throw themselves on us, and rip us open. They will do it quietly. The same with the rhinos, with their horns. Ah! I would have fun seeing you, Tumbo-Rumbo, split in two by a rhinoceros' horn, you complete clown! Right, Waungwana, my brothers, it is understood. Single file, everyone calm, no noise, no coughing, no sneezing, no speaking, no whistling, and no spitting!"

After this brilliant piece of impromptu oratory, the caravan set off in perfect order. Unfortunately, after some twenty paces, a porter got caught by a root and fell backwards with his load on his neighbor, who in turn fell backwards on a third porter, as if it were a game of skittles; there was laughter and shouting to make the whole place echo. The guide got angry, repeated his harangue, and order was reestablished, only to be troubled from time to time, when, for example, a man fell asleep when marching and collapsed under his load.

It was a thrilling march, however, on such a night, across that forest, and in that silence. By our feet, we could scarcely see the path, the sky above us was lit by countless stars, and the clouds which moved in front of the moon gave us at one moment shadow, at another, light. The trees seemed to turn into fantastic shapes, our glances around told us of mysterious and unknown depths, around us there was everywhere the varied croakings and hummings of insects, gentle, sharp, staccato, and monotonous; it was a real concert.

Sometimes we heard the cry of the hyena, something like a long giggle, coming to us from far away. There was also, nearer and more sinister, a dull sound, indistinct, something like a growl, a drawing of breath, and then a trampling down of grass, which made us suspect the presence of some big beast of the forest. And the silent caravan glided patiently on its way, naked feet treading the narrow path, like a long procession of shadows.

Then the mind was free to reflect, and the soul turned of its own accord toward him who made all these things. He who from the beginning right till today has been with them as they developed through the centuries, and who is still protecting them through his fatherly providence.

The universe never sleeps. While in his humble yet supremely confident liberty the missionary advances toward the heart of Africa along paths lit by the moon, the grass is absorbing the night air and the tree is slowly growing, insects chirp, birds rest, the wild beasts look for food, and the African villagers dance to the sound of drums.

Elsewhere in the world, where there are big cities and prosperous countrysides, one man sleeps and another works, the sick man yearns for morning, the workman is at his task, the soldier is on guard, the financier is occupied with his accounts, and while the monk prays, the unbeliever blasphemes.

At that very moment, when I was planting my feet on the path in the silence of the night, nameless horrors were taking place. One man enjoys a life of self-indulgence, another ties round a nail the rope with which his hopelessness leads him to hang himself; a baby is born, and an old man dies. In one

Euphorbia in Guruva desert

place, all is flattery, in another a conspiracy is being planned; here everybody dances, there a man cuts his throat.

What do I really know and who can give us the grand total of all that passes on the earth at one particular moment, while the moon shines on one side of it and the sun on the other? When time comes to an end, God will do the arithmetic of these thoughts and words and actions. What matters is that our account should be in the black, not the red.

Near midnight, we got to a big clearing, where we halted. Immediately, fires were lit all round, everyone found himself a makeshift bed, and, within a quarter of an hour, impressive snoring was already evidence of a determination to sleep. At three o'clock in the morning, Mgr. de Courmont was already up; every day, he said mass on his portable altar. When he had finished, the francolins were already clucking in the long grass, the porters were stretching themselves, and Selemani produced a black potion which he claimed to be for internal consumption; it was what he regarded as coffee. We drank the clearer part of this beverage, and the sun had not yet risen behind us, when we started the march.

The coolness of the morning did not last long. There was no dew on the leaves. It would be a hard day. Moreover, the further we went, the gloomier became the landscape. On our right, there was always the same chain of mountains: but here it rose up like a wall, without anything which would introduce some variety into its desolate monotony. The plain had a very similar appearance. Everywhere sand which had been carried down from the mountains was mixed with iron ore. This was a painful path to walk on, passing through the beds of dried streams, where the water had passed as though they were canals, and we got quickly tired of gazing on these barren wastes, covered with rust, and paved with iron. There were some thin tufts of grass growing here and there. Some acacias, which could serve as parasols against the sun grew, each on its own in the desert, their heads almost green. Sometimes treelike euphorbias, which have adapted to such a wilderness, were also growing there.

A rather special range of flowers has managed to adapt to this hideous land, but the scorched, shriveled leaves, whose very appearance was unpleasant, told us enough about their sufferings. We did not see any animal running about in these plains, we did not hear any bird beating its wings, no insects enlivened this gloomy landscape with their humming, and even the breeze fell silent.

As the day went on, the sun blazed more fiercely, the overheated track burned the soles of our feet, our wearied gaze could only distinguish before it a strange shimmering of colors, the redness of the soil, the greyness of the

CHAPTER 9: TRAVELLING THROUGH THE DESERT

bush, and there, up above, the sky, like an enormous silver shield, seemed to reflect the merciless rays of the flaming sun.

The caravan was no longer marching in a straight line but consisted of individuals and little clusters of men. It advanced downheartedly, slowly, without a word spoken. Only, from time to time, a porter at the end of his strength threw down his load and fell upon it. The poor fellow had found the shade of an acacia, and he hoped that it would rest lightly on him, just as a grave weighs lightly on the one buried there. Alas! The shade of the acacia is really too light to give protection from the sun. But anyhow, it was an excuse to get back one's breath, and we have taken this excuse ourselves sometimes.

Gradually, the soil seemed to become more hospitable to the vegetation which grows on it, and toward midday we had pointed out to us what seemed to be a green line on the horizon.

It is Kitivo and its river, where we had been told we ought to camp; now was the time for courage. The bravest of the porters began to move quickly, and, when they had got there and quenched their thirst, we sent them back with the calabashes full of water to revive their exhausted comrades. By evening, everybody had made it to the camp, we had crossed the Guruva Desert.

Chapter 10: The Valley of the Umba

The Sources of the Umba and its Course. The Valley, its Appearance, and its Inhabitants. How a Meeting was Marked by Divided Opinions. Islam.

From Kitivo onwards, the country looks completely different. Here, the rivers come down from the mountains and they bring with them freshness, fertility, greenness of vegetation, joy, and sometimes also fever. The Umba River gathers water from all its tributaries, gives plenty of water to whoever wants it, and carries the remainder into the desert which it cuts in two. From then on, the river water is only useful for satisfying the thirst of the herds of wild animals, and, when it approaches the sea, in fertilizing the fields around Vanga.

The real source of the river is on the Sambara plateau high up in the big Handei Forest. It runs down the side of the mountain in a gorge which can be seen very clearly from below. Three sizable rivers flow into it—the Ngwelo, the Kivingo, and the Mbaramo—which in turn take water from many other streams. At Kitivo, the aneroid barometer recorded a height of 389 meters. With such plentiful water, all these valleys have very rich vegetation. In the patches of the forest you can walk bare-headed on safe ground. We can feel that the sun is there, but we do not see it. The only obstacle on the ground are the creepers, which can be enormous. You can see their feet, but you cannot say where all their strands, looking like cables or ropes or threads, spread out to. They tie themselves around the tops of big trees, which they climb up in order to get some sunlight, and up there they disappear from human sight.

The rich humus left by the vegetation is made use of by the local people. Every year, they clear whatever is growing in a section of the forest and leave it to grow again. They cut the undergrowth, they cut the grass, they cut the creepers, and really they cut everything for which the scythe, the knife, the pruning knife, and the axe are serviceable. But the big trees cannot be cut down by small tools like these. So they remove a ring of bark from around the tree and let it die. If the tree takes too long to die, one piles up at the foot a heap of dry branches, grass and leaves, and starts a fire. We have gone through a forest treated in this way; the soil had nothing growing in it, and the big trees stood dried up, as straight as masts, magnificent in the way they stood, without a leaf or a green twig, without a bird perching on them, white and sad in their nakedness. This was a painful sight; but in Africa one never has pity on trees, only rarely on animals, and even for human beings, only occasionally.

The population of the valley is very mixed; there are Sambara villages, and also Zigua and Kamba ones. Sometimes you get people of different tribes living in the same compound. Each group of villages has its own chief, and his permission has to be sought by any stranger who wishes to settle in this fertile arcadia. However, naturalization is easily granted. Moreover, the different villages are fairly similar. They are surrounded by a stockade with generally an impenetrable hedge of euphorbias and thorns. Outside of this, there may be an open shed, sometimes replaced by a tall tree, giving plenty of shade, which serves as a meeting place for the men who gather there during the heat of the day to talk, joke, discuss, philosophize, and exchange gossip while weaving mats, and sacks, and baskets. Meanwhile the housewives are sheltered by the verandas of the houses, as they shell peas and wipe the children's noses, as happens everywhere.

The houses are round. In some places, the village has a tree trunk holding various grains, packets of maize and beans in bags, which are kept in the open air. At the entry to the village, before the gate in the stockade, a long pole, equipped with a shell, has been put up to protect the inhabitants against enemy raids. Unfortunately, this scare warning can suffer the same fate as scarecrows put up in the fields; some unscrupulous birds come to rob the field and mock the straw man.

These people eat very little beef because they do not want to attract the Maasai, for cattle attract the Maasai just as milk appeals to snakes. They have goats, sheep, chickens, and small dogs. Their menu is sometimes enriched by a desert antelope, or a forest boar, or an ordinary field rat, and they accompany their meals with an excellent kind of *pombé* which is made with sugar cane juice.

We could see from this valley the high plateau of Sambara, which is home to the Mbugu, a little-known people. I am told that they speak a mixture of Pare and Maasai, and their main occupation is raising cattle. They are handsome people—slim, almost skinny—but they seldom come down to the plain, through fear of fever. Alas! When shall we be able to meet them face to face to give them that which they lack, and which alone is absolutely necessary?

Our porters by now were doing better than they had been. The coast has a very harmful effect on these Swahili ruffians; we saw it, we knew it, but we could do nothing. Now that the desert lay between Vanga and ourselves, we no longer feared that they would leave us, and, indeed, they were very much at home in our company. Most of them have already traveled into the interior with European explorers—Stanley, Thomson, Teleki, and so on—and their backs are still marked by the whips used by their previous employers. This time, they were rather astonished not to have received treatment of this kind. But we did not make any promises that this would always be the case.

Everything, then, went well between them and us, but they quarreled among themselves. This quarrel began with a theological argument. It had begun a few days before, and had started with a goat. I must, then, go back a bit. We had been given a harmless goat by a friendly village, and, through kindheartedness, had given it to our men. Selemani only kept a leg for us, and, seeing the state of his jaw, a piece of liver for himself. All the rest had to be divided among the Kambi or teams of the caravan, numbering five:

> Fardyallah's team, composed of eight old slaves, Muslims from the country around Bagamoyo, calm, not very intelligent, but not at all ill-natured.

> Mpenda-Safari's team—young men from the hinterland, restless, noisy, only recently arrived at the coast where they have gone through the form of a conversion to Islam.

> Nderingo's team—people who joined us for various reasons.

> Mbega's team—pagans who do not accept the Quran, and who were happy in a rather childlike way.

> Finally, Hamis' team—recruited from Mombasa rogues, claiming to be strict Muslims, and the purest of the pure.

And so, each team had its leader, its plan for camping, its way of doing things, its principles, and its cooking pot. When we gave out glass beads and linen, we gave to the leader to divide among the team members. When something went wrong, it was to him that we had to speak; when an animal was killed, he took the part assigned to his group, which is always dependent on the group's number.

This first goat had been handed over to the caravan. Ali, of the Mombasa team, the Ali who at Vanga had shown himself to be Sampson's equal, took hold of it, cut its throat, and divided it up, with the modest justification that he and the other members of the team were really authentic Muslims, and therefore the goat must be killed by him, or be rendered impure. However, when the animal had been divided up, it was noticed that it was a very odd goat with neither heart, nor liver, nor lungs, nor hooves, nor head.

The next day, a chief had made us a similar gift of a sheep, and the converts of the Mpenda-Safari, happy to kill the animal and to share it out, cut its throat. This produced uproar. The men from Mombasa shouted, "Dirty carrion, killed by impure hands. Better to die than to eat it." The old Bagamoyo slaves longed to get their teeth into it, but, being a bit afraid of the Mombasa men, said that they could not eat it with a clear conscience. Nderingo's team felt that the meat was quite all right. Mbega's team rather shockingly said that even if the sheep had been four days dead, they would not shrink from eating it for a minor scruple. An argument broke out leading to quarrelling and insults.

Another time, we were given an old billy goat. The righteous souls of Mombasa cut its throat, but the others spat on it as a revenge for the way they had been spoken to. On the day when I was speaking, the quarrel flared up again. The men from Mombasa regarded any animal which has not been killed by their hands as being entirely unacceptable. Mgr. de Courmont, seated on a tree trunk, read his breviary. Fr. Auguste was showing Selemani the way to peel onions without having to cry. I myself listened to the debate and was gradually drawn into it.

"So, lads, you only eat ritually pure meat?"

"Yes, always."

I asked, "And ritually pure meat is?"

"It is the meat of an animal which a true Muslim has killed while turning toward Makka (Mecca) and saying 'Bismillah!'"

"So that is it. If I turn a pig in the direction of Makka . . ."

"Oh, not so, whichever side you turn it to, it is still worth nothing."

I asked, "Are there then clean animals and unclean?"

"Oh, yes."

"Rats, cats, dogs, monkeys?"

"Unclean," he answered.

"The camel?"

"Pure, as pure as possible; it was Mohammed's meat."

"The hippopotamus?"

"Pure . . . no, impure . . . well."

I had asked an embarrassing question, and opinions were divided. Hamisi, the team leader, came to the rescue, and laid down the principle.

"Please listen carefully," he said to me. "Here is the rule which you can follow. An animal is pure, if having eaten, it chews the food like that," and he imitated a cow ruminating. "But not the others."

"Then," said I, "Why do you eat chickens?" This question greatly perplexed the apologist. The Muslims seemed rather upset, the pagans were delighted, and my friend Mbega pressed the question triumphantly.

"That is it: Why do you eat chickens?"

"And why," broke in someone else, "do you not cut the throats of fish?"

Hamisi had recovered his self-confidence and said, "Fish are not animals, and, as for the chickens, they are ruminants."

I asked, "Are chickens ruminants?"

"Oh, yes," he replied. "It is absolutely certain; they do a bit of chewing. But we do not see much of that, as they only do it at night."

"Really," concluded Mbega, in a rather mocking tone. "That can happen with them from time to time, when they are suckling."

I went ahead from that ingenious suggestion and said, "Hamisi, let us ask ourselves, who made all these animals, both the pure and the others?"

"It was God."

"Quite correct, it was God. Now God is almighty, all perfect, and all good. Can he make something which is essentially impure? He could not. If you make something impure, you are impure yourself. So when Hamisi, and you, Ali, and you, Abdullah, you say about the animals created by God, 'this one is pure, but not that one,' you are calling God's work into question and you are blaspheming. Everything God has done, he has done well; but it is up to us to see what is suitable or unsuitable for us in the way of food, medicine, drink and so on."

Two Maasai warriors

An embarrassed silence followed. Ali, who was a smart fellow, replied confidently: "It is not we who have made the law, it was Mohammed. That being the case, there is no more to say."

I replied, "There is a lot more to say, Ali. Who was Mohammed to comment to God on the animals God had made? Will you say Mohammed received this law from God?"

"Exactly, master," said he, "I had not thought of that."

"Well, if it was God who gave him that law, Mohammed should have been able to prove that it was so, by working miracles and raising the dead to life. Instead of that, he just raided caravans, dreamed that the moon came into his sleeve, and that he had ridden up to heaven on a mare. After which he said, 'If you do not believe me, I shall break your neck.' Is that how one should do things, if one is really sent by God?"

Everybody kept silent. The pagans smiled in an amused way, but the Muslims were shocked. I began again: "Since you cannot reply, I shall do it for you. Please listen carefully. Long, long ago, God created the world and all that is in it, both above and below.

Camping in a village

And everything that comes from his hand is good, at least for the purpose for which he made it. He put man over the stones, the lead, the iron, and the silver, over the grass, over the animals, and said to him, 'All this is for you. Make use of it, for food, or for medicine, or to decorate your home, which might otherwise be rather gloomy. But do not exaggerate things; take what is useful for one occasion and leave the rest for later. There is a woman, just one: she will be your helpmate in life, but not your slave. The goats go about in a flock, led by a billy goat: but for human beings, everything starts with the family, father, mother and children. And you must be brothers and sisters to each other, and you will adore me and serve me, and you shall not kill, nor steal, nor commit adultery. And when any human being dies, I shall judge him on what he has done during his life." Make an effort to listen, pumpkin heads. "And so, my friends, human beings became numerous, and, as they became numerous and scattered, each group developing its own way of life, some became whites, others yellow, others again black, but we are all from the same father and mother whose color I have never seen. It is the same as with peas: there are grey peas, red peas, and white ones, small peas, middle-sized ones and fat ones, but they are all the same peas." (General agreement). Then I continued: "Only, as people became more numerous they became less good."

"It is always like that," said one of those present.

"And God chose one tribe on earth to keep his commandments, and, in that tribe, a leader to guide it. Now the tribe was the Jewish people, and its leader was called Moses, Musa, as you say it."

"He is quite right," said some of the porters. "It is incredible, his knowledge of our religion."

"Ah," said Ali, "as to our religion, they know it better than we do, but they do not accept it. Their hearts are hardened."

"No, my poor Ali, our hearts are not hardened. I have studied your religion and I have studied my own; that has been the big thing in my life. And if we have a very thorough knowledge of them both, it is because we want to save our souls. It is because we see the truth, and so we are not Muslims, but Christians."

"But what about Musa?" someone asked.

"All right. God said to Musa, 'One day, I shall send someone into the world who will give it the perfect, final revelation for all mankind, and there will be nothing more to add to it. People will recognize him by this and that sign. But, while waiting for his coming, you, Musa, will be the leader of this tribe and you will give it a code of law which will distinguish them from all the others.

"And so it was. And in the law which Musa gave the Jews, they were forbidden to eat fish without scales, the owl, the hare, the pig, as well as animals dead from disease, or suffocated with the blood still in them. Why? We do not need to know that. Perhaps he wanted to train those people in obedience and to separate them from the surrounding pagan tribes. Moreover, these rules had a great deal of value for the health and the development of the people.

"Later on, God himself sent him who had been promised: it was Jesus whom you call Isa."

"It is true," said the porters. And then they muttered, "This damned European knows everything. He must have read the Quran."

"And people knew for sure that Isa was sent by God, because all the prophecies that had been made about him for hundreds and thousands of years were fulfilled in him. Moreover, to prove that God was with him, in God's name he cured sick people with a single word, he raised the dead to life, and he did the most extraordinary things.

"Then, he said, 'Until now, you have had two guidelines, religion and law. The Christian religion is for the whole world, and it must be taught to all the peoples of the world, both whites and blacks.' This is what has been done; it was taught first to the whites, and now the whites are coming to teach it to the blacks. And that is why we are here, we three have come among you, my dear friends. (Signs of astonishment. The pagans smile happily; the Muslims are visibly upset)

"And so, the religion of God and of Isa is for the whole world. As for the Jewish law, well, it is the law of the Jews. The Arabs, who are their brothers, have accepted part of it, and that is why they will not eat this or that kind of meat. But neither you nor we are Jews or Arabs; we are not therefore obliged to follow the Arabs or the Jews. Every tribe has its own customs. The Banyans do not kill their fleas. Does that mean that you should not kill yours?"

Somebody exclaimed, "Well, I kill all my fleas."

This revelation brought a wave of laughter. During it, I tried to see the effect of my homily on the men who stood around me. Ali whispered in his neighbor's ear, "Let us get out of here. He might destroy our faith."

I cut in. "Destroy your faith, Ali? It is a long time since you became good friends with me, from your feet up to your hair. Come now, what gives a man a pure soul?"

"Never eating impure meat," replied Ali.

"No, Ali," I said. "Bad meat is only bad for the stomach. You are mixing up your stomach and your soul, Ali! (The pagans and the uncommitted roared with laughter and expressed noisy approval)

And so I continued, "We harm our soul when we act against the laws established by God.

For example, when God arranged the marriage of Adam, the first man, how many wives did he give him?"

"One," said somebody.

"Well," I said, "why do you Muslims give yourselves four wives, and, on the side, take as many as you can get?"

"It is," replied Ali, "a privilege."

"Yes, a privilege which Muslims give themselves, but God does not permit it. That is what corrupts the soul! Again, the soul is corrupted, when, for example, you go into the hinterland, sack peaceful villages, steal ivory, group together defenseless men, women, and children, chain them up and then sell them at the coast, as though they were herds of animals, people who are your brethren and God's well-loved creatures. What corrupts the soul is all these thefts and adulteries. Again, you corrupt your souls when, as I know you do, you say things to each other which would make monkeys fall upside down. Hypocrites, you wash your body by day and by night, and, by day and by night you dirty your soul. Isa spoke rightly about you when he compared you to the tombs in your cemeteries which you take care to whitewash: seen from the outside they are dazzlingly white; open them and you find only rottenness and disease."

My opponent, after a long silence, said, "With all this talk, we are forgetting to go and have something to eat."

"Yes," I said, "I understand that, but first give me an answer."

"Well," said Ali getting up, "it is easy to give an answer. When a Muslim has sinned, he just washes his hands while repeating the summary of his faith—*'La ilaha il Allah, wa Muhammad rasul Alla'* (There is no god but God, and Mohammed is his prophet). And so his sin is wiped away. As for these bush people of the interior, God has given them to us as slaves, for it is written, 'The pagan below, the Muslim above.'"

But scarcely had Ali given us this proud slogan with an air of superior satisfaction, than my good friend Mbega took up a fistful of cow dung and threw it at the speaker's face, shouting, "Liar, the Muslim below, the pagan above."

That was the summary and conclusion of the controversial meeting which ended just as it might have done in Paris—in an exciting punch-up. Well, readers, that is Islam. Certainly, we have a great deal of respect for the old patriarch Abraham, he who begot Isaac and Ishmael, *unum de ancilla et unum de libera* (one from a maidservant and the other from a freewoman). But while keeping all appropriate respect for this episode of sacred history, we can agree that these sons of Abraham, represented today by the Jews and the Arabs, have caused a great deal of worry to us gentiles, miserable descendants of Ham and Japheth. On the one hand, the Hamitic Africans combine their rather jolly temperament with a feeling of relative inferiority and a certain sense of humiliation caused by their skin color. On the other hand, the descendants of Japheth, the Aryans, let us say Europeans, dazzled by the brilliance of their material civilization, are conceited, self-indulgent, certainly intelligent, but also absent-minded, and, above all, extraordinarily naive.

Finally, at the side of their younger brothers, or among them, the Semites are steeped in a hypocrisy so deep that it looks like loyalty, in a dishonesty so natural that it can be mistaken for easygoing good nature, and in a confidence of their supernatural superiority so fundamental that nothing so far has been able to weaken it. And, in their relation to us, blacks and whites, they crush the weak and undermine the strong, in their conviction that everything is permissible or even praiseworthy, against those human beings who are not "believers," that is to say, who are not Jews or Muslims. That is their strength.

And here is something astonishing. These hypocrites and unrelenting enemies have allies among us. Many politicians, public speakers, writers—and talented ones too—say that we must favor Islam in Africa as providing a step toward civilization.

Let us define our terms. If, by "African civilization," we understand a state of things in which Africans wear long white dresses, Islam may indeed help to bring this about; but, if we define civilization as combining intellectual development and moral improvement, Islam is disastrous for Africans. After having brought about some modest advances, and suppressed some pagan practices, it imprisons Africans permanently in an arrogant fanaticism, a hostility without any prospect of reconciliation, a supreme hypocrisy, and an immorality fit for scoundrels.

Pagans, fetishers, cannibals, savages, or whatever you like to call them, may be hostile to European civilization—and this is hardly surprising considering the behavior of some "civilized" Europeans in Africa—but, basically, they like Europeans. If a European takes care to behave always among Africans as befits someone who is just, decent, and kindly, they love him enthusiastically. The African pagans are a fertile seed-bed for faith and civilization. Muslims are a barren field. That is the difference, and every real friend of progress can see it.

But, say these gentlemen who spin theories, when Islam gets the upper hand in an area of Africa, it puts an end to deplorable evils—drunkenness, for instance, or cannibalism. As to Islam suppressing drunkenness, the best evidence to the contrary is that in Zanzibar town, with its Muslim population, entire shiploads of gin and adulterated alcohol disappear at a frightening rate. But it must be said that this serious drinking takes place at night and at home; passing Europeans see nothing. They are the ones who collapse in the street. As to cannibalism, you should not think that it is found everywhere in Africa. This horrible custom is found in some rather exceptional tribes, who are well known for it. The Muslims respect these tribes and understandably so.

A rat trap

But if Islam really reduced, even if it could not suppress, these criminal or wicked customs, would it really be a civilizing factor if it replaced them with this implacable fanaticism, this degrading immorality, and these shameful diseases, fatal to the peoples infected by them and of which it has a sad specialty? And from another angle, can anyone tell us, where do we find the greater number of victims: among these cannibal tribes which must soon change their ways under increasing European pressure, or at the hands of the Muslims themselves who always regard "unbelievers" as herds of people to be exterminated or enslaved, to be captured, exported, and sold? There is another prejudice. People think that it is normal that Christian missionaries and Muslims detest each other because of the conflict of their religious values. On the other hand, a free-thinker who knows how to make concessions to, and, if necessary, approach, the doctrinal positions of the sons of Muhammad, gets on well with them. I understand perfectly. A free-thinker who objects firmly to the practice of Christian faith and charity will be most respectful toward Muslim propaganda; he will encourage it, and he will reward it. Well, our freethinker—who I may say in passing, not only has his own dogmas, but holds to them, in a very intolerant way of which he is quite unconscious—will be manipulated in a very smart way. Muslims, in fact, respect, admire, and even have affection for Catholic missionaries whose faith and devotion they know.

But, Muslims are full of the deepest contempt for apostate Christians, some of whom put on a bad imitation of Muslim practice, and others have the most complete indifference toward God and religion, even though these apostates may be useful to Muslims. How often have people said to us, "You, the Padres, you will certainly be saved through the great mercy of Allah. For you believe in him, you serve him, you invoke him, you even adopt in his name a way of life of which even our greatest saints would not be capable. But these European brothers of yours, who never pray, how do they differ from animals? And how can God, whom these unbelievers have never wished to recognize during their life, recognize them at their death? Well, God has cursed them and believers despise them."

That is the truth. And yet the Muslims have charming manners; they can be gracious, hospitable, foreseeing, helpful, generous. These are displayed when the opportunity requires them. And they always trap naive Europeans. One of their most typical and most popular proverbs says, "If you cannot cut someone's hand off, you had better kiss it." The Muslim way of dealing with you and me and all unbelievers is contained in this proverb.

Chapter 11: At the Mbaramo Pass

On Guard against the Enemy. Facing Danger.
On the Mbaramo Pass. A Night of Misery.

By now it was the third of August. The last village where we stayed was built on a little river which came down from the mountains and which ran to join the Umba at some distance. There we had been told:

> Look out, the Maasai will be on the way you are taking, coming to make war on the Digo and steal their cattle. Be ready to stand up to them, for when the Maasai go to war, they attack anybody they meet.

The people who were telling us this were messengers who claimed to have seen the enemy. They seemed to be sincere and we had to take our precautions against anything untoward. We made a special distribution of cartridges to those of our men who had repeating rifles. The rest, armed only with muzzle-loaders, were given an additional supply of powder, bullets, and caps. After that, we had to lay out our program, have some practice firing, and, of course, an encouraging speech.

> Men of Bagamoyo, of Mombasa, and from wherever you come, listen well. People have told us that the Maasai will be on the way we are following. That is their responsibility, but we shall be there also. We shall march together, one behind the other, for the whole of the journey. There will be a stop every hour; apart from that, it is forbidden to fall behind or to move away in the bushes. Keep silent as you march; no shouts, no songs, no making a din. The guide will go twenty paces before us, with two men just behind him. As soon as you hear him shout, "Look out!" you will all halt, and, in a calm and orderly manner, in the place which I shall show you, you must form a circle, with each man close to his neighbors, standing behind his load. And so, you will be crouching down behind the boxes and the packages of cloth, and you must allow the Maasai to come with

CHAPTER 11: AT THE MBARAMO PASS

their spears, and, when they have got close, and the command is given, then fire! They will fall like rabbits . . . my friends, when I signed you on at the coast—here is my list—you have all given me men's names; however, if by mischance there is a woman among you, let her say who she is. She will stay here; and we, the men, will go to battle!

This speech was greeted by enthusiastic applause, as though it was some great historical event. I began to feel the thrill of military glory, and I had the idea of adding, like a heroic Haitian general, that at the moment when battle would begin there would be more that forty monkeys gazing at them from the tree tops.

However, I consulted Mgr. de Courmont, who thought that such a piece of classical rhetoric would have an unfortunate effect, and so I just said: "Let us have a practice."

We practiced what we would have to do, and, as it went all right, it was theoretically clear that, if we were attacked, we would cover ourselves with glory. It was midday. We marched on. As we came out of the fertile valley of the Umba, the country through which we had to pass became much less attractive, but not as unpleasant as we had experienced in the Guruva Desert, which had left us with an unhappy memory. Here and there, there were baobabs (*adansonia digitata*), ebony trees (*dalbergia arbutifolia, dalbergia melanoscilon, dalbergia saxatilis, dalbergia bracteolate*), strychnos trees (*strychnos spinosa*), and thick brushwood, where, among the thorns, euphorbia trees and creepers (*euphorbia tirucalli*) are mingled with thick quadrangular wild vines (*vitis quadrangularis, vitis crassifolia, vitis mossambicensis*). There are beautiful groups of adenium (*adenium speciosum*) with splendid red flowers, and everywhere this strange passion flower with bristling thorns, which we have met already and of which a single foot creates masses of green vegetation. We went on, in an unworried way, up to a pass through which we had to go, the Mbaramo Pass. The sun was not hot. On the left, there was the mountain; on the right, the plain. And there was not even the shadow of a Maasai.

So we kept on going, always moving upwards. Suddenly the guide, twenty paces ahead of the caravan, stopped, raised his hand very high, signaled to us to stay where we were and crouched down on the path. We had to form a circle. There was right beside us, a small hillock which was just the thing for our defense, and was moreover covered on its far side by thorny brushwood, which reduced the area which we would have to defend; but, to tell the truth, our men were now much less ready for battle than they had been at the practice. There was no need now to tell them to keep silence; none of our warriors disturbed it, even by his breath.

Then, seeing that the guide kept on looking at the path, as though he had been hypnotized at some precise point, we began to wonder if he was engaging in some form of fortune-telling. Step by step, we quietly went up to him.

"What is that?" we asked him.

With an extremely worried air, he pointed out to us . . . a cow pat! A great roar of laughter greeted this astonishing revelation.

Rather annoyed, he retorted, "Do not be silly, there could not have been just one cow here."

This was really a very sound point to make, and it was justified by our seeing, soon after, a lot of footprints and hoofmarks. We were soon convinced that the guide had been quite right by the evidence of nibbled grass, broken branches, and, finally, little paths, newly opened, which ran down to the plain of the Umba. That very morning, some Maasai had passed that way, bringing with them, as they always do, some cows to give them milk, and it was at that point that they had left the track to go into the wilderness and take a straight line to the river.

When we had come to this conclusion, our brave warriors, breathing noisily, spoke all at once, laughing triumphantly, and saying to each other, "What a pity! We would have wiped them out." We continued our march, still going higher, and soon found ourselves on the crest of the mountain buttress which we had to cross. There, we had a really magnificent view.

Behind us, after Bwiti, we had left three semicircles of mountains, running as a whole from southeast to northwest—the first from Bwiti to Bombo, the second from Bombo to Panga, and the third from Panga to the Mbaramo Pass, where we had then just arrived. The plain, grey and vast, ran far into the distance. To our north, there were the picturesque Taita Mountains, whose blue outline blended with the blue of the sky. Before us, there rose the chain of Pare Mountains, which we had to reach, crossing a great plain.

We sat down on the stones, happily free from contact with the Maasai, and were delighted to see this new land where we would have work to do, and which lay open to our gaze. We were glad to rest in the shadow of the slender mountain bushes. Unfortunately, there was nowhere we could draw water, and the very stony soil provided nourishment only for a big euphorbia tree, picturesque in a wild sort of way.

The landscape on the slope down which we now had to go was richer and more cheerful. All the time, flocks of quails, francolins, and guinea fowls were going past in full flight, and we all marched happily toward the camping ground where Mgr. de Courmont had already set up his tent. This was in the middle of the wilderness, where only a few acacias spread with their thorny branches and their loosened leaves on this side and that. There was no water and no firewood. We stopped, because the fall of night did not allow us to go further, and we settled down as well as we could, hoping at least to have a good night's sleep.

And then, the clouds which covered the sky seemed, without making much noise, to come down toward us, and then dissolved into rain, gentle at first, and then heavier and heavier. What would become of us? Where we were, there were neither trees nor bushes nor brushwood. Gradually, the rain put out our camp fires. The porters gathered in little groups and crouched down, leaving their backs to the falling rain; others, more venturesome, slipped into our tents, and we lacked the courage to chase them out. They became bolder, they pushed in, and then they curled up; it was like a cluster of rats in a hole. But they were so tired that they managed, all the same, to sleep with occasional wakings up, rolling on top of each other amid the boxes which were falling down and the packages which people tried to grip onto with some idea that they were irritating and stubborn sleepers. And the rain kept falling on and on the cluttered-up tent until morning.

Chapter 12: At Gonja

A Maasai Encampment. The Village of Gonja. Medicine for the Devil.

Getting up, for those who had managed to sleep, came without delay as did breakfast and the preparations for departure. Everybody was eager to get on the road and to wake up bodies sodden with rain and numb with cold.

Gradually the grey sky became brighter and we once again saw the Pare Mountains before us, rising up like a gigantic wall.

Right in front of us, but at a higher level, we could see a long white streak which stood out against the dark green of the forests. It was, we were told, the Mkomazi, which runs down in waterfalls, and which we had to cross that same day to arrive at Gonja. We were now crossing a plain which had really no variety. It was flat everywhere, generally black in color, with fissures here and there, and wretched, with some outcrops of thick pieces of white quartz which seemed to stick out with a certain amount of determination. Elsewhere, the plain was covered with various light and short species of grass, among which, at certain points, one sees rather unusual kinds of asclepiad plant, and the only shade is provided by various acacias and mimosas, which, further along, form forests of thorns.

The guide began again to warn us about the presence of Maasai. But, since the porters had seen him get worried by a cow pat from a Maasai cow, they no longer gave him their respectful attention; he just was not listened to. He, annoyed by this, marched on, grumbling. Then suddenly, we saw him stop; leaning forward, he swept the horizon with a glance, and, with an outstretched arm, pointed to a reddish line which, down below from us, seemed to be moving through a woodland of sparsely scattered acacias. The caravan behind him stopped and gazed.

"Children, here are the passing cattle: Hide your red pinafores." (French Nursery Rhyme). This time, they really are the Maasai cattle. They go past, past, continuing to go past, following each other in long lines, which move slowly. There are hundreds of them, no, thousands.

CHAPTER 12: AT GONJA

As soon as the stragglers have caught up with us, we set off again along the path, marching as a unit, as though it were a procession. The leader was the guide who spoke sufficient Maasai for a meeting, followed immediately by Mgr. de Courmont and Father Auguste; then the caravan, and, finally, behind the last porter, I brought up the rear. We went on, very serious and quite silent; suddenly we found ourselves facing the Maasai encampment. The guide gave the greetings, he was answered, and the caravan passed on.

I must say that there is a complete contrast between the young Maasai warrior out on a raid, of whom we had only seen the signs, and the peaceful Maasai in his encampment, with elders, children, and women, just as we found them there. In my rear-guard position, these famous desert pirates seemed to have such peaceful intentions, and meeting them seemed to promise me such excitement that I absolutely had to go toward them, without any protection, except a very long stick, an outstretched hand, and a smile on my lips. Straightaway, people are all around me. What magnificent nomads! The fairgrounds in Europe which like to parade "Africans from the jungle" have nobody to compare with these. Near to me, in front of their tents of cattle hide, dear old grannies, wearing leather clothes and laden with copper and iron ornaments, were cutting up a sheep. Smiling, they gave me their big hands streaming with blood. I responded cheerfully to their greetings and was almost tempted to get myself invited to the pantagruelian feast which they were preparing. On the nearby trees, families of crows, marabouts, and vultures waited patiently for the feast to begin, and below the trees delightful little children, snotty-nosed and sticky-eyed, were waiting also. I have to admit that the children looked at me rather disdainfully, with also some interest, but not fear; rather, as in Europe, the children of the gentry might, one fine day, see on the grounds of their father's manor house, a stranger with a rather dodgy look. But their parents seemed more favorable to my vagabond self, and when the guide, frightened by the careless way in which I mixed in with people whom I did not know at all, came to pull me together, a little sharply, we parted with happy feelings on both sides.

An hour later, we had reached Gonja. Gonja is a well-built village at the foot of the Pare Mountains, almost at the middle of this chain, on the much-travelled route from Pangani to Kilimanjaro and the Maasai country. To the east there flows the Mkomazi, a little river which joins the Ruvu, a little in front of Maurivi, and which we saw, as it came down from the mountain, falling in rapids. The banks, which have been formed over the centuries by a gradually accumulated humus, are extremely fertile and reminded us of the Umba Valley: the same patches of forest, the same productive banana groves, the same crops, and the same greenery.

We put the river between us and any foolish moves on the part of the Maasai, and so settled on the far side, near the village. The village itself was protected by a stockade of tree trunks, further strengthened by bushes, euphorbias, and a little kind of asclepiad (*sarcostemma*) plant, which has an abundant sap. This is extremely corrosive and squirts out even when given a very moderate tap. If it gets into the eyes of the man who has touched the plant, it blinds him, and makes him helpless.

Some of the houses are round as in the African hinterland, others are square as on the coast, but in general they are not well looked after. It is here, on the road to Pangani, that we find the furthest point of Islam's penetration. It is here the last place where one sees the long white shirt which symbolizes Islamic civilization. However, the fact of it being white, and the fact of it being a shirt, covers up far more uncleanness than the cloth or skin covering worn by the "bush" people. However that may be, the present population which has conquered the country from the Pare is a mixture of Zigua and Sambara, speaks fluent Swahili, mixes a certain amount of Islamic ritual with the traditional African religion, and accepts the authority of Mwasi, one of the sons of Semboja, who resides further down at Mazinde, and has become the most widely recognized Sambara chief.

When we were there, Mwasi had gone down to the coast, and we could only see his *akida* or deputy. This was rather fortunate, since we had only to present him with a sheep, rather than a bull. For, if you are given a bull, you have the obligation to give a bull, or the value of a bull, in return; for a goat, you give a goat, a chicken for a chicken; an egg for an egg: and if you are given nothing, you give nothing.

However, there are exceptions, and when your feelings have been touched, you find yourself making little presents. For example, that evening, three well-built young men came to see us, followed by two small children. They were Maasai; one of them in particular was certainly more than six feet tall, with limbs looking as though they were made of cast iron, an African Apollo with a black skin; his hands gripped magnificent spears, his shoulders were covered with a calf skin. Five or six days before, they told us, they had taken a bullock and gone to make a picnic in the forest, in the way good friends do. By this time nothing remained of the animal except its skin, which they were dragging behind them. Having heard that there were white people travelling in the country, they came to pay them a visit. They had crossed the river very quickly, and here they were in our camp, gazing at everything with intense curiosity and a touch of ill-concealed envy.

CHAPTER 12: AT GONJA

Two old Maasai men, Pare

Then suddenly, these big young men seemed to tremble, then they jumped in the air, and, at the same time, a strangely accented song rose from their throats. After ten minutes of this dance, simple yet strange, the guide put around the young men's necks some red linen, and gave the children some blue pearls. Our visitors left us, promising to bring all their age mates to see us the next day, a promise which we did not take very seriously. Such was our first encounter with this extraordinary people, the Maasai. We were to meet them again later.

However, this was not all that the day held for us. I do not know if I was the victim of a run of bad luck, or that a talkative porter had given people the idea that I possessed supernatural powers, but late in the day a big villager approached me, begging for my help. He explained that his poor old wife had been possessed by the devil for a very long time, and that I would do the two of them an enormous service if I could eject this unwelcome stranger. A crowd of a hundred or so people were there to back up what he said, and they added that the ablest exorcists of their country had consistently failed, faced with the incredible tenacity of this devil.

So they brought the patient, a woman of about fifty, big, strong, holding herself straight upright, rather stiff, with reddish eyes and regular features. I stood facing her, gazing straight at her, and prepared to question her about the beginning and development of her illness, which I felt must be some kind of neurosis. Then, lo and behold, little by little, without saying anything and without any change of attitude, the good lady started to tremble gently, then more strongly, then very strongly, then to jump, and then to dance, but there seemed a continuity in what she did, as though she were driven by some internal force; really, she could have been a cardboard puppet in a Punch and Judy show. To be honest, I began to feel very embarrassed by her performance.

"Come on, solve her problem," cried Mgr. de Courmont.

"It is your specialty," added Fr. Auguste Gommenginger.

I was being mocked by my superior and my confrere, from whom I should have received the staunchest support, and also I had to face the worried crowd, anxious for a cure. I felt that if I did not immediately take the initiative, I would lose my credibility. While the woman continued her capers, I started to explain that this state of mind was in no way caused by the devil—really, I did not know where it came from. But if one continued to make sacrifices to the devil to get him to come out, he might turn up and stay permanently. I added, as something which the occasion seemed to demand, a short explanation of five or six basic religious truths. Finally, I said that, unfortunately, I had not brought with me the appropriate medicine. I said, "However, mother, I shall not let you down. If you drink this medicine, tonight, before the cock crows, you will feel a complete change, and you will get up very quickly. Villagers, see that she has the door open for her!"

And there and then, I gave her the drink; she swallowed it as though it were something sacred. Now, this medicine was a strong laxative. In the morning, people came to tell us that the devil had gone out during the night.

Chapter 13: Pare

The Pare Chain of Mountains. A Musical Greeting. At Kisiwani. The King of Creation. In Sight of Lake Jipe. The Local People.

From Mombasa to Vanga, we went consistently from north to south. From Vanga to Gonja, the caravan turned west. From Gonja to Lake Jipe and to Taveta, we needed to go northwards, following, first of all, the foothills of the Pare Mountains. For the most part, the Pare Mountains are a granite chain, similar to the Sambara massif on the east and the Nguvu massif to the south. They divide into three sections separated by gorges, which enable the local people to pass through. Pare, properly speaking, is Pare-Usangi, and Pare-Ugweno. To our right there were also some mountains which formed a kind of large corridor—dry, stony, and unattractive—and which took us five days to walk alongside.

Do you remember that when we were at Vanga we received a young man from Pare into our caravan? He was called "Pure," that is "Maize Seed." As names go, it is a nice name. Maize Seed had found among the Muslims of Buriti four cousins of his who were on their way to the coast, where honest businessmen would have had them taken to Pemba and sold, pretending that they were being given a cruise at sea.

These young men—very simple, very naïve—have done us good service in taking the place, from time to time, of those of our porters who, from fatigue or sickness, could no longer do their work. And now we got to their home. Their village is the one we reached after Gonja, and Maize Seed is, as he told us, the son of the chief, old Kimbute. How happy the fine old patriarch was to see his son again. But there is also the tremendous disappointment of knowing that Mbaruku of Gasi, a man whose fame had spread very widely, far from sending him the wonderful presents he had promised, had kept his calves and had wanted to sell his children.

But what are we hearing there? Our young men from Pare had scarcely laid down their loads in the village square, when they were surrounded by their relatives, friends, and acquaintances. And then, what seemed like little sighs were drawn out to make delicate and touching songs, *piano, pianissimo* (gentle, very gentle). It made me think of the gentle voice of a music teacher, who, in a well-run boarding school sets the tone for his pupils, and to whom his pupils respond. It seemed that fifty voices of varying ranges joined in.

It was really the Pare way of greeting. Oh, how can I praise for you that greeting? Close to me stood Maize Seed, whom his wife had just recognized. He had just arrived with his packet of cloth, sweat running down his forehead; she was on her way to the spring, with a pitcher on her head. When the two saw each other, they both put down what they were carrying and moved toward each other to take the other's hand. Then they turned their heads, he to the east, she to the west. Neither said anything, they did not even smile or show any sign of their feelings; they began to sing that music beyond description which was truly a humanized warbling. As they sang, they swung the other's hand which they took first of all near the wrist, then they leave it, little by little, touching in turn the palm, then the finger-bones, then the tips of the fingers. After that, they looked at each other, they smiled at each other, they chatted, and they became a man and a woman again. The rules of etiquette having been observed, human nature took over.

The next stage of the journey brought us to Kisiwani (the island), where we stayed for two days to stock up on provisions, for there are no villages between Kisiwani and Taveta.

Kisiwani is, like Gonja, a fertile, inhabited place. As at Gonja, this is thanks to a river that comes down from the mountain and then takes its rest in a large hollow in the land, a hollow cluttered up with papyrus plants. As we know, the ancient Egyptians used the thin membranous layers of the side of the papyrus plant to write their food accounts and their memoirs. However, the people of Kisiwani, who are not very interested in archaeology, do not seem very interested in the past history of this famous plant found all over tropical Africa.

In the rainy season, it seems that the river, which is called Mbaga, sometimes flows into the Mkomazi, but the maps are quite wrong in making it turn toward the desert. They are equally wrong in claiming that an imaginary river starting from Ngurungani flows into it. But at Ngurungani itself, there is only a little rain water conserved in stone basins.

A village at the foot of the Pare Mountains

At Kisiwani we were 600 meters above sea level. The surrounding mountains make us feel the cold sharply enough. During the night, the thermometer fell to 8 centigrade; it had been 30 degrees when we left Zanzibar.

On the 8th of August, we had been told that a five-hour march would bring us to a camp site somewhere at the foot of the mountains, near to which we could perhaps find water. We set off at six in the morning and we kept going till two o'clock in the afternoon. We crossed a large plain which was grey and dried up, with the only interesting object in the landscape being the sight of some herds of antelopes and zebras. The soil was barren, the sun merciless. Finally, our tired state and our disillusion made us fall down under a small tree, thorny and stunted, as are all trees in this gloomy country. The guide, who had lost the way but was afraid to admit it, set off to explore the mountainside, with orders to fire a rifle shot if he found water.

An hour went by. Some of the porters caught up with us; the shot could be heard, though very far off, and we went in its direction. We found the remains of a camp site and settled in. There was water nearby, in the hollow of a rock where it flowed down in a crystal trickle, overshadowed by a big sycamore. Providence had provided this delightful watering place for the herds of animals that inhabit this wilderness and for the men who, by chance, pass through it. When we got there we had to ask some gazelles to make room for us; it was they in fact who, by the tracks they had left behind them, had enabled the guide to find the basin of clean water.

CHAPTER 13: PARE

There was nobody living there. After some time, however, we managed to make out, much further up the mountain, some squares which seemed to be fields, three miserable huts, and finally, toward evening, a little cloud of smoke which rose timidly between the brushwood and the rocks, revealing the presence of man, the king of creation. What an impoverished ruler!

On we went! That morning, as we got up, people said to us, "Today you will see the big lake toward which you are hurrying, you will see the Jipe." After the grim march of the previous day, hope seemed to give us new legs; we still had the plain before us, mountains to our right and left, and antelopes everywhere. At last, three hours after having struck camp, I climbed up a tree on the side of the path, which seemed to be there precisely for giving views, and down there, just at the far end of the desert, above the leaves, beyond the plain, there was what looked like a long mirror, lying along the horizon, among tall grasses. Dear reader, it was the Jipe. Three cheers for the Jipe!

Straightaway, our porters started firing their guns, each in his own time, as in revolutions at Paris. But here our porters had two aims—to make the place echo with the joy of their arrival, and to tell the locals of the joy which they would have if foodstuffs and water were brought. Rifle shots are the signs employed by all the caravans from Pangani which come to seek ivory in the far interior.

After less than an hour had passed, the local Africans came down, dressed in a very picturesque fashion, bringing everything we needed: cool water in the big calabashes that they carry on their backs, held in place by a strap which they pass around their heads, packages of chickens, baskets of beans. They wanted in exchange linen, pearls, and brass wire. Both they and we were satisfied.

Here, Pare from various villages who had not seen each other for some time came together as at a market and, naturally, the songs of greeting, which are a specialty of theirs, began again. Our merry porters shook hands all round with the locals, and greeted them in African fashion. This playful comedy ended in great bursts of laughter, a sign that both sides felt they had done well.

The Pare people are extremely interesting. They are spread along the whole chain of the Pare Mountains, but have withdrawn onto the higher ground for very sensible reasons. They wanted to avoid the Maasai, who come to the lower-lying ground to raid for cattle, but who scarcely dare go up the high ground through treacherous and little-known passes. They wanted to get away from untrustworthy neighbors—to be found on all sides—mainly the Zigua, the Sambara, the Chagga, and the Arusha, who, under pressure from the coastal Muslims who are ruthless slave traders, have, every so often, raided this simple and ill-armed people. Finally, they wanted to develop the high plateau, which is cooler, more fertile, and more profitable in various ways than the valleys and the slopes where the dryness of the neighboring desert is already to be felt.

The Pare, black in skin color, not ill-shaped but generally small, thin, and nervous, belong to the great cultural and linguistic family of the Bantu, a word meaning "people," which, lacking any other term, one has given to a great range of peoples with a common origin spread over Africa between the Atlantic and the Indian Oceans and from the Cape of Good Hope to the Sudan.

The Pare were formerly spread over a wider territory than they have today, for elements of their language are to be found to the south, on the high plateau of Sambara, and to the north in the plains of Arusha, Kahe, and Taveta. This language is, as we would expect from their being Bantu, agglutinative, with prefixes indicating the categories, or, as is sometimes said, the classes, and with similarities of grammar and vocabulary to the languages of neighboring tribes from Zanzibar to the Congo.

They are both farmers and herdsmen living in villages or in isolated families, and they irrigate their crops with very well-made canals. But the water which is not necessary for their use is generally allowed, when there is not too much of it, to drain off into the forests and on to the rocks, where it soaks away, so that, down below, the Maasai should not be attracted by the clear flowing water. If they were, they would bring their herds to drink and would take the opportunity to increase them at the expense of the Pare.

This plateau is cold and damp; there are crops which cannot grow there. However, there are a great many banana trees, maize, beans, yams, sweet potatoes, pumpkins, and so on. As for animals, there are chickens, goats, sheep and cattle. One can enjoy the company of a dog, a fierce little red dog, with pointed ears, who does not bark, but squeals, bites, and hunts. There are many bees, half domesticated, half wild—well, you might say the same about the Pare. They set up beehives made of hollowed-out tree trunks which one then hangs from the branches of trees to which they are tied by creepers. The bees establish their seat of government there, they keep their families and their possessions there, and when everything has gone well, human beings take what they want.

To the north, the Pare-Usangi Mountains have a great deal of iron ore and the local people work very skillfully with it, making their own pickaxes, knives, spears, hatchets, and arrowheads, and providing them for their neighbors. Each district of the mountain chain has its own chief, sometimes indeed each village. Despite the fascinating music with which they greet visitors, quarrels are frequent, outbreaks of jealousy are by no means rare, and wars seem never to stop. Really it is just as in Europe and everywhere else. Moreover, we find here the taste for finery, the sense of what is good taste, the demands of fashion and the varying degrees of excitement aroused by these motivations among children, young people, mothers, mature people, the old, and the decrepit. Then there is the need to dance, to make music, to gather for feasts where sometimes people forget the limits imposed by that cardinal virtue, temperance. There is also the respect for the supernatural, the obedience to the moral law, the more or less complicated rites of passage for birth, puberty, marriage, and death. All of this is to be found among the Pare, for it all comes from human nature, even if it is something of an ideal.

It is not without difficulty that cloth reaches these high grounds; it is indeed appreciated, but in an unfanatical way, and if it is unavailable, there is no difficulty in replacing it with skins which have been tanned and made ready for wear. These well-prepared skins, resistant and solid in bad weather, outdo the best products of Manchester. The women adorn the edge of these skins with shells and glass pearls, with various colors, making patterns which show a certain artistic sense. As for copper and iron necklaces, big and small, fashion puts them everywhere, on necks, on arms, around the loins, on the knees, on the feet . . .

The men also like to make sacrifices to the Graces, as they said so well in the last century (eighteenth), between two applications of the guillotine. First of all, if there is any linen in the house, they take it *à tout seigneur, tout honneur* (to every lord, every honor). The young men are, moreover, regular in dressing their hair in little cords, which, at the same time, they smear with red earth, which they have mixed with castor oil. This vegetable product, whose name by itself recalls to whoever has used it rather difficult experiences, is, throughout this part of Africa, highly appreciated for external use. Wherever the castor oil plant is grown, the fruit is gathered to be boiled in water, then it is squeezed as much as is necessary, and then the oil which floats on the surface is gathered drop by drop to prepare various cosmetics and to use for rubbing on the body. This is something really necessary for Africans; substances with fat content lubricate the skin and protect from daytime heat and night time cold. Mothers feel that this type of care for their children is almost as important as keeping them fed. So tribes which lack agriculture like the Maasai, use butter; and those who have neither farms nor herds, like the Ndorobo and the Boni, use the fat of animals which they killed while hunting.

All Pare men wear a pendant earring; we must also mention, to give a full account of Pare male get-up, some bracelets and necklaces, a long pipe, a bamboo snuff box, a knife carried in the belt, a bow, a leather quiver filled with arrows, and sometimes a spear. Finally, for people who have a good dose of self-respect, there is an item which deserves special mention. It is a seat, but a seat which accompanies its owner everywhere; it is marvelously simple, unquestionably useful, and strikingly ornamental. This seat is a part of Pare dress and makes other kinds of seats—such as stools, benches, stalls, chairs, armchairs, sofas, divans, rocking chairs, love seats, wing chairs, Voltaire chairs, and different kinds of thrones—quite unnecessary. If a forward-looking and intelligent manufacturer introduced it in a civilized country like France, it would be immediately patented with a government guarantee. It consists of a thick cattle skin, cut into an oval shape, of the size desired, and kept in place by an ordinary bit of string which ties it on to that part of the body which a man never sees, but which, throughout the inhabited world, he knows is there to be sat upon.

Such is the way of life of this friendly Pare people. Alas! All that we can do for them is go past their mountains, praying God to hasten the day when we can come to tell them the story of God's love for them.

Chapter 14: At Lake Jipe

The Lost and the Found. Among the Antelopes.
The Happiness of Simple Living. A Difficult Stage of
Our Journey. Double Alert. The Jipe and its Edges.
The Devil in Our Guide's Body. A Sunset.

By climbing up a tree, we had been able to get a good view of Lake Jipe, but actually to get there would require marching for ten or twelve hours; it was out of the question to do this all in one go, our caravan and its men being heavily laden and weary. We reached a decision that, having got back some of our strength by halting at Mdimu, we should continue on the way forward and sleep in the Kizingo Desert which lay before our eyes; this would make the next day's share of the journey shorter.

Allowing the majority of our porters to take their time over their meal and follow it by a siesta—the latter completes the former—we decided to go on ahead with some of our more reliable men. It was two o'clock in the afternoon. We had been told that there was only one path which we could follow till sunset and, sooner or later, the rest of the caravan would catch up with us.

Trusting in the information we had been given, we went ahead, feeling quite happy. But this wretched path went so far toward the left that we began to wonder if it was the right path. We stopped to rest and to consider what to do, when, lo and behold, the guide ran up shouting, even when he was still quite a distance away, that we were lost.[1] We quickly started searching for the right path which should lead us across the desert to Jipe. Happily, the grass is not too high, walking was fairly easy, and crossing a landscape which was from time to time enlivened by meetings with herds of wild animals, we ended by getting on to the right path. But simply seeing these animals is annoying. We were ahead of the main caravan party; our

---

1. The edition that Fr. Adrian translated continued: "Without noticing it, we had taken the path for Arusha which passes through Le Njaro, between Sanghi and Gweno." Fr. Florentine Mallya pointed out that this location is unknown. And indeed, the sentence does not appear in the 1928 edition.

provisions were running short, it would be marvelous if this walking dinner could be made really useful. Mgr. de Courmont permitted me to try my hand; well, it was all in a day's work and I set off.

Little by little, I began to feel the passions of my hunting forebears. I found myself alone, far from our encampment, near to a herd of the big antelopes called pofu (*bucelaphe canna*). There were certainly fifteen or twenty of them, and their leader was a magnificent male with a black coat, his mane fluttering in the wind. Straightaway, I moved toward them, hiding myself behind the bushes, the clumps of trees, the ups and downs of the landscape, moving with the wind, now sliding, now crawling. Humiliations are the price man pays for his victories over the animal world.

Finally, I reached a dry stream bed, and hid myself there. The herd of antelopes was no more than 200 meters away. I fired; all the antelopes ran for their lives. The handsome male ran toward the mountains, abandoning in cowardly fashion his interesting family which ran off toward the lake. I went off after them, and as I ran I saw that one antelope was running by herself, dropping out of the herd. Then she stopped for a rest, set off again, took another rest; she had been wounded. Though she was some distance away, I fired again at her. While the others ran off helter-skelter, the poor creature took a few steps forward, slowly and as if worn out by tiredness, then calmly took a last mouthful of grass—like a prisoner condemned to death taking his last breakfast. Then she looked at me, and lay down in the long grass.

There she was; a superb animal, a little bigger than an ox, but less fat, with greater freedom of movement, slenderer and more elegant, with a red coat with white spots, with long straight horns, great black eyes entirely damp, and at the point nearest to the heart a little stream of blood, the color of a red rose. I felt a kind of pity, which was almost remorse, but very difficult to define, as I quickly took her life. Everything was finished.

But what was I to do next? The caravan was well behind us, even the advance guard had not appeared, and I was afraid that, if I went to look for it, I might not find my antelope in this wilderness where really nothing stands out as separate from the landscape. I tied a large red handkerchief to the mouth of my rifle and lifted it in the air. I climbed up onto the rump of the antelope—and I stayed there, making signs to attract attention. Now, almost immediately, the bulky form of Abdallah appeared on the horizon; he had heard the rifle shots, he had thrown down his load on the track and ran "as fast as he reasonably could," as the books of rules put it, holding a long knife.

Without too much fussing about whether the animal was alive or dead, Islam's faithful son tried to find the north—the direction of Mecca—decided to look southward, and, muttering the prescribed invocation, which he nearly forgot in his excitement, cut the antelope's throat. Gradually the caravan caught up with us, and there was an outburst of singing and dancing—everybody was happy. No more squabbles about the correct ritual, no more arguments or controversies, no more hair-splitting over what is pure and what is impure. I said to a devout Muslim, "That is not good meat, the animal was already dead when its throat was cut." To which he replied with conviction, "Oh, it was dead outside perhaps, but surely it was still alive inside."

We slept in the desert, since it was in the desert that Providence had provided us with our supper. With tremendous gusto, the porters got their loads together, and organized our camp, putting up the tents, searching for firewood and cutting up the antelope. The shares of meat were quickly divided; each porter got meat for at least three days, if he kept it till then...

Unfortunately, a supply of water was lacking, and we simply had the water we got at our last stop. It did not matter. As night fell on the plain, our men lit huge fires all around, epic-size pieces of meat were put to be grilled on the charcoal, while elsewhere long strips of meat were being smoked; everybody could do cooking according to his own ideas, men gathered round the fires, they chatted, they laughed, they told stories, they shouted, they poked the fires, they sang, they ate, they lay down in the long grass. Meanwhile the wind blew from the mountain, and the smell of the cooking was blown by the wind to mingle with the scent of the fragrant wood used to make the fires. One's inner feeling of the great wilderness, of our marvelous freedom, of a way of life appropriate for this country, gave all this African scenery an atmosphere which combined grandeur with gentleness.

We others, we Europeans, have so complicated lives, above all in this late nineteenth century, that living has become very difficult. We are always searching for happiness, indeed our search has something crazy about it, but we insist on so many ingredients for happiness that some of them are bound to be missing. A simple life brings happiness; the so-called primitives know what peace is. In Europe, smart young people go to the theatre, taking with them the boredom, the miseries, and the pointlessness of their lives. In the salons of high society, one has a duty to have fun; one can show off what one is wearing, the social whirl spins one round, and one can enjoy dancing. But here, we experience the happiness of early man; God is over us, piles of meat lie at our feet, our souls are at peace. Surely this is real freedom.

So time passed. Our men, who in these circumstances had really been enjoying themselves, had slept very little or not at all, and we gave them a surprise when we got up toward three o'clock in the morning to attend the mass which Mgr. de Courmont said, as usual, in his tent. Those, who had been awake all night, tried then to get some sleep; it was a bit late to start, but finally at five o'clock, everybody was moving, each one carrying a piece of smoked meat in his load.

The next part of the journey proved to be very demanding. When we got out of the Kizingo Desert, we entered the old basin of Lake Jipe. The water seems to have disappeared from there a long time ago, but it has left very visible traces. This was surely a very large lake; little by little, the area holding water had shrunk and perhaps is still shrinking, and in this it is similar to

CHAPTER 14: AT LAKE JIPE

most of the other big African lakes: the Ngami,[2] the Tanganyika, and even the Victoria Nyanza. For we have to accept this conclusion: Europe is becoming colder, and Africa is becoming drier, a conclusion which is particularly bad news for those who will live in ten thousand years' time.

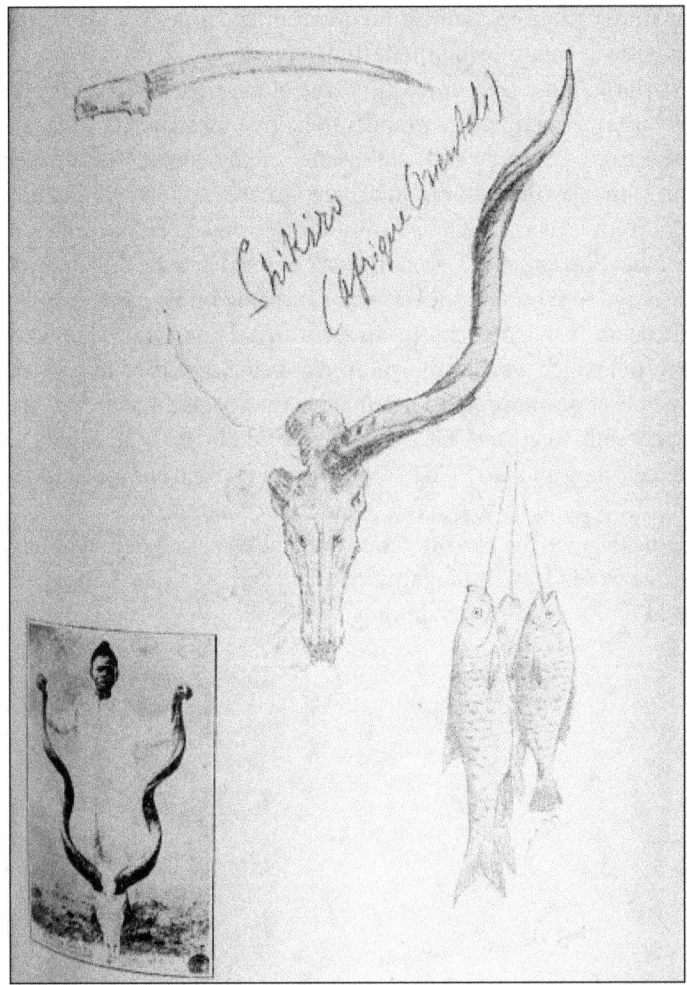

Here, in the old basin of the lake, the delicate grasses give way, little by little, to a rather special and inhospitable kind of vegetation, whose fruits pricked, whose leaves cut, and whose thorns got into our feet. All trace of the path has disappeared; we chose to take risks, aiming at a clump of trees, which the guide has pointed out to us, and which from afar looked

2. A lake in Botswana.

like a little round hill. But if we kept too close to the lake, we were liable to fall into large holes hidden by the grass, and we had to make a big detour to arrive finally, before midday, on solid ground where we checked on our numbers, six in all—three missionaries, old Selemani, the guide, and a child. The rest were scattered, some in the desert, some among the long grass or under the trees, and some down in the holes. I prayed that their guardian angels might bring them to us.

We started off again, one behind the other, tired, silent, our eyes fixed on the clump of trees which would surely give us some cool place to rest. We experienced a burning sun, the absence of any breeze. The air seemed to shimmer with heat, the soil was quite bare. But we kept on, without any stops. Suddenly from under a wretched mimosa tree on our right came a muffled sound, rather like somebody groaning. What seemed to be the shape of a wild animal started to move, and it was soon standing on its paws, giving, to our astonished gaze, a magnificent specimen of an old lion, with yellow skin and a big mane, but which was clearly annoyed at being disturbed in his siesta, and whose whole appearance was daunting. He then took three or four steps forward, apparently to get into his stride, he waved his thick tail calmly enough, and uttered a long and terrifying howl. We had to place our souls under God's protection and stand up to our foe. I said to the guide,

"Quickly, give me my rifle." But the guide, feeling perhaps that giving me the rifle would leave him empty-handed, was very slow to obey. "Do you see," cried Fr. Auguste, "he is slipping away."

Mgr. de Courmont added, adjusting his lorgnette, "What a splendid creature."

The lion, king of animals that he was, seeing these six human beings, standing their ground, and these dozen eyes looking into his, felt that things were against him, and slipped slowly—all right, very slowly—but finally he did slip away, while we six were very happy to see his failure of nerve. But we were all agreed that things would have gone differently if we had been fewer, or, if one or other among us had tried to run away.

Now that the lion was gone, we started on our way again, talking this time, and, forgetting the sun, our tiredness and our thirst, we exchanged impressions. We congratulated ourselves on not having yielded ground, not even knitting our brows—but, speaking in confidence, it was perhaps because we were taken by surprise. However, we had not gone very far when once again something stirred in the grass; the guide, really frightened, halted. Something rushed between the legs of poor old Selemani, who in his alarm fell backward, dropping all together—his basket, his saucepans, and his gun. It was a hare!

A quarter of an hour after this double alert, we reached a cluster of acacias. Their leaves formed a kind of dome and the clump had served as a landmark from afar. Little by little our porters caught up with us; they were weary but none of them was missing and we pitched camp. We deserved a break. We took it the next day, a little beyond where we had encamped, in a spot where the lakeside was largely free of the long grass and the reeds which surrounded it. It was here sufficiently accessible for us to take a bath, with the hippopotamuses for company. As we looked at them, they snorted as if they were welcoming us.

Lake Jipe[3] is a sheet of water, rather shallow, about five kilometers in width and sixteen kilometers in length, from north to south. It is 737 meters above sea level, and this figure will serve for the Ruvu River in its course in the hill country. The Ruvu is fed by the various streams coming down from the south side of Mount Kilimanjaro and reaches the Indian Ocean at Pangani. We can say that Lake Jipe gets its water from one of the tributaries of the Ruvu, the river which the Chagga call the Lumi and the Taveta call the Mfooro. This river receives the overflow from the Taveta oasis and receives also the Kitito River which flows into it on its left side, and in the rainy season, another river, the Le-Njaro, which comes down from the Taita Mountains. The Ruvu turns north while it is flowing though Lake Jipe and leaves the lake flowing more or less in the same direction with a slight inclination to the west, creating a marsh which is only crossed with difficulty. That is why people travelling past the lake do so on the eastern side, where we had camped.

---

3. The original had: "Lake Dyipe, or as the Taveta people would say, Lake Jipe."

On this side, the plain extends to the Taita massif, with only some limestone hills toward the northeast. On the opposite side, however, there are the beautiful Gweno Mountains, with rich soil which is farmed by the local people, and which are wooded on their higher slopes. Elsewhere, everything is part of the plain, and the plain is dry and desertlike.

There is little to be found on the banks of the lake except acacias, big mimosas with scented flowers, delicate leaves, and strong thorns. Then, in the water, there are small bushes, reeds, papyrus, and various cyperacean plants (*cyperus, scirpus, sclera*, etc.). There were a lot of interesting cockleshells, some of them not previously documented. There are plenty of good-sized fish, but they are rather similar to each other, and are not very tasty—cyprinoids and siluroids, the same kinds of fish which can be found in the rivers that come down from the mountain to form the Ruvu. Crocodiles are certainly to be found, just as they are to be found in Lake Chala which fills an ancient volcano crater above Taveta. As for the hippopotamuses, they are entirely free to frolic, and at nighttime they roam around among the reeds and the long grass. The tracks which they have made are useful to our men when they go to draw water from the lake. This lake water is thick, muddy, greenish, and altogether disgusting. In order not to drink it as it was, we filled a bucket with this water, threw into it a thick pinchful of ground alum, and stirred the bucket with a thick stick, and all the rubbish in it was thrown out. So, to the astonishment of our porters, who did not understand this piece of magic, we could drink clean water. To anybody travelling in Africa, or lacking a satisfactory filter, I would venture to recommend the use of alum.

As for birds, there are flocks of egrets, plovers, ducks, pelicans, and wild geese. But we have never seen so many guinea fowl anywhere else. There are flocks of twenty, thirty, even fifty guinea fowls to be seen, with mother guinea fowls looking after their chicks on the banks of the lake among the short grasses and on the dry and sandy ground which suits them.

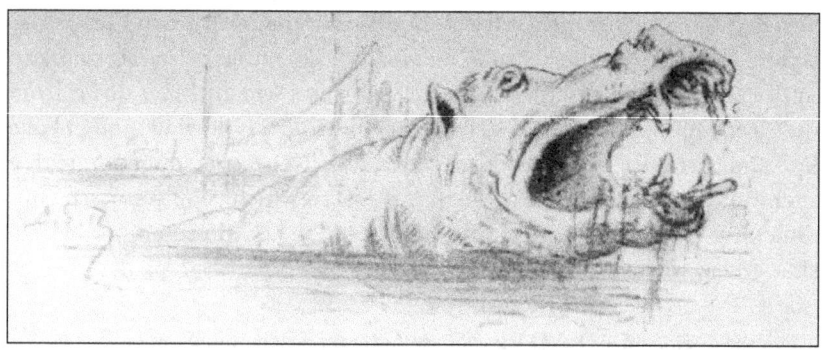

CHAPTER 14: AT LAKE JIPE

They call to each other, they cluck, they peck, they run about, and they flutter about. At night, they shelter on the trees. We killed some of them, but it would have been easy to make a massacre.

Moreover, the country around Lake Jipe is really a hunter's paradise. On every side, except for the Gweno and Taveta Mountains, there are vast plains, unsuited to agriculture, but which provide animals with a safe home.

While the herds of animals are scattered over these vast plains, they have a common meeting place. This is the lake, where at night they come to slake their thirst, before returning, each to his own patch of ground. And so, the banks of Lake Jipe are grazed and trampled on like those of a pool where big herds of cattle come to drink every day. When we took a stroll under the acacias which surrounded our camp, we woke up not just one buffalo, and fearing an attack, for which we were not adequately armed, we beat a retreat in good order. In the frightful march across the Kizingo and beyond, we frequently saw the strange form of giraffes, the gleaming skins of zebras, the various species, sometimes so attractive, of the African antelope (Grant's gazelle, Kobe, the Natal cephalophe, *Ccpahophe raseur, tragelapke des bois, apyceros molampus, nesotrague musque, electrague des roseaux, agocere noir, strepsicere coudou, boselaphe canna, taceblepas grious*, etc.); now and then there were ostriches, who always stayed a long distance from us.

These ostriches, it may be helpful to mention, are a new species (*struthus danaoides*) which has only been recognized in recent years.

Now here is something surprising. These animals have very regular habits which fit in perfectly with their needs. Can we say that they live in society? Perhaps it would be better to say that they have family life, for it is rare that one finds two adult males together—they clash and one kills the other or chases him out or enslaves him. This is why we meet these isolated individuals, who are to be found quite often, and whom hunters know well. These solitary animals have been driven into exile, and their outlook has become embittered by their vagabond existence. Theirs is a world unfriendly to the old. As to the herd leaders, they have ten or fifteen or even twenty followers, who give the leaders obedience and respect. They guide the herd, they signal any kind of danger, but also when they are calm, the young can freely gambol.

People think that when night falls, the animals simply hide in the woods. In fact, they gather in an open space, far from any clump of trees where one or other enemy—lion, leopard, or human being—could organize an ambush. There, pressed against each other, they rest, ruminate, sleep, and wait. Sometimes in the evening, sometimes in the morning, they go to drink water; but the paths they follow always avoid unsafe places. They go to graze by the first light of day, they come back toward ten o'clock, to find shelter under the trees, and reappear in the afternoon, toward four o'clock. However, there are always animals who act as lookouts, taking position a little in front of the herd, with stretched-out necks, with heads held high, and ears turned to the wind, only taking a mouthful of grass from time to time, in order to have something to do, while the bulk of the herd grazes peacefully, the old rest, and the young enjoy themselves.

When a cruel rifle shot brings down the chief, who is both leader and sultan, the herd wanders confusedly about; but soon the most vigorous, perhaps the most ambitious among the young males, sees that there is a power vacuum, and as happens in every house, or republic, or principality, or kingdom, or empire, he takes over and the reorganized family continues its journey in the wilderness.

In an alliance, there is always some question of interest. One quite often sees two or three species of antelope together, and usually it is a case of a small herd joining a bigger one, looking for safety in numbers. Antelopes are also ready to join forces with zebras, since the zebra's fine sense of hearing and its height give it the ability to warn against any threatening danger. A giraffe, looking only at its size, could really function as a semaphore; but it seems to be regarded as not really capable of doing this—frankly, it is rather stupid, and so it is not seen as a useful ally. The buffaloes, a crowd of quarrelsome characters, only welcome the company of a bird, which frees them from the vermin that covers them, with the greatest dexterity, mateyness, and perseverance, and an extremely relaxed approach, and, of course, provides itself with a delicious meal. The same applies to the rhinoceros and the elephant; they are, moreover, such big landlords that they cannot accept the presence of poor and small-sized relatives. But the ostriches, and especially the crowned crane, move around through even the biggest herds in entire liberty, among the excrement which provides them with their daily sweet course. Lions travel alone, or with their nuclear families, as do leopards. But both of them are closely followed by the hyena, who delights in collecting what the big beasts have left; hyenas are the rag-pickers of the wilderness.

It was here, and in the previous year, that a herd of zebras adopted a donkey, in a rather surprising display of hospitality. The donkey, a magnificent creature, a pure-bred Mascate animal, had been bought at the coast by German officers posted to Arusha. Then, one day, inspired by the great open spaces he saw before him, he dreamed a dream of freedom and escaped. After a great deal of fruitless searching, the German officers had forgotten him, thinking that he must have become a lion's dinner. But, lo and behold, he was seen several times in a herd of zebras, who seemed very fond of him. The officers tried several ways to bring him back, but all their overtures were in vain. Another example of a civilized being preferring liberty in the wild to a refined slavery in a high-class stable.

The European travelers who have passed by Lake Jipe have spoken unfavorably of it; perhaps they did not camp in a suitable place. We, the missionaries, and our men felt ourselves fortunate to have a two days' break on the lakeside. The guide, who was particularly stressed, was delighted to have brought us so far, safe and sound. However, the Africans, both men and women, seem to suffer diseases which one would think could only affect people from very developed countries. A fine young man of about twenty-five—lean, nervous, easily impressed—was one evening seated by a fire where some antelope meat was being grilled, when suddenly his friends noticed that he was talking nonsense. They shook him, they pinched, they called him, and they might have been dealing with a tree stump. There could be no doubt; the "spirit" had seized Mwalimu. An old man, the oldest of that group ran to me to tell me:

At Teveta, after fishing

"Father, be so kind, give me an earthenware cup."

"A cup, Fardyallah?" I replied. "And must it be earthenware?"

"Yes, to give Mwalimu a drink."

"Surely Mwalimu can drink today in the way he has always drunk."

"Oh, but . . . you see . . . the devil has entered his stomach and is moving up to his head."

I asked, "The devil, Fardyallah?"

"Yes," replied Fardyallah. "We know that, we Africans. If you will excuse me, white people just do not understand. And to get the evil spirit to leave him, you have to give him cold water in an earthenware cup, if you will excuse me."

"Is it really the devil, Fardyallah?"

"It is the devil, Father."

We got up, at once, very eager to see at close quarters the veteran enemy of humankind. Poor Mwalimu was there, sitting at the foot of his tree, clutching his knees with his outstretched arms, with his hands crossed. His whole body sagged, his eyes did not move. He chanted syllables which sounded a bit like Maasai, but did not make the slightest response when we called him, nor to the gentle pinches which we tried on his skin. The supposed devil was quite simply an attack of hysteria. We did not give him a cup or anything earthenware; we left him, without making a fuss, till the following morning. When morning came, there he was, lively and ready for work, having completely forgotten the possession episode of the previous evening.

But where is Kilimanjaro? It is so big and yet so difficult to see. How can it have chosen such dimensions and yet show itself so rarely? We began to recall the tradition of the Arab travelers, according to whom this is an enchanted mountain which hides itself, changes position, only to reappear and then hide itself again.

Admittedly, we did see it. It was at the moment when we had left the last mountains of the Pare chain and were entering the wilderness. The guide stopped the caravan, and, pointing leftwards with his hand, toward the northwest, exclaimed, "Look over there." We did look: there were only clouds, some certainly black and threatening, then, up above, very far up, in a break in the clouds, there was something small and entirely white.

"Well, what is it?" I said.

"That shining point, that is Kilimanjaro," replied the guide.

And, straightaway after, another cloud which had moved like a veil pulled by an invisible hand hid the summit of Kibo, for that it certainly was. Since then, we had often gazed in that direction: but all we saw was the sky, carpeted with grey.

We then decided not to gaze on Kilimanjaro until we actually got to Kilimanjaro. However, at the end of the second day of our break, a little before sunset, we ventured again into the waters of Lake Jipe. At that time of day, bathing your feet is really enjoyable. But we scarcely passed through the line of reeds which blocks the view of the lake itself, then we had to utter a cry of spontaneous admiration: Kilimanjaro!

What I was seeing was the sort of experience which you can never forget. There, before us, against a background of blue sky, the huge outline of the marvelous mountain stood out, as though it were the work of a vigorous artist. I could see two summits: the one on the left, somewhat rounded and dazzling in its brightness, which is called Kibo, the African giant, which raises its snow-covered head to more than 6,000 meters; the other one on the right, closer to us, jagged, dark, and rather frightening, with only a few white patches, this is Mawenzi, which is only 5,300 meters above sea level, but which from Lake Jipe appeared to be as high as Kibo. Because of the position where I was, the plateau which links the two summits was practically invisible. I could not see any of the details of the landscape of the massif—neither forests, nor valleys, nor individual peaks. The two craters seemed to be supported by an enormous pedestal, formed into one by the flow of lava, as though to serve as a candelabra lit in the course of centuries to the glory of the Creator. Alas! It is almost the only homage that he has received in these lands, and it has been given to him by his own hand.

However, the Maasai, who lead their flocks over the African savanna and see this wonderful mountain which rises before them on their horizon, have called it "The House of God." May we be empowered to make it an altar to God! Moreover, at the time I was at Jipe, everything combined to justify this idea of mine about Kilimanjaro. Lower down, on the inhabited foothills, one could see fires of dry grass burning, lit by the local people in their fields. Long clouds of whitish smoke rose slowly in the calm and clean air of the evening. They made me imagine them as a number of dishes placed at the foot of the mountain.

Here, nearer to us, on the other side of the lake, a great sun, such as one sees in Africa, was going down, like a red disc pulled down by its weight. I saw it sink rapidly behind a long line of picturesque hills, covering some with the darkest indigo, others with bright sky blue. Elsewhere, on the first foothills of Kilimanjaro, along the Pare chain, on the line of trees along the lakeside, and in the vast unclouded sky, it spread a marvelous range of colors, sometimes merging, sometimes passing from one color to another, and giving shades of an unlimited delicacy: green, blue, purple, violet, orange, opal—everything could be found. Then, to complete this superb picture which the hand of the Creator has painted and repainted at the same place over the centuries, there was before us the huge form of Kilimanjaro, reflected in the calm waters of Lake Jipe as in a mirror. Meanwhile, on the top of the mimosas, the insects were preparing, a little timidly, to practice their night song, the lake-dwelling birds passed slowly over the surface of the lake as they returned to their nests, spreading their great wings, and, from the depths of the distant savannahs, animals advanced in their herds, thinking, perhaps correctly, that it is for them that providence has prepared this watering-place.

This silent solitude, the increasing darkness of the evening, and the stillness of this world of tropical nature, combined to cover this unforgettable scene with a religious and meaningful calm. And, through this silence, how well our prayer rose to God, who had called us from so far away to give now his name and his word to those peoples who for centuries have known these marvels of his.

Chapter 15: Taveta

THE OASIS OF TAVETA. ENCAMPING AND WELCOME.
AN AFRICAN EDEN.

At six o'clock in the morning we left this delightful lakeside encampment. We turned away from the river to our left, whose course is marked by a green line of tall trees including quite a number of palm trees, and struck straight across the wilderness. Here the thin grass is nibbled as in a meadow, seemingly too straight to satisfy the herds who are looking for food. There are only some rather odd-looking euphorbias and dwarf passion flowers which escape being chewed by the animals.

On the horizon, there is what looks like a rampart; it is the forest, it is Taveta. This word, which the coastal Swahili and, after them, European travelers, pronounce Taveta, and which the local people call Taveta or Tooveta (from the Kwavi word, Ndoveta) is the name of an excellent oasis which all travelers have described very favorably. It lies to the southeast of Kilimanjaro where there is a dip in the landscape, filled with riverine benefits carried down from the great mountain, thanks to the river to which Thomson and Johnston have given the name Loomi, which is in fact used at its source in Chagga country, but which seems unknown to the Taveta people; these call it simply Mto or Mooro, "the river." This has its source in the forests which surround the lower slopes of Mawenzi, crosses the plain, leaving the greater part of its water in the subsoil. Here and there one sees springs rising up, and almost everywhere one has only to dig one or two feet in order to find water. This is the secret of the fantastic fertility of this stretch of ground, and, especially for strangers, of its definite unhealthiness. If Chagga people from Kilimanjaro stay here for any length of time, they get fever or rheumatism or dysentery.

This oasis has a triangular shape, with the top toward the north and the base is on the south side, running along Lake Jipe. From the summit to the base is just over eleven kilometers, and the width is, on average, two or three kilometers. The population is only about 2,000 or 3,000 people. Between the fertile zone, whose fertility is really quite remarkable, and the neighboring desert, whose lack of water is really frightening, the boundary marks a sudden transition, with no intermediate zone. Where the soil sinks in sufficiently to receive the outpoured water, you get the tropical vegetation at its most exuberant; but where its height blocks the possibility of receiving water, what you get is the barrenness of African soil, burnt by the pitiless sun.

Here we were then at the entry to this Arcadia. On the track we were taking—for you can get there by another track coming from the Taita country—a river, the Kitito, sharply separates it from the desert. This river passes sleepily under the cover of century-old trees and thickets which make passage impossible; the water is sludgy, there is mire and mud, and rotting tree trunks, and uncountable shells under the leaves of trees which, having fallen, remain in the river.

We halted on these unattractive river banks and then crossed through the forest by a pathway which was narrow, winding, and gloomy. Then there was another river to cross, this one more attractive, and finally we saw the big banana plantations, whose green leaves provided shade for everything. The farms which have been made are extremely neat, there are irrigation channels which run everywhere, and round huts scattered here and there in this green labyrinth. These give this man-made landscape an air of freshness, prosperity, and magnificence which has impressed all who have experienced it. Very soon there was an exchange of greetings under the broad banana leaves, and the welcome given to our white faces and European dress showed us that we were dealing with a people different from the other tribes. Here, nobody hid, nobody ran away; on the contrary, everybody—men, women and children—ran to see us, to greet us, to clutch our hands. More than one old lady grabbed hastily a bunch of bananas and brought it to us. They claimed that they wanted to sell them, but this was not to be taken seriously. They just wanted an excuse for taking a really good look at us, while showing us their wobbly teeth and their ears, which touched their shoulders.

We were shown a clearing in that forest of banana trees. The guide told us, "this is where all the Europeans camp." The British travelers, Thomson and Johnston, travelled this way, as did the Maltese Martini, the Hungarian Count Teleki, the American abbot, without mentioning a Russian prince, a Polish count, and perhaps others. But we were the first Catholic missionaries and the first Frenchmen who had the honor to pitch camp there. As such, we attracted the attention of the Tavetan population; crowds gathered to see us, weigh us up, speak to us, and, after this process of assessment, there was a general agreement that the new arrivals came from an interesting and highly civilized tribe.

The camping ground had a number of big huts, built in Swahili style, by our worthy forerunners, professional explorers, hunters, adventurers, princes, lords, or ordinary millionaires. Our men settled in without difficulty, while we, as we were accustomed to do, set up our tents, which protected us from a lot of things, notably vermin.

We stayed two days at Taveta, resting, buying provisions, paying the porters with cloth and pearls, but also getting to know the country and visiting the people.

The country was just as has been already described; its exuberant fertility is really superb. The banana trees are carefully cultivated, looked after, irrigated, and freed from dead leaves. Thus they grow exceptionally large and provide the local people with the bulk of their diet. The botanical name is *Musa paradisiaca*. Here, more than anywhere else, one reflects that it seems this was the plant which sheltered Adam and Eve at the very dawn of human life. Then, after the disaster from which we have never fully recovered, this was the tree that gave them their first dinner and their first clothes. Certainly, this was a long time ago; but here, taking a stroll under the great green leaves, gently swaying in the breeze over our sinful heads, one has to look sadly backwards, and recall our far distant origins. Taveta is, alas, an Eden, but an Eden where the serpent's suggestions are taken up even more readily than in the first Eden.

In a lot of countries, the banana is simply regarded as a fruit for dessert, and the banana tree is simply the plant which produces bananas. But at Taveta, one sees things differently: the banana tree can provide everything. To begin with, the trunk, green and cut into thin slices, provides excellent food and drink for the cattle, the sheep, and the goats. The dried leaves are used for providing huts with a roof. As for the bananas themselves, they can be eaten raw or cooked or roasted: there are ten or fifteen ways of making them eatable. At the very time when these lines are being written, the American newspapers announce, with a certain pride, that a citizen of that businesslike country has found how to make flour out of the banana. What a wonderful discovery! The people of Taveta have been doing just that for

CHAPTER 15: TAVETA

centuries: the banana must be plucked just before it gets ripe, it should then be cut in two, then dried in the sun, just as cassava is, and it should then be crushed in a mortar with a pestle. That is not all; here, as in Chagga country and Buganda one can make an excellent beer with bananas. Such is the wisdom of providence. For it is providence that has spread through the world foodstuffs which the people who consume them regard as necessities of life, like bananas at Taveta, the coconut palm on several African coasts, the bamboo in Burma, tea in China, wheat in Europe, rice in India, the breadfruit tree in Oceania, pepper in the West Indies, cod in Newfoundland, pigs in Chicago, macaroni in Italy, sauerkraut in Germany, garlic in Provence, and apples in Normandy.

However, bananas are not the only crop at Taveta. They also cultivate Angolan peas, maize, guinea corn, sweet potato, yams, pumpkins, sugar cane, and so on. One catches the river fish with a net, but some people fish with a rod and line, in the best middle-class manner. They search for honey enthusiastically, and to get it they set up hives made of hollowed-out blocks of wood, which are tied to a branch of a tree with a hook and a rope; but the wood has to be hollowed out with care, even a certain artistic skill, for nobody can get married unless he has shown previously that from time to time he will bring some honey to his home. They also have cattle; but the cows are not allowed to wander about grazing, not only from fear of the Maasai, but even more from fear of horseflies and other flies, including the terrible tsetse fly. They are fed at the house, as has been said, on banana trunks cut into thin slices, and this is perhaps something to recommend to cattle breeders in Africa, who are attempting to reintroduce them in places where, up till now, cattle have not been able to survive.

Moreover, not all the cultivatable land is actually cultivated, and one can still find quite a lot of patches of ground where the virgin forest can still display all its original magnificence. What trees! What columns! What branches! On a day, when one remembers how the sun is burning the wizened leaves in the neighboring desert, it is delightful to wander under these splendid canopies, walking along a barely visible footpath. There the light only came, sieved through the marvelously outspread foliage of these magnificent trees. On them, creepers spread as though they were living ropes on gigantic masts. Here and there, flowers grow whose bright colors contrast with the dark greenery of the leaves. The river also delighted me with its constant bubbling and the volcanic rocks which interrupt its flow, its sides carpeted with delicately shaped ferns and its great trees. The branches of these trees on both sides of the river came together high above it, forming majestic arches. Among the palm trees, we have to note the wild date palms, but even more remarkable are the raffia palms which grow in superb clusters, shedding their enormous leaves in picturesque and chaotic heaps. With their leaf stalk, people make light ladders, doors, girders, and sheepfolds—in fact anything that one wants.

The population of Taveta is made up of ethnic groups which were originally separate, but which now have the same way of life and culture, the same language, and even the same physical type. There are Taveta people in the strict sense, brothers of the Kahe and Lower Arusha people, whom we shall see later; they were joined by the Chagga, the Taita, and the Kamba. There is even here a small settlement of the Kwavi, brothers of the Maasai. Physically, the Taveta tend to be intermediate between the Kwavi and the Africans who speak a Bantu language, more thickset than the Kwavi, and more handsome than the Bantu speakers. On the whole, people here have advantages compared with those farther south, being better-looking, more welcoming, more communicative, politer, more intelligent, and more artistic. Everybody speaks Swahili fluently; but, rather unfortunately, European travelers have been overgenerous, and this makes them expect more than is reasonable.

Islam has made some converts among them and it would be unfortunate if, in gaining ground, it closed this attractive people to Christian influences. The Taveta people would have been glad if we had settled down there, and already several children offered themselves for education, each offering to bring a friend, who in his turn would bring someone else. But we had to go on to a more distant horizon. Alas! How many times is a missionary on his travels obliged to repeat the words of the Savior: "*Misereor super turbam*" (I have pity on the crowd).

With quite a lot of caravans passing through Taveta on their way to get ivory in Maasai country or coming back from there, the local people could today have all the cloth they want, but they handle animal skins so well, and give them extremely artistic decoration with glass pearls that they are little bothered by strikes in Liverpool or Manchester. People also adorn themselves with little chains, ear pendants, and bracelets. The men, especially the young men, are quite happy to dress in the Maasai style, plaiting their hair with care, and making at the back of their head a kind of tail with a strap. It is this, surely, that has produced the strange story of "tailed men" in the interior of Africa, which received much publicity thirty years ago. This report gave great pleasure to certain dogmatic scientific writers who found this a clear proof of man's monkey origin. "There you are," they cried, "we were quite right. There still exist men who lack the ability to sit down without relying on their tail." In fact there is a taillike object, but it is a product of art rather than nature and it is not in the place appropriate for a tail. There are a lot of gaps in the popular scientific writings of these gentlemen.

CHAPTER 15: TAVETA

Another curious fashion is the dressing-up of a young wife when the time comes for her to give birth to her first-born. We met this custom at the house of a neighbor of our camp, who had very politely invited us to share a calabash of milk in his home. We three missionaries, having arrived in the house, sat down on a bull's skin, stretched out tightly and functioning as a settee or a bed, according to the time of day. It was the old lady of the house who had shown us in to her sitting room. In a corner, a cow was chewing something. Near to her, her calf, firmly planted on its hooves observed us with much amazement: it was surely the first time that he had seen white people. We exchanged the usual greetings, and then passed the calabash full of curdled milk from hand to hand. Mgr. de Courmont just touched it with his lips, Fr. Auguste only left three hairs from his beard in the calabash, and it came to me, with, very unfairly, the order to swallow it all. Finally, I managed it, and we had got up to take leave of our courteous hosts, when a noise which sounded very like a rattlesnake stopped us right on the threshold. A baseless fear. It was not a snake but a lady, loaded with iron from head to foot, with her face veiled by chains, and the small chains on her chest, her loins, her arms, her feet, and her ears. Then there were copper necklaces on her shoulders, on her arms, and on her legs. As well as these, there were glass beads everywhere, bits of iron as well, bits of iron wire, bits of brass wire, really the contents of an ironmonger's shop. Then the old lady said, "She is his new wife," and made a rather special kind of face.

But while young wives and mothers are thus honored and protected, we have to admit sadly that new-born babies risk a very unfavorable reception on entering the world. Children who are born feet first, whose first teeth appear in the upper jaw, twins, cripples, and those begotten by an uncircumcised adolescent are ruthlessly strangled. Circumcision is here the custom, as it is in many other African tribes, without there being any Muslim influence. Boys are circumcised when they are between sixteen and eighteen, and they can marry only after circumcision.

Polygamy exists; but it is expensive and therefore limited. Each new wife needs a bride-wealth of a good number of heads of cattle, not to mention the honey, the cloth, the pearls, and so on. In the Taveta way of thinking, woman has to obey man, she is his inferior, and on this subject they have a legend, told me by a young man in a long conversation in which he told me many other things.

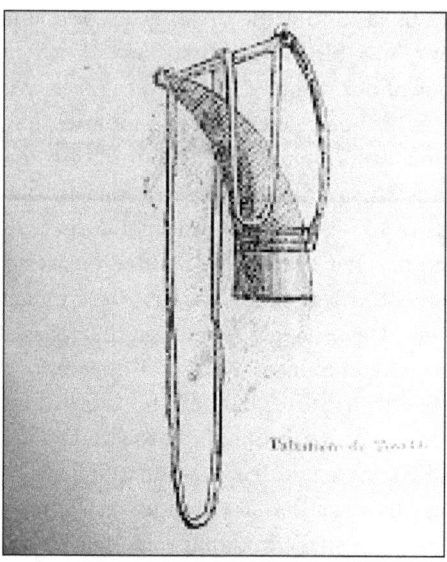

Snuff container, Taveta

"In the beginning," he said, "God wanted to try the heart of man and the heart of woman. And so, he took the man aside, gave him a knife, and said, 'Listen, tonight, when she is asleep, you will cut your wife's throat, as I tell you.' And then God took the wife aside, gave her a knife, and said to her, 'Listen, tonight, when he is asleep, you will cut your husband's throat, as I tell you.' That was that. Then the man went away very sad, thinking, 'Cut the throat of my wife, who is like a sister to me! It is impossible, I shall never do it.' And he threw the knife in the river, and, if he were asked, he would say he had lost it. The woman also went away. When night came, she took the knife and went to kill her sleeping husband, when God reappeared, and exclaimed, 'Wretched woman, as you are so wicked, you will never touch iron again. Your place will be in the fields and in the kitchen.' Then, turning to the man, he said, 'Your goodness has made you the master and given you the right to use weapons.' That is why, added Kombo, my informant, even in Europe, so we are told, it is the women who do the cooking and the men who do the eating."

There are no slaves at Taveta. Everybody works, but, as the soil is very fertile, everyday work is not very demanding. All ages and both sexes have plenty of time for chatting, strolling, drinking, dancing, and enjoying life. Moreover, there has been a very strong Maasai influence: for example, unmarried young people live in separate quarters but, they do not have a special way of life, as do the young Maasai, nor are they given military training, since they are not expected to engage in war outside their own territory.

Villages do not exist; everyone lives in their family's compound.

With regard to the political system, the Taveta people have a republic. It is interesting to note that this is a republic of a kind which was once proposed for France, a republic without a president. There are two assemblies, the assembly of the elders, and the assembly of the young men, the elders being a calm body of men, while the young men are more inclined to stir things up. In principle, a consensus between the two assemblies should be established when a consensus is possible. When it is not possible, the senate of elders, which has more authority, more moderation, and more experience, solves the problem by yielding. I am sure that you understand I am talking about Taveta.

When a stranger travels through Taveta, he receives a deputation composed of members of both assemblies; both the elders and the young men expect presents. We had to accept this ancient custom, and as this entry fee was requested politely, we did so cheerfully. Many European travelers have complained about this custom which is to be found among many of the tribes of the African interior who feel that they have the right to ask payment for the use of their roads. Perhaps these travelers have a case, but perhaps also they do not understand how government works in European countries, since they object to these payments in Africa.

Let us change the roles and imagine three or four Africans with charcoal-colored skins arriving at Marseilles in their customary get-up with arrows and spears, bringing foodstuffs, ivory, nuggets of gold, diamonds, parrots, monkeys, and other African products which are very interesting to Europeans, and who are followed by a hundred individuals recruited from here, there, and everywhere, who are their porters, their domestics, and their soldiers. This crowd arrives and straightaway camps down in the Cannebiere (a big street in Marseilles), and starts the cooking. Oh, dear, what a row. Immediately, the prefect, the police, and the city council will send a crowd of representatives, employees, police sergeants, customs officers, and gendarmes to tell these ill-informed people that they had first to pay their immigration fees, and secondly to find elsewhere to stay. I even suspect that some of these officials would try and get a personal present. Now, if these Africans, as their response, take these bureaucrats by the beard and twirl them round in the air, what would we, Frenchmen and Frenchwomen say? We must be honest and recognize that tolls, customs duties, and taxes are among the most recognizable signs of a functioning human society.

PART TWO

To Kilimanjaro

Chapter 16: On the Mountain—Kilema.

August 14, 1890

Here we are on the fourteenth of August. For a long time now, Mgr. de Courmont has been wanting to reach the foot of the mountain for the fifteenth, so that the first mass offered on the mountain should be said on that day when the Assumption of the Blessed Virgin is celebrated.

There was nothing to keep us any longer at Taveta. On the morning of the fourteenth, after a rather cold night, we forded the river by means of black stones which were slippery and unreliable, and more than one of our men took one of these health-giving, albeit involuntary, baths so highly recommended by modern medicine.

As we went on, we continued to see banana plantations, and when there were none to be seen it was because their place was taken by a stretch of remaining virgin forest. Water was everywhere, often forming streams and deep pools at the sides of which grew marvelous raphia palms; but a lot of these palm trees, which have leaves that can be ten meters long or more, have been damaged by the local people who, as has been seen, use the veins of the leaves.

Then we had a difficult crossing. It was a kind of river, deep and muddy, with no very clearly marked bed. We had to cross it on big tree trunks thrown across, which were as slippery as greasy poles. What a trial for people who, like our porters, are carrying loads of thirty kilograms. If any one of us falls into this abyss, will it be possible to fish him out? So we took off our shoes, rubbed our feet and hands with sand, and with prudence, patience, and humility, on hands and knees, all of us managed to make this dangerous crossing without leaving anything behind. A little further on, behind a low doorway, the forest came to an end. The earth rose up suddenly. It is the desert, the desert with its fiery sun, its hard and unrewarding soil, its thin grasses, its grey coloring. Then there are the little trees, spaced out and twisted, their leaves burned by the sun, its creeping euphorbias, its strange asclepiadees, its thorny acacias, in short its thoroughly unpleasant character.

Sycamore and waterfall

To the right and to the left, there are chains of reddish hills, with some gaps, some hillocks, each standing by itself, and some cone-shaped hills. The British traveler Johnston suggests that all this goes back to a period of volcanic eruption. When both Mawenzi and Kibo were active volcanoes, the two enormous craters at the top were blocked by the tremendous amount of molten matter; then the earth, finding it necessary to expel this lava from its interior, threw up these secondary hills, just as a sick body covers itself with inflamed boils.

There were three sights at which our eyes rejoiced: on our left, Lake Jipe, Kibo in front of us, and finally, after I had vainly chased a herd of antelopes, the sudden appearance of a little river flowing in the shadow of a double hedge of splendid evergreen trees. It was half-past eleven: we pitched camp.

Water! Everywhere in Africa one is delighted by the sight of water. But this time the water leaping and bubbling before our eyes is water from Kilimanjaro; we've got there!

The next day, August 15, was the day when the Catholic Church with the worldwide presence of its churches, its priests, and its faithful, sings the praises of the sinless Virgin through whom the Savior came. We, three missionaries, on the edge of the known world, came together to join our prayers with hers. At the foot of the marvelous mountain, whose shining summit seems to dazzle us, here for the first time we add our voices to those of our fellow Catholics scattered all over the world: "Come, let us adore the King of Kings, whose Virgin Mother is today taken up into Heaven."

This is a fascinating river. We camped near an old sycamore tree, not far from a waterfall whose noise informed us of its existence. We had an afternoon and then a whole day to explore its banks. The river still flowed strongly near to where we had encamped, but further along it got lost in the deposits of lava, gradually disappearing. There were herds of antelope wandering close to the river. I chased some of them until I got tired, and came back with some of our porters in the deep, but by then dry, bed of the river where we suddenly came across a family of buffaloes which was resting in the shade. When we had managed to dodge them, we came back slowly, looking for insects which were very common under the bark of fallen trees—wildlife certainly, but less dangerous than the buffaloes. Near just here, what is that stick whose black color stands out against the green grass? I stretched out my hand to take hold of it, when suddenly the stem straightened out like a spring, hissing and swelling. It was an asp, the same kind of frightening snake that killed Cleopatra. Had I come closer, I would have died like that famous lady, of whom Pascal said, "If her nose had been shorter, the world would have been a different place." After a moment of alarm for the snake and for me, the man and the reptile went back to where they had been, but when I returned to the attack, this time armed with a stick, the asp had gone.

On the morning of the sixteenth, we set off again and having crossed a nearby big river, the Kilema, we took the mountain road which ran decidedly to the right, the Chagga road, for that is the name given to the southern side of Kilimanjaro. While we were making arrangements at Mombasa for the departure of the caravan, a young man approached us one day, who was originally from this area. I had known him previously and had cultivated his acquaintance. He now asked to join us in order to return to his homeland. It was providence that had sent him to us missionaries. Nderingo was immediately accepted. He kept on asking us to let him lead us straight to his home area, Kilema, which he claimed to be without equal for happy living, and to introduce us to the king, Fumba, with whom he had played at leapfrog in his childhood. But in the last four days, his urgings had become more and more pressing, and in the end we yielded. We left behind us various districts, where magnificent forests and standing crops could be seen at a distance, and began to mount the lower slopes of the mountain. These are fertile, with plenty of shade, but their only inhabitants are herds of buffaloes and elephants, whose tracks we often saw.

The Gates of Kilema

Here we were at the gates of Kilema. These were a kind of building with beams placed on top of each other and tied together, with, at the bottom, a narrow hole kept closed by pieces of wood that could be removed. Nderingo went in front of us and, faced by the unusual and rather unattractive way in, his first act was to fire a rifle shot. Immediately, the woman who kept watch inside asked, "Who goes there?" Nderingo recited our ranks and our merits, and made himself known, giving the names of his father and mother, of his uncles and aunts, of his brothers and sisters, and of his male and female cousins. He spoke sharply to the doorkeeper who was striving to remove the pieces of wood, and finally slipped into the hole, through which we could pass. It is a real mouse hole for human beings, but it was impossible to enter anywhere else, because of the impenetrable hedges of spiny creepers which protected a chiefdom at war.

Behind this door, which was immediately shut when we had entered, we saw a long path, twisting its way between two hedges of brushwood, and spreading out at the end on a shady lawn which seemed to take us back to dear old Europe. Before our eyes there was abundant grass, cool, green, and short. There were beautiful trees, which provide changing patches of shade, little shallow pathways running between the hedges, slopes which surrounded the gardens and the fields, but also we saw something that reminded us very strongly of home. This was just like the little valley where we dreamed of what our future might be, learning some Greek words and taking a quiet doze after studying the books of the great writers. It is here we have the tree where the magpies nest and the blackbirds sing! And there the stone with a carpet of moss, where granny loved to sit in the first fine days of spring. Dear granny, whose wobbly jaw and hairy lip used to fascinate us so much. Truly, how far away all these memories of the past are, and how happy one feels when they return.

After a few minutes' rest, during which we exchanged cheerful greetings with the local people, we started off again on a narrow, stony path. We kept on up the mountain, the air became cooler, there was a greater variety of flowers, and as the birds sang and the streams flowed we found ourselves on some level ground. Here, suddenly, we were greeted by a loud volley, to which our carriers responded with their rifles. It was a noisy and splendid greeting for us. For the woman who guards the entry to Kilema had announced our arrival.

When the guns fell silent again, a big fellow, nearly six feet tall, young, well-proportioned, with an upright posture, came away from the group of riflemen. He was carrying on his shoulders a nice tablecloth, and wore on his head a felt hat covered with a cotton cap. This is what one wears on really big days.

Nderingo whispered in our ears, "That's Fumba, the king."

The chief came forward and gave each of us a vigorous handshake. To stress his welcome, he was careful to grasp our hands three times, putting all he had into it. Then, having looked at us with frank curiosity, he showed the guide a place where we could camp and went away.

Nderingo followed him and surely gave us a warm recommendation. We had in fact told him to explain the motive for our journey, and prudently to make arrangements for us to stay in the district. A little later the chief sent us a plump cow for our supper, much to the joy of our men; we in turn gave a present to mark our arrival. Soon the local people, having heard the gunshots, crowded round us. They gazed at us, listened to us speaking, gently touching our clothes, running their hands over our heads, and pulling our beards, in playful curiosity, to see if they would come off.

This is a very beautiful country. Behind us, the two dominating peaks, Kibo and Mawenzi, only appeared occasionally above the veil of clouds which provide the mountains with a shifting belt. But we could see clearly the vast virgin forest, the enormous lower slopes of the mountain, the seemingly bottomless ravines from which the muffled sound of distant waterfalls came. Around us we saw the luxuriant greenery of fields and gardens, the large leaves of innumerable banana trees swayed in the wind, and these little enclosures, surrounded by dracoena trees—each the home of a family, free and independent—called up dreams of country life at its best, gentle and picturesque. On our right hand, and on our left, a little further away, were two hills, which would be regarded elsewhere as mountains. On them there were many white blotches, which move about. They were herds of cattle whose far-off mooings we could hear. In front of us, and down below, there were the quiet waters of Lake Jipe and the blue mountains of Gweno which stand out against the endless extent of the sky. There are also many rivers meandering in the plain and the great Kahe Forest, where they come together, and the vast desert, which one can see stretching a very long way, till sky and land seem to fuse, in the far-off and unclear horizon of the Maasai country.

Meanwhile, in the afternoon, we went to pay a courtesy call on King Fumba. Nderingo, who had been in the royal presence since our arrival, went before us as he had to introduce us. Mgr. de Courmont was tired and could not come, so only Fr. Gommenginger and myself went. This is just as well since the king was completely drunk. Apparently this was the result of his happiness at our arrival. And there he was, seated on a small, well-carved wooden chair, in front of an elegant house, a well-built wicker building. It was the storeroom for food and drinks. Facing us was his palace, a big wooden house, oblong in shape. On one side there was a kind of big shed for holding meetings. Then, scattered about, there were houses belonging to his wives and his servants. The whole set of buildings was surrounded by a bright green hedge.

CHAPTER 16: ON THE MOUNTAIN—KILEMA.

Fumba and his wife

As we approached, Fumba tried to get up; he found it difficult and was unsuccessful. He sat down again and tried to get back his strength in having new supplies of beer brought. This was a beer made from bananas and millet, and we had to share it with him. This was in fact a very good drink, much better than the ordinary *pombé* made from guinea corn which the lowland people drink. A lot of sympathy for the chief was expressed, but the more that people sympathize, Fumba, who did not seem to have difficulty in finding where he could spit, mumbled, wept, dribbled, and stammered in a really awful way.

Suddenly, Nderingo spoke with democratic bluntness, telling the prime minister, "He's as drunk as a full jug can make you."

"What's that?" said the king. "Is that you, Nderingo?"

"Quite true," replied our man. "You're reasoning like a calabash."

"Oh."

"Like a pumpkin."

"Eh, a pumpkin."

"We can't talk business now, you'll only say something foolish; you don't see things properly, you're spitting all over the place, you are making yourself look ridiculous."

"Then have a drink yourself, Nderingo. It's a pleasure. . ."

"No, your majesty, go and sleep. We shall come back tomorrow morning. We shall kill a goat, and then we shall make a binding alliance."

"Ah, how fond I am of you," said Fumba to end the discussion, shaking our hands vigorously. "Stay with me: we shall have a splendid time every day."

The next morning, we got word that the chief was capable of discussing things with us, but Mgr. de Courmont, who did not wish to make an agreement with him too quickly, sent the two of us (Gommenginger and Le Roy) to see the king. This time, he met us at the door of his main house and talked to us in a way which was both very friendly and very sensible. We explained who we were, why we had come, and what we wanted.

Fumba replied, "I quite understand you. For a long time, I have wanted to have some Europeans who would stay here. We have had white people who come for trade, or for hunting wild animals, or who want an adventure; but none of these stay. They make us stand in line so that they can photograph our faces with their cameras, and then they go home and show the photographs to their wives, telling them, 'Here are the Kilimanjaro people: they have heads like cooking pots.' But you are quite a different kind of European. Everywhere in the world there are some decent people. Your aim, so we have been told, is to give black people education and to share your way of thinking with them. It is a good idea. Here, we know that God exists, but we are not sure of what he wants us to know."

Nderingo broke in, as a zealous convert. "He has told us not to drink."

"Well," said Fumba, "I did not know anything about that. Don't you see, Nderingo, that everybody has his own way of drinking? Some people hardly drink at all, other people drink enough to stumble when they are walking. As for me, when I settle down to drink, I really must get thoroughly stoned."

Then he turned to us. "The first thing we must do is to become blood-brothers."

"Blood-brothers?"

"Yes, it is a custom of our country. Don't think that we are savages. You will eat a bit of me and I will eat a bit of you. It is the simplest thing imaginable."

The bishop was not with us. Fr. Auguste, using a questionable argument that I was his senior in the priesthood, said that he could not accept the honor, so it fell to me.

Near there, a splendid goat, totally white, looked after by a child, waited a little impatiently: it was the goat of the covenant. One by one, the elders went up to it, and spat on a fistful of grass and the goat's head. They said, with the seriousness of men performing an act of worship, "I give you to God, I dedicate you to God." It seems that, once this ceremony is completed, the goat cannot go back to the herd; it now belongs to God, it is sacred; if it is not sacrificed as part of the ceremony, it must be allowed to wander in the woods.

As it was to be sacrificed, the goat was brought to have its throat cut; its liver was shown to the people participating and pronounced both healthy and pure; then the breast, which had been passed rapidly through the fire, was brought to us on the end of a wooden skewer. As for the rest, some was burned, some was thrown to the birds, and some was eaten; for it was a true sacrifice, a sacrifice to the Creator and Master of the world. It was a sacrifice such as was offered by the early descendants of Adam and Noah. How strange, but also how enlightening to find these acts of worship among this isolated mountain people who have lived, down to the present time, without any Jewish, Muslim, or Christian contacts.

But let us get back to our business, I mean, to our goat, for the ceremony of blood-brotherhood was just about to begin. I tried to be serious, but respect for the truth makes me confess that my fellow missionary (Fr. Gommenginger) standing behind me, roared with unliturgical laughter. There we were, facing one another, seated on a bull's hide. Fumba clutched my arms very firmly and I did the same to him. An elderly uncle stood beside the king. My guide (Nderingo) stood at my side. Then the king's sponsor, rubbing his long index finger along his nephew's forearm, like a pork butcher sharpening his knife on a stone, solemnly uttered these words:

"The white man of the French tribe—oh, what is your name, your real name?"

"Fr. Le Roy."

"Hm, Mapere-rua?"

"That's it."

Immediately, everybody tried to pronounce this extraordinary name, which had come from so far away. Nobody managed it entirely correctly, but it was accepted as a real name. The old man started his introduction again.

"The white man of the French tribe, Mape-Rua, the man who reads, writes, gazes at the mountains, cures the sick, speaks to everyone, and prays to God, Pe-Rua has come to Fumba. And he has said that he will build his house at Kilema, that he will live there, and that there he will do good. And that is why he wants to be the king's brother."

Everybody repeated, "Yes, the king's brother."

"But if Lape-Rua is a liar, or a thief, or a traitor"—and the elder turned a terrifying glance at me—"may he die."

The crowd repeated solemnly, "May he die!"

"When he goes away, may his eyes be looking backwards."

"Looking backwards!"

"When he tries to look at something, may his eyelids be sewn together."

"Sewn together!"

"When he walks, may his legs creak and crack like a worm-eaten stick."

"Worm-eaten!"

"When he moves forward, if he moves forward, may he move like a flooded stream!"

"May he move!"

"If he climbs a tree, may he do so feet upwards, head below."

"Feet upwards!"

"If he goes for a walk, may he walk on his hands, with his feet in the air."

"The feet in the air! Ah, his feet in the air!"

"When he eats, may his food choke him."

"Choke him!"

"When he drinks, may his drink flow through him, as though he were a bamboo."

"Flow through him!"

"When he spits, may nothing come out."

"Nothing!"

"Or if he does bring something out, let everything come out."

"Everything!"

"And may he be turned inside out from top to bottom just like a sack."

"Like a sack!"

"May he be strangled by a leopard."

"So be it!"

"May the lion devour him."

"So be it!"

"May a snake bite him."

"So be it!"

"May the hyenas divide him up."

"So be it!"

"May the vultures tear out his eyes."
"So be it!"
"May the sun cook his entrails."
"So be it!"
"May he be poisoned by drinking milk."
"So be it!"
"May drinking water burn him."
"So be it!"
"May fire devour him."
"So be it!"

The old magician stopped, but then finished still more energetically with a final curse, which had better be left in the local language, but, if translated, should be kept in Latin.

Well, that's it, keeping a stiff upper lip before these frightening possibilities is useless, even a really macho man would be worried, thinking of the dreadful state he would be in if any of the prophecies came true. For instance, if one woke up one morning to find oneself turned inside-out like a sack.

I felt much relieved, when the magician, having finished his litanies, spoke directly to me on behalf of Fumba.

"Mapera, do you wish to drink my blood?"

I replied, "That's all right by me."

"If you vomit it, you are my enemy: if you swallow it, you are my brother."

"I agree."

It was now the king's turn. My sponsor, taking over the ceremony which I had had to accept, said:

"You, Fumba, king of Kilema, listen to me. And all of you, likewise, listen to me. If the Father here, or his brother over there (Fr. Gommenginger) settles here, or travels around here, in any part of your territory, and if you, Fumba, or if someone under you, does them some harm: if you steal from them, or let someone steal from them, if you cut off their water, if you won't let them have land, or wood, or foodstuffs, if you do damage to their houses or their fields or their flocks and herds, if you prevent people coming to them for trade, and, above all, for learning to read the word of God, and to recite the prayers of which God approves, and to see the sacrifice of the mass, if they have to say one day 'Fumba has deceived us,' death to his father, death to his mother, death to his wives, death to his children, death to his uncles, death to his goats and sheep and cows."

"May all his banana trees die off."

"May the stream of his mountain dry up."

"May his fire go out for ever."

"May his beer become a poison which kills him."

This last curse caused Fumba to tremble unwillingly, but he recovered himself quickly and uttered a vigorous "So be it!"

At that point, the king's uncle took a local knife, a sort of two-edged dagger and with difficulty made cuts in the king's forearm and in mine; pressure was applied to the cuts and his blood and mine squirted out. Fumba took a bit of meat, cut from the goat's half-cooked chest, rubbed it vigorously on the cut in his plump black arm, asked me to open my mouth, and then pushed it down into my throat. Lord have mercy! If only the chunks of meat were smaller, and if my confrere, Fr. Gommenginger, didn't find it so funny.

I was given blood-stained meat three times, but despite everything, I managed to cope. The pieces of meat were duly swallowed, and the public was happy to see that.

"The depth of my heart is as pure as heaven."

Now it was my turn. Three times I served Fumba huge mouthfuls of meat with my blood as the sauce. They went down as though falling into a pit.

The king, with an extremely friendly smile, put on my index finger a kind of ring made of goat's skin: I gave him a similar one, and everyone got up to go.

The ceremony was over, and so we were brothers. Fumba, radiating good will, took our arms straightaway, saying that he could not hide anything from us. He invited us to go with him and see everything in his house; he showed us his rapid-firing rifles that he was given by an American traveler. He also showed us a watch which just refused to go, although, he told us, he had repeatedly banged it against the wall. Finally, he introduced us to his respected wife, a tall, calm, intelligent woman, who came with her handmaids and her two children.

The king asked, "Do you want snotty-nosed kids like them for your school?"

"They're just what we want, but they needn't be snotty-nosed."

"We'll give you them: we have swarms of them."

Later on, we had a formal exchange of gifts. Fumba sent us three spears, all absolutely magnificent, made by local craftsmen, each of which would, among the Maasai, have been worth a head of cattle. We, in turn, gave him linen, woolen blankets, an axe, and glass pearls.

The rest of the day we spent going round the boundaries of the capital, to see where it would be best to site the mission. Fumba gave us guides, and as dark clouds seemed to be appearing over the plain, he immediately sent for a well-known rainmaker, who could keep rain from falling or

CHAPTER 16: ON THE MOUNTAIN—KILEMA.

make it fall, according to need. The specialist promised to drive the clouds away, and so we set off.

This is a marvelous country: there are splendid valleys, delicious dales, rivers with high banks, irrigation channels remarkably well laid out, big banana plantations, well-looked-after crops, and little paths hollowed out in the shelter of the trees. The little private farms are surrounded by hedges of growing capis bushes, there are dracoena enclosures and baskets of greenery and flowers at the entries to gardens, and the houses are well looked after. Above us, there was the mighty mountain; below us, the vast plain. Everything combined to make an atmosphere of happiness, beauty, and fascination. The population was large and full of good will. The children who flocked round us followed us about and watched whatever we did. They will be easily tamed! Many of the men were away, in a war against Sina, chief of Kibosho, to the west of the mountain.

We returned, but already the clouds had invaded the place, climbing up the valleys and covering everything. It was a damp mist, cold and piercing. When we got back to Fumba, we were soaked, like mice in a tub. "Well, what about your rainmaker?" The chief, a little ashamed, replied, "Unfortunately, he could only hold back half of the rain that was coming. If he had stopped it all, it would have meant a whole year's drought, all the rivers would have dried up, and you would not have had anything to drink."

Kilimanjaro chameleon

Chapter 17: On the Mountain—Moshi

A View of Kibo. Over Hill and Dale. M. d'Eltz and the German Station. The Anglican Mission. At Mandara's. The Mists and by the Fire

The following night was cold despite the woolen blankets on our camp beds. We had all suffered from it and slept badly. At four o'clock in the morning, Mgr. de Courmont said mass in his tent. Fr. Augustus, in his tent, was talking to our old cook, Selemani, whom the priest had accommodated in his tent. Selemani, not knowing how to keep his old bones warm, had pushed himself into the sack for onions.

I got up and went out. But scarcely had I put my nose out of the door than I was captivated by a fascinating sight. Up there, under the vast vault of an absolutely clear sky, sparkled the magnificent Kibo peak, like a dome of burnished silver. How beautiful it was, free of clouds, majestic and sublime, in the dignity of its total stillness.

The intense whiteness of its snow is dazzling, but little by little, as the day goes on, a gentle golden light can be seen on the snow which changes from yellow to orange and from orange to red with, sometimes, shades of green and blue. It is the sun which, from far away, sends the first rays of its splendor to the great mountain, whose frozen face dominates the hot lands of Africa. Later, when the evening star has appeared, the mists of the great virgin forest rise up in clouds, and, in a little time, the high plateau and the magnificent peaks are covered by them as though by a veil.

We leave at ten o'clock, having repeated our promise to return in a short time, as the chief had insisted. My poor dear brother Fumba, till when shall we be faithful to each other? We took the road to Moshi, a small state in the middle of Chagga country, lying to the west of Kilema. It is here that the famous Mandara is king. There is a German station there, directed by M. d'Eltz, who has long been giving us very pressing invitations to "come down," if one can use this expression when what we have to do is to climb up to the station, which is 1,200 meters above sea level.

CHAPTER 17: ON THE MOUNTAIN—MOSHI

Moshi[1] is separated from Kilema by the chiefdom of Kirua, with several rivers with high banks, enormous ravines and awe-inspiring steep slopes; it was a rough journey for the three of us, and for our men. Happily, it took only four hours.

As we were walking along the narrow paths which the local equivalents of engineers have skillfully cut on the sides of the hills, we met the Kilema warriors who were returning from Machame. Things went well, it seems. They numbered about 1,000 men altogether, but they were divided into small groups of ten or twenty. They were relaxed, without military formality, some still carrying their weapons and wearing military dress, others in everyday clothes which were rather skimpy. Some of them were driving cows and calves before them—their share of the booty. Others brought as captives women and poor little children. The women scurried along the path, the children, too young for that, were clinging to their mothers' backs, with anxious looks in their big, frightened eyes. They were not quick enough to escape in time, and so the poor little creatures were taken as slaves.

Finally, we got to the German station. It was a house of wooden boards, with some huts with clay walls, elegantly situated in a grove of tall trees, from which a magnificent view stretched before us. But M. d'Eltz was not there. A Christian Sudanese sergeant, who with some coastal Africans had to guard the house, told us that he was living at lower Arusha, two days' journey from Moshi on the plain in front of us, with a European NCO, Mr. Kayser, and a small group of soldiers and workmen. The next day we sent him a letter with our greetings and the news of our arrival. He came to meet us on the 22nd.

For us, M. d'Eltz was far from being an unknown quantity. He was born in Poland of an aristocratic family which has some members living in France. Much of his youth had been spent in Russia, in the Ural Mountains and Siberia. Later on, he came to Africa, and when he was at Bagamoyo we had different occasions to benefit from his straightforwardness, his trustworthiness, and the integrity which marked him as a true gentleman. He had often urged Mgr. de Courmont to commit to founding a mission on Kilimanjaro; but circumstances had made him postpone the project, so, as it seemed today that it must be realized, M. d'Eltz was particularly happy.

However, immediately after our arrival at Moshi, the first thing we needed to do was to send our greetings to Mandara, the local ruler and the principal chief among the Chagga. But, because of the thick mist which surrounded us, we could not go to him ourselves. Our emissary apologized for

---

1. The text has, "Motchi (and not Moshi as it is written on the maps)." A native speaker assures us that the word "Motchi" does not exist in the Swahili language today.

our absence, and the visit was returned by a minister of the king—a rather shrewd, lean old chap, wearing a rather dirty cotton bonnet—with whom (I mean the old chap) we had an interesting conversation in Swahili.

Kibo	Mawenzi
(6,100 m)	(5,300 m)

The following morning, we had fine weather. Mgr. de Courmont was tired, so Fr. A. Gommenginger and I went down to make the official visit on his behalf. On our way, we came across the Anglican mission, founded here in 1885 by Bishop Hannington of the Church Missionary Society, whose East African base is at Mombasa. We went in, and I had the good fortune to find Dr. Baxter who was in charge of the medical work of the mission and whom I had known for some time.

The director of the pastoral work of the mission, the Rev. Mr. Steggal, was not there. He had received a hurried message from Mombasa that "a party of Romanists" was on its way inland. He went quickly to make arrangements with the Taveta people. We had been warned of this—so without further delay, he had built a hut on the banks of the river so as to show these terrible "Romish priests" that the place was already taken by the Anglican Church. Frankly, we must admit that even if we had wanted to start a mission in that oasis, we would have been rather frightened by the warning sign that our well-intentioned friend had put there.[2]

---

2. The next two paragraphs, indented, are not found in the 1928 edition.

CHAPTER 17: ON THE MOUNTAIN—MOSHI

Mandara

Perhaps I could mention that in the sultanate of Zanzibar there are two important Anglican missionary societies whose doctrine and whose outlook are in sharp contrast. One of them, the Universities Mission of Central Africa at Zanzibar, makes very sincere efforts to draw closer to the great Catholic family—almost all of whose doctrines it accepts. But the other mission (the Church Missionary Society) at Mombasa seems to belong to the time when it was believed, with the firmness of a dogma, that all Roman Catholics worshipped idols, that their priests were possessed by the devil, and that the Pope had cloven hooves, proof that he was the Antichrist.

It is taken for granted that every issue of their main periodical, the *Church Missionary Intelligencer*, contains some hackneyed old accusation against Rome which has gone stale two or three centuries ago, but which can always be trotted out again. It cannot be said, however, that these good people are uninterested in progress. The most recent volleys of the Anglican Church against Catholic superstitions, as everyone knows, have been fired in Uganda from up-to-date Maxim machine guns. Leaving that aside, I must quickly add that Dr. Baxter has never, to my knowledge, quoted the Apocalypse against us. Indeed, during our stay in Chagga country, we not merely got to know each other better, but had some very friendly outings together.

At this time, the mission of "our separated brethren" just consisted of two huts with clay walls, rectangular in shape, architecturally unimpressive. When the Rev. Mr. Steggel is there, he explains biblical texts to some children and Dr. Baxter gives devoted care to all the sick people who come to him. Mandara himself is one of Dr. Baxter's patients, but the patient and the doctor are not very happy with each other, the patient because he has not been cured, and the doctor because he knows only too well that his medicine gets thrown out of the window.

Finally, we arrived at the palace of the famous Chief Mandara who, like Mirambo of the Nyamwezi, Msere of Katanga, Makoko, and Mutesa, has had the glory of gaining the interest of European travelers who have written their African names in their books. As soon as our arrival was announced, we were brought into his presence. The house had a rectangular shape and was divided into three rooms. It was built in Swahili style by workmen from the coast. I found it less impressive than Fumba's house, but perhaps I am biased in favor of everything done by my blood brother.

Mandara lives in the central room, seated on a bed he never leaves, wearing a long robe of white cloth; on his head, he has a cotton bonnet, a French national identity marker, whose use by the kings and people of central Africa I found very flattering. His feet were covered by a blanket of white wool. Around his neck hung a necklace of blue pearls. On his right wrist he had a copper bracelet, and that was all. The man himself was tall and well proportioned and seemed to be about fifty. One of his eyes has sunk back into the socket, but the other, which does the work of two, has a marvelous sparkle. His nose is rather aquiline, though broad at its base, and the beardless face is very well shaped. All the Europeans who have met Mandara have noted two outstanding qualities in him: a very keen intelligence and exceptional craftiness. We have seen him on several subsequent occasions, either by ourselves or with Mgr. de Courmont, and we share the same general impression and are very impressed by his features: so quick to show what he is really thinking, his polished affability which distinguishes him, and the really interesting conversations we have had with him.

CHAPTER 17: ON THE MOUNTAIN—MOSHI

He was too young to have known Rebmann, the first European to have visited Kilimanjaro. But he recalls perfectly the visit of Baron Van Den Decken in 1862, of the Englishman New in 1873, Thomson's visit in 1883, Johnston's in 1885, and later on some German travelers. On practically all of them, he could give stories as surprising as those which they have told about him. He had, he told us, heard the French spoken of, but he had never seen any of them and we were happy, in presenting ourselves as such, to correct some of the historical information which had been given to him about this interesting tribe. In return, Mandara without any hesitation, gave us very detailed accounts of life among the Chagga, the people, their way of life, their beliefs, and their system of government, and an equally detailed account of his own life. He spoke Swahili very fluently, as well as Maasai, and we enjoyed conversations with him that lasted for two hours without a moment of boredom. Surely no European crowned head could do the same!

Moreover, Mandara has a friendly contact with the German emperor and he is very ready to talk about this distant kinsman. Some time ago, he allowed three young countrymen of his to travel to Europe in the company of a German traveler. They were shepherds, but the newspapers eagerly described them as princes, ambassadors, and ministers plenipotentiary, whose mission was to lay Africa as a whole, and Kilimanjaro in particular, at the feet of his Imperial Majesty, Wilhelm II. We had a meeting with these courageous young men who had undertaken, without incurring any expense, a very interesting expedition to the white people's country. We were naturally eager to learn what their impressions were. Well, what was it that had most struck these simple souls in Berlin (they had only seen Germany)? It was the enormous number of cattle that they had seen on a market day. As for the rest, they had returned completely disillusioned. They had always taken Europeans to be rich and wise people, a species of demi-gods.

"But, just imagine, you can see white people there, real whites, sweeping the town streets, carrying water, shaving dogs, picking up horse dung! However, there are also rich people, such as the man who owned all those cattle, but these rich people never come out. They live in big stone houses, in rooms which shine like mirrors, and they sit, from morning to night in chairs with cushions stuffed with linen. Beside them there is a little box, filled with sawdust, for spitting into. Truly, these people are happy: all they have to do is stuff their hands in their pockets all the time. But the Europeans who come to our country, they suffer and sweat. Certainly, they don't have chairs with cushions full of linen; they come at other peoples' orders and must be very unhappy."

Mandara roared with laughter at this summing-up by his ambassadors. Thus our first visit came to an end, with our being shown the gifts given by the emperor: a ring, woolen blankets, and silk sheets, two breastplates, cannons, rifles, watches, trumpets, two sewing machines, and cardboard model animals. He asked us our opinion of them all, and of course we said they were worthy of an emperor.

And so we had some happy days at Moshi, which we spent in paying visits, collecting information, and buying supplies. There were delightful moments in the afternoon and the evening, when the sun set behind the immense pyramid of Mount Meru and when the herds slowly returned, mooing as they came along the tops of the hills. But there were also rather grim mornings, when the thermometer went down to 8 centigrade or even lower. Sometimes we were enveloped by a thick fog, and now and again the fog's icy humidity became a fine yet piercing rain which made us feel frozen. We seemed to be no longer in Africa, but back in Europe, experiencing the worst kind of autumn days, when everything is mud, mist, coldness, and melancholy. Our men sheltered in the huts round the station, huddled round small and unsatisfactory fires.

But the man who seemed to suffer the most was our poor old Selemani. Since our arrival at Kilimanjaro, he had always stayed in his kitchen. Crouching down, he occupied himself with poking the smoldering brands and passing his hand—his big, gorillalike hand—over his ravaged face. It was a long time since he had washed—the water being much too cold—and, as he had rubbed his long fingers in the charcoal, in the soot, in the ashes, in oil, and in grease, and then applied them to his head and his face, he had finished by making his rugged head into an extraordinary work of art. Right in the middle of the layers of primitive painting with which he had unwittingly adorned himself, his eyes alone seemed alive, black, bright, and shining, like rosary beads. The rest was a confused mixture of meaningless stains, with something like a hump and something else like a hole, that is, the huge nose, and the toothless mouth. You could say that it was a ball for playing skittles which a child had decorated. Moreover, he seemed to me to spend a lot of time in meditation, and as meditation sometimes brings on drowsiness, he was generally to be found dozing on his knees until he was woken by the sound of his own snores. He would then look round, as normally happens in such cases, and throw an onion rather carelessly into the saucepan, poke a brand under the pot, run his hand full of grease and charcoal over his head, and start dozing off again. Poor old Selemani! We sincerely sympathize with his sufferings, especially as in these conditions all his dinners were disasters.

Chapter 18: On the Mountain—Machame

The Journey to Machame. Revolution and Civil War. A General View of the Country. A Startling Adventure. Face to Face with Eternity

Our conversations with Mandara, as well as the knowledge we had acquired from other sources, had convinced us that only by visiting the western side of the mountain could we claim to have explored Kilimanjaro thoroughly.

On August 24th, we took the road, but this time accompanied by M. d'Eltz, who was kind enough to help us, not only with his knowledge of the country and the respect which he commands there, but also with his cook and his bodyguards. All those in our party who were in poor health—including poor old Selemani—remained at Moshi while on a cloudless afternoon we went quickly down the mountain slopes, turned westward, and crossed the lower end of the district of Uru. Finally, having crossed the River Rau, we decided to camp for the night near a stream where elephants had left many signs of their presence. Here we saw enormous droppings, nearby we saw footprints in the mud, elsewhere broken-down trees in the forest, and often a cluster of hairs on the trees which they had used for rubbing themselves. Incidentally, one of our African companions told me that these famous pachyderms, when they are really big, cannot get up again when they have lain down to sleep, and that is why, when they want to sleep they lean up against big trees.

The next day, after a rather difficult march across a barren strip of land involving the crossing of three big rivers—the Umbwe, the Makoa, and the Weru-Weru—we left the districts of Kibosho and Kindi on our right. We climbed sharply toward the north and found ourselves in a thick forest, where fortunately two guides sent by Mandara led the way. There was no road; at least, we could not use this word for the narrow track that ran rather haphazardly under the branches and among the creepers. We are no longer walking, but rather, as far as is possible, we creep, we slide, and we jump. The porters have a still worse time than we, with their loads which are constantly caught up in the bush. We are making for Machame, the largest and the most beautiful of the Chagga chiefdoms it would seem, but which at that moment was torn by war and revolution. The previous king had gone to join his fathers, but his two sons were available, both equally anxious to serve the happiness of their people. They were Ngameni, supported by Mandara of Moshi and, against him, Shangali, the protégé of his neighbor Sina of Kibosho. The allied warriors of Fumba, Mandara, and Ngameni had gone on campaign a few days before; but, disappointed at not scoring a decisive victory, they had gone back home, taking some cows and their calves, some women and their children, and leaving the country a little more disorganized than before and nearer to ruin.

CHAPTER 18: ON THE MOUNTAIN—MACHAME

M. d'Eltz, in view of his responsibilities, wanted to get a clearer view of the situation, and we travelled with him because of our own interests. We feared an attack by Sina, and that was why we had to go through the forest. After a long march, we reached a point where we could see along the narrow path, in a seemingly unending line, the remains of the little fires of dry twigs: they marked the former encampment of the warriors of the triple alliance. They had passed the night there, lying down in a long line, better protected by the impenetrable forest than they would have been by building pillboxes. At last, we came out of the forest and could see the country which was just magnificent.

Ngameni, who had been contacted by a messenger, sent a small escort to meet us and earnestly asked us to camp near his compound, "For" he said, "the country is on fire and there is a great deal of danger."

We went down a slope where we could move quickly, as it was rather like a staircase, beside a powerful river flanked by large embankments. This was the Kikavu (literally, "the Dry River") which flowed with a great roar between two enormous natural walls. We crossed it, not without difficulty, by a ford; we went up the other side, and there we were at Ngameni's.

The poor boy, who was his father's eldest son and who had expected to be his successor, had found himself an exile in his own country. What had happened was that his brother Shangali had occupied the upper part of the chiefdom, while his uncle, also in revolt, is practically independent on the west; to the east, Sina's soldiers occupy everything, and he (Ngameni) only holds lower Machame, where many of his people were waiting to see which way the wind would blow so that they could submit to the strongest contender. The central part of Machame, where the deceased king used to reside, was for the time being abandoned and had become a battle-ground for the opposing armies. Definitely, being a king is not always enjoyable.

At Machame, as in the rest of Chagga country, there are, strictly speaking, no villages. Each family has its own household in its own enclosure, which is surrounded by its farmland. In peacetime, the system is perfect. But when war breaks out, these individuals can be massacred or captured, one after another. So, on the banks of rivers with very deep beds that cannot be blocked or diverted, huge camps have been cut out of the ground where the population can take refuge, piling themselves on top of one another, with everything that they can bring along—furniture, provisions, and livestock. These camps are surrounded by big ditches, at least three to four meters in breadth and six to eight meters in depth; one can get to the village of refuge by a gangway which can be easily withdrawn. These ditches, which seem to reflect an enormous amount of work, are created by a current of water, directed to soften and then remove the earth and, in addition, big pieces of wood are used.

The encampment, where Ngameni was living, consisted of about 300 hastily constructed huts. Facing it, on the other side of the river, there was another similar settlement. We visited it several times: really, it was sad. All these poor people are literally on top of each other, and we could scarcely find space to put our feet. Added to that, there were many sick people, some of them dying from dysentery or smallpox, an extreme lack of any comfort, and an environment of horrible filth. In the midst of all this wretchedness, we had at least the happiness to baptize a few dying children, the first fruits of Kilimanjaro: may the souls of these innocents, when they entered heaven, intercede for their country, to bring it God's mercy and his saving power.

Ngameni, who seemed to be about twenty, did not seem to have the gifts of a great warrior or of a great diplomat, despite the long piece of red cloth in which his disputed majesty was covered from his head to his ankles. In any case, he received us as real saviors. Without any arguing, he accepted all the proposals made by M. d'Eltz; and when he understood that we, the missionaries, might perhaps agree to settle in his country, he was delighted; his ministers and counsellors and the whole population shared his happiness.

Unfortunately, in such circumstances, was this wise? Was it even possible? Mgr. de Courmont, who had the ultimate responsibility, was afraid of some catastrophe. Fr. Auguste and I, people with less claim to wisdom, thought that this was a situation which could turn to the advantage of the mission, and in the three days when we waited there, Mgr. de Courmont permitted us to explore together the land and meet its inhabitants on condition, however, that we did not go up into the danger zone.

We followed this ruling; little by little, however, we were bold enough to go a bit further, and on the third day, we set off in the morning, more alert than ever. Our intentions were of the best; we had only two men and a rifle with us, plus a satchel for the botanical specimens, a flask for the insects, and a net for the butterflies. We did not take anything to eat. Then, cheerfully enough, we went up alongside the river. We saw the banana plantations, which had been ravaged, the trees cut down, everything in chaos. The irrigation channels had been blocked, houses overturned and the wooden posts which supported them burned. The cooking utensils had been broken. Here and there, we saw a skull half gnawed by the hyenas. It was painful to see all this; that is what war is! And those poor people, who had lived happily enough in these enclosures, what had become of them? Alas! Put the question to the Muslim slavers on the coast, to the well-to-do people of Mombasa and Pangani, or the planters of Pemba.

CHAPTER 18: ON THE MOUNTAIN—MACHAME

But, despite all that, what a beautiful country it is! We no longer had, as at Moshi and even Kilema, these ranges of hills and ravines, one after another, thrown together in a tiresome disorder. Rather, from the foot of the mountain, the ground rises up in an easy continuous slope to the wide alpine meadows which can be seen up there, below the huge virgin forest from which water flows in rivers of different sizes, in torrents and in streams, to give life and abundance to Machame's vast and fertile terrace. We could also see that marvelous Kibo, whose calm majesty dominated the landscape, was nearer to us and seemed more covered with snow than before. On the far horizon, the jagged summit of Mawenzi seemed to cut into the sky with its black profile. To complete the picture, there were, quite close to us, just behind the green plantations on the other bank, light white clouds floating and rising, like an immense veil of gauze, neatly stretched out.

So we kept going.

"Say?" I said, "Shall we go down to the river?"

We went down. The water was rolling noisily across enormous blocks of black lava, and here and there, at the points where it ceased to rush, groups of silver-colored fish swam past, following each other.

Then I asked, "Shall we go to the other side?"

We saw a path going up and took it. There was nobody in the fields or on the paths. The entire population had gone away, leaving to whoever wanted to take them the marvelous bunches of icy bananas which were to be found everywhere, just ripe, sometimes carried on tree trunks of the size of a man's body, sometimes fallen on the ground and rotting there. Sometimes also we saw some deserted houses.

And so we kept on ahead. In a grove of tall trees, we suddenly came across ruined houses surrounded by a formidable stockade with beams very carefully carved; it was something quite out of the ordinary. The dwelling places have doors, made of planks which are nearly a meter wide. All around, there were cooking utensils, huge vessels for brewing millet beer and broken drums. In the center of the village, there was a small stream, flowing down like a waterfall and its unceasing gurgling was the only cheerful note in the solitude of these tragic ruins. Later we learned this was where the former king had lived, his palace in fact, and that it was the site which, if we decided to stay with him, Ngameni intended us to have, together with the surrounding banana groves. We could say it was the Tuileries[1] of Machame.

"Shall we go up to this plateau?"

And so we went up. I must tell you that Father Auguste is a man of very sound character, we always find ourselves in agreement. In the long

---

1. A royal palace in Paris.

grass, we found man-made holes as we walked through it. Apparently when a war breaks out, the Chagga take refuge in these hiding places where they can avoid being attacked by the enemy, and, if need be, they can wait to ambush the invaders. We stand at a point where we can see the whole country stretched out, as it were, before us.

"Perhaps now we could go to that hillock that you can see a bit further up?"

Then suddenly, strange cries, several times repeated, could be heard from across the river, reminding us of those warnings which the ancient warriors of Gaul used to send through broom shrubs; a little later one man comes out of a nearby banana grove and immediately goes back. In less than three minutes we have been surrounded by a large group of tall, sturdy, young men armed with spears, arrows, rifles, and clubs for head-smashing. They wore an extraordinary variety of clothes.

They all spoke at once; then they started harassing us, pressing close to us, giving us pushes, jostling us, even searching us, and we soon understand some of their cries: "Wizards! Spies! Let's kill them." A huge beanpole of a man turned himself round, screamed ferociously, and repeatedly threw his spear forward, but, happily, it only hit our clothes. Finally, he stopped.

"I believe," said Fr. Auguste, "that we must prepare ourselves for death."

Turning pale myself, I said, "Let us wait till one of us falls; the other will give him absolution and in turn receive it."

Happily, we did not show what we were thinking. Anyhow, since the missionary, like the soldier, must someday fall in the battle for which he has volunteered, and Kilimanjaro is as good a place as the coastal swamps, a spear thrust is no worse than a bout of fever, and for the poor rag bag that we call our bodies, the friendly shadow of the big banana trees is preferable to that of weeping willows and lean cypresses. Here, at least, we would have come to journey's end in acting as missionaries (even if with a bit of the smuggler about us), seeking a new place to raise the cross of our Redeemer and set up his altar. This would give us a right to first-class treatment at the gate of heaven.

But the two men who were following us seemed to be thinking very differently; they were as silent as fish, dumbfounded and shaking. We put on an appearance of being very astonished by all this row, and to seem calm, and even, as far as possible, smiled and asked people to be quiet, and they accepted. A man who knew Swahili—an African interpreter to the slave traders—came out from the excited crowd. He had been one of the wildest among them; but, after all, we could with him find out why we should be speared, information which would of course make us very happy.

He asked us insolently, "Who are you?"

"You can see for yourself. We have come from far away to see your people, but you managed to receive us in a very ill-mannered way."

"So you are travelers?"

"Oh, yes, men who have been told that this country is really beautiful and so we are walking around it. If we cannot come here to look at this mountain, you have only to tell us; we would have observed it from further down."

"Do you not know that Machame is at war? If you want to go walking, you should choose another time. Why did you camp at Ngameni's place?"

"We have to camp somewhere. The other day we were with Fumba, yesterday we stayed with Mandara, today with Ngameni, tomorrow with Sina. We go everywhere."

"Tomorrow with Sina?"

"Oh, yes, Sina is a big friend of ours."

"How good they are at pretending to be innocent. But just wait; we have conclusive evidence against them. Look, what are these gadgets for? Can't we see that they're only for working bad magic on the country?"

There were mutterings in the crowd. "Ah, ah, that's got them. They'll never be able to wriggle out of that."

We answered, "Gadgets? You're a clever man, you speak excellent Swahili; don't you see that they are for collecting butterflies and herbs? Take a good look. You silly man. You don't know how to use these herbs, but we Europeans can make medicines with them."

And I turned toward Fr. Auguste, speaking to him in Swahili, so that people could understand me. "How distressing it is that these people deal with us like this when we are travelling to help suffering humanity!"

"True," he replied, "It's not encouraging; so much the worse for them if, next month, smallpox carries them off!"

The interpreter broke in again. "You are spies and behind you there are hidden soldiers; well, isn't that so?"

"Have you gone crazy or do you think we are crazy? If we had wanted to spy on you, we would not have come in the daytime and we would have got guides from among Ngameni's men! Are we making war on you? Just wait, here is all the powder and shot which we still have."

And, having said this, I handed to the crowd a bit of powder and shot which I happened to have in my pocket. This little present, which might have seemed hardly helpful to us, disarmed them. They spoke with each other, exchanged their impressions of us, and took counsel together. There was a young man, whom we found later was Shangali himself, the brother and enemy of Ngameni. He seemed to enjoy weighing us up, and on our side, we saw him as a very decent sort. In other circumstances, we would

CHAPTER 18: ON THE MOUNTAIN—MACHAME

have struck up a real friendship very quickly. After a quarter of an hour, which was not exactly amusing, the discussion ended with the following proposal being made to us: instead of killing us straightaway, without even knowing who we were and what we wanted, one of us would be sent back to our encampment and the other would be kept as a hostage.

As there was no better choice, we agreed to this. But then the two of us argued as to who would stay and who would go. Finally, Father Auguste, understanding that there was the same danger in taking the road back as in staying with the warriors, accepted to go with our two guides, accompanied by a platoon of soldiers, while I would have the honor of staying a prisoner of war until there was more information. Actually, this arrangement did not annoy me, as I felt I could get on very well with these brave country people; to begin with, I would teach them a game of forfeits. I would tell stories from my own country. I would even poke them in the stomach for fun and so on.

Then I began to think how embarrassed Mgr. de Courmont and M. d'Eltz would be by my being held prisoner. I changed my ideas. I said with a slightly worried air, "I would be delighted to stay with you; you seem to be such nice people." Then I pinched, in a matey way, the commanding officer's shoulder, "However, I must tell you that I am terribly hungry and my white man's stomach isn't used to your food. Even the birds do not all eat the same seeds. What will you do with me? And supposing I fall ill? And, if I die? There are animals which cannot stand even one day's captivity . . ."

Taking up this line of argument, Hamisi, who is a master of putting a case, but who had hitherto been too frightened to speak, hastened to add that he had neglected to tell them that if I die in their hands, I the first European to arrive here, it will be a scandal which will give Chaggaland a bad name, from Mombasa to Kavirondo. Goodbye to our herds of cattle! And the banana plantations! And the rivers, above all the rivers! Ah! Machame! Machame! You have eaten the skin of the first white man who came to greet you! After that, do what you will! We shall see!"

The valiant warriors looked at each other intently, and, after a short silence, the oldest among them cried, "Go quickly, all of you, and take your gadgets."

Calmly, we retraced our way, and as we were being watched, and perhaps we might be followed, as soon as there was a hedge between the people watching us and ourselves, we slipped across the fields, then very quickly crossed the river and got back to our camp. It was almost dark. Ngameni's soldiers, who had, from midday on, been sent to look everywhere for us, were gradually coming back. As we ate the supper that was waiting for us, we gave a rather unsatisfactory explanation of our late coming, but at least our appetite made it clear that, thanks be to God, we were still alive.

Chapter 19: On the Mountain—Kibosho

*At Kibosho. Chief Sina. In the Lion's Den.
The Warriors' Dance, Prelude to Battle.
Final Agreement. How We were Saved.
The Joy of Living.*

From the time of our arrival, M. d'Eltz, seeing that the core of the problem was at Kibosho, with Sina, had sent two messengers to say that he would like to have the opportunity for a friendly chat. This approach had worried the formidable king.

"If I refuse," he said, "it may mean war with the whites. If I say yes, it may mean a considerable loss of power." After thinking things over, and having had the court diviner apply various tests to M. d'Eltz's messengers, Sina sent them back with, as answer, the word, "Come."

We decided we would all go together, for we all wanted to see this man who had managed to hold in check the cleverness and the armed forces of Mandara and his allies. Add to this that he is the main seller of slaves to the Arabs and that no European had managed to see him in his kingdom.

We had to cross again the three rivers—Kikavu, Makowa, and Weru-Weru—but going up closer to their sources this time. Then we followed a straight line, leaving the fertile lands of Machame on our east, and so reached a large uninhabited plateau, where we could see the paths the elephants had taken in the long grass. We crossed another river, from which we had a magnificent view of Kibo. We entered the district of Kindi, very beautiful, very fertile, but all of whose inhabitants had been killed or captured or driven away by Sina. This happened twenty years ago. Such is the richness of the soil and the power of the sun, that, between then and now, the land had become the site of a huge and beautiful forest of tall trees. Now we were on the banks of the river Umbwe; it is the boundary of Kibosho, which we then entered.

In Kibosho, we met messengers sent by Sina, who were waiting for us with presents, namely, a goat and a spear, both, in their way, of equal beauty.

CHAPTER 19: ON THE MOUNTAIN—KIBOSHO

Kibosho is less of a unit than Machame and less rugged than Moshi. It is composed of a series of little hills which provide a number of plateaux and valleys. The country as a whole faces south and is very well watered, with the water supplied by irrigation channels, and is very carefully cultivated. As we go, we see blacksmiths' forges, women working in the fields, and children driving herds of cattle and flocks of sheep before them. The very beautiful banana plantations are weeded in a very tasteful manner, and something absolutely new in Africa: they are nourished with manure from the cowsheds.

But there, on a large plateau, was the palace of Sina the chief. It is a kind of big rectangle, protected by a deep ditch which ran for two hundred meters in front of us. A wooden bridge provided the entry. In the first interior courtyard we had been ordered to remain without crossing this rubicon, but beyond the bridge the lawn appeared so green and so good, and then it was so distasteful to seem to bow to the wishes of an unhelpful monarch that we crossed the bridge and went, quite cheerfully, to camp on the inner lawn. We settled in the shade of a big tree, near a little traditionalist shrine, in the middle of which, stuck into the ground, there was a fine elephant's tooth. In front of us, a growing hedge of dracoenas rose high and dense, and it and seven other similar hedges behind it blocked our view of the royal residence, of which we could only see the very summit which had a white flag hanging from it, the flag of Sina.

But here there was nothing of the hurried, sometimes enthusiastic welcome which we had received elsewhere. Everything is cold, silent, and almost solemn. A few locals passed before our camp without stopping or saying anything. When our men asked them for firewood for cooking, they told them to go and buy it themselves; when they wanted to buy provisions, they were told that there was nothing to sell.

At last, after a rather long delay, Chief Sina deigned to show himself. His bodyguard went before him, a child accompanied him, carrying his chair, and an interpreter followed him—the same man whom we had met in the uplands of Machame. He entered by the little door which had been cut in the dracoena fence, and came slowly toward M. d'Eltz, who received him with equal dignity.

Sina himself is a solidly built man of the mountains, about forty years old, with a round-shaped strong head, on top of which he has a sort of bonnet—an ox's bladder, ornamented with glass pearls—which fits his head exactly. His beard is short and covers his neck like a necklace, his face is thickset, rather gloomy, and harsh even, with two big bloodshot eyes; his limbs are short but strong, and he wears a red cloak which covers him completely. People say that he is a usurper; he had been a minister of the king of Kibosho, and one fine morning he got rid of his master and took his place.

Since then, nobody having dared to suggest that he retire, he has ruled over all the western side of Kilimanjaro. Some years ago, he even managed to force Mandara into a temporary exile, and up until then, he effectively counterbalanced the German colonial forces which had penetrated the rest of Chagga country. Something that happened recently can give an understanding of Chagga political ideas.

The ruler of Machame, which has a common boundary with Kibosho, had died, and Sina felt that this gave him a great opportunity for extending his influence. He got the support of the second son of the deceased chief by clever promises, and thus needed an excuse for making war on Ngameni, the legitimate heir. He therefore sent him a secret agent, who, having greeted him with the utmost submissiveness, spoke more or less as follows:

"I've some really big news. Sina had a stomach upset yesterday and he died in the night. You know how much we regret the passing of the real chief whom Sina dethroned. Come quickly and make one of his predecessor's sons the new chief. People will welcome you and you can take half Kibosho for yourself. It's a chance that will never come again . . . "

A little later, other messengers came to confirm this exciting news, and Ngameni made a sudden decision to invade Kibosho. Alas! Sina ambushed him in the Kindi forest, drove him back and came to Machame, where he gave his backing to Singali, Ngameni's younger brother; there was now a pretext for war.

But, as I said, here was Sina in person. M. d'Eltz spoke more or less as follows:

"For a long time now, I have been wanting to see Sina and to sort out certain questions. So I came to Machame and went to see Ngameni. There and then I learnt that Sina is making problems for Ngameni, and is launching military attacks against him. I am not quite happy about this. Why should soldiers from Kibosho invade Machame?"

Our visitors at Kibosho

Sina replied, "Ngameni has attacked me. I am only defending myself."

M. d'Eltz answered him, "But now I am friends with Ngameni."

Sina insisted, "If Ngameni is your friend, Shangali is my friend. Ever since Mandara came on the scene, he has made war against me; I have to defend myself against him. If Mandara and Ngameni stay peacefully at home, I shall do the same."

They went on talking for some time, in a fairly calm way. M. d'Eltz managed to keep cool, Sina could not altogether conceal his anger, backing up what he said with vigorous gestures, brandishing a rhinoceros horn which seemed capable of smashing someone's head, and appealing to the crowd crouching around him for support, which they gave very readily. Finally, he got up and said he would think about it, and, the following day, give his definitive reply.

The remainder of the day passed like this. We began to think we would have done better to remain on the other side of the ditch, but now that we had crossed over, we could hardly move elsewhere; people would think that we were frightened and we would be lost. Now the locals came up, but instead of mixing with us they kept at a distance, squatted down in line, wrapped themselves in their long pieces of cloth, and, with their spears planted in the ground, gazed at us in silence. That night, M. d'Eltz took care to post sentries at the doors of our tents, and by the grace of God, we went to sleep. Nothing happened during the night, except that in our carriers' quarters a rifle had been stolen, plus a powder horn and some cloth.

In the morning, Nderingo, the young man from Kilema who was travelling in our caravan, and who was useful to us as guide, interpreter, and intelligence gatherer, told us that Sina had sent for his *wasoro* (counselors) to hear their advice.

From early in the morning, we saw strange-looking warriors, dressed for battle, arrive in little groups. On their heads they wore large and tall leopard-skin bonnets with long monkey hairs on the back as decorations; on the back, a kind of thick cover, made of vulture feathers, ox-skin worn round their hips; they also had necklaces, bracelets, and leggings; a sword hung straight down each man's side, while a head-smashing club hung from each girdle. One hand grasped a big shield, the other a spear, one of those magnificent Maasai spears, made entirely of iron. Many of them had rifles, including rapid-firing rifles. All these people passed before us, glancing at our camp, and then slipping away through the little gateway facing us. When women and children appeared on the scene, they were harshly driven away: they had no place in the battle which might occur.

Soon all these warriors came back again, grouped themselves in four companies, and started a series of exercises, which were certainly impressive. There were about a thousand men, and among them quite a numbers of Kwavi from Upper-Arusha who seemed to be the officers in charge of training, all uniformed and well armed.

We had with us forty African—some of them the carriers of our caravan, the others the soldiers under M. d'Eltz's comman—all armed, likewise, with repeating rifles, it is true, but then not all were heroes. Our caravan leader, for example, when he saw this military muster, had a sudden stomach upset, just like the Duke of Wellington at the Battle of Waterloo.

CHAPTER 19: ON THE MOUNTAIN—KIBOSHO

M. d'Eltz sent a message to Sina to ask what he was planning to do, why these soldiers had been paraded near us and what was the purpose of their exercises?

Sina replied, "Don't be worried; my young people have to be allowed to enjoy themselves."

Really, they enjoyed themselves enormously, Sina's young people. If we had been watching them from a rather safer position, we would have been quite fascinated. It was a real military review, with exercises and maneuvers. The exercises were performed exactly as they were intended and formed a marvelous overall series, but there was nothing that outdid the beauty of the war songs which we heard them singing while these extraordinary soldiers sang as they paraded, now forming into platoons, now dispersing, and now coming together as a unit.

Everything that happens in a battle was acted out, not only through dramatized imitations but also by songs. Everything combined to make a marvelous harmony, with a wonderful degree of mimicry.

It began like this. Scouts are sent out, they report the enemy's presence, the warriors try to avoid being seen, they crawl along the ground, advancing cautiously; all is in total silence. Suddenly, there is a shout; it's the attack. Both sides seem to be fighting with songs, just as much as with weapons; now and again, a soldier, wearing a rather unusual uniform, leaves his group and, with a crazy fury, seems to be ready to attack on all sides. He runs through an imaginary enemy with a spear, but when we saw the way he hurled himself toward us, apparently challenging us, we did not feel it was purely imaginary.

Then, when the drama was over, the four companies formed up again in several rows and the song of victory began, the spears were lifted and lowered in a thrilling way, with the sunshine reflected on them in military splendor; the shields, held above the soldiers' heads, formed a covering recalling the tortoise shells of the ancient world. The choir of deep African voices led by a soloist amply developed a song where everything the soldiers had experienced was expressed. The song started with the calm courage of the beginning, the sudden surge of excitement, then the surprise given by the enemy, straightforward fear, then the fortune of battle swinging back to inspire the final victorious effort, the tragic laments over those who had fallen, the vengeance taken for their deaths, and the final triumph. With men dressed like this in such a setting, I can say that this outdid by a long way the best concerts that I have ever heard in Europe.

Moreover, the show was absolutely free of charge. But it went on for so long, and with something of a hidden threat in it, that it finally became rather irritating, even though very beautiful. Our men watched in silence and seemed to be thinking it over. M. d'Eltz seemed a little worried, mainly because of the responsibility he felt he had for our safety. Mgr. de Courmont seemed to have been enchanted by the marvelous music; Fr. Auguste Gommenginger was walking up and down, arms behind his back, evidently anxious. As for me, I was busy in my tent, arranging the boxes and bundles of cloth to make a barricade, preparing rifles and cartridges, and secretly seeing that all our men were armed. In addition, M. d'Eltz's Sudanese were on the alert, and M. d'Eltz himself was ready to use on Sina's valiant warriors his enormous gun for hunting elephants and buffaloes which looks like a cannon.

That was our situation; what did the future hold? Toward four o'clock in the afternoon, M. d'Eltz sent another message to the chief.

"We are tired by all this noise. If Sina wants peace, let him say so. If he wants war, let him be honest. In any case, now that his soldiers have surely finished their exercises, we shall begin ours, with all our guns and all our machines.

Sina replied to this rather ironically. "I have never spoken of war . . . As for other matters, I have finished listening to my advisers, and I am coming."

A little later, he did in fact arrive, accompanied by his retinue. But he wanted a face-to-face dialogue with M. d'Eltz, admitting that the big hats worn by the missionaries were for him a bit frightening and that what he had heard about them made him fear their influence. M. d'Eltz was very ready to meet Sina privately, but he refused—and wisely—to follow him behind the dracoena hedge where Sina wanted their meeting to be. They therefore held their discussion in one of the corners of the square where we were encamped. Sina agreed to be friends with the Europeans and make peace with Mandara. As for Machame, Ngameni would rule the lower part of the chiefdom and Shangali would have the upper half. M. d'Eltz accepted these conditions and it was agreed that we should leave the next day.

When the discussion was over, Sina once again spoke to his soldiers and, once again, we heard the soldiers' songs, but this time there was no challenge directed at us so that we could relax and enjoy them. Yet there was something strange in the air and we had to be on the alert. That night, mysterious groups which roused our suspicions kept on moving around our camp, but, all things considered, nothing serious happened.

We dined, and then on 28th August, led by two guides provided by Sina, we went back by the Kindi road, and then went straight down to the south. We found once more, at about six in the evening, the river Umbwe where we settled down as well as we could, on an island in the river, overshadowed by trees; with night falling. Soon fires were lit and food was being prepared, when Nderingo slipped into my tent. "Father," he said calmly, "we have escaped from the lion's den. Last night, after the peace agreement, were you aware that people wanted to cut our throats?"

I said, "Only cut our throats?"

CHAPTER 19: ON THE MOUNTAIN—KIBOSHO

"Yes, and make a thorough job of it. The interpreter who stays in upper Machame came to me on purpose, and I found that they're not much worried about killing Sumburi (M. d'Eltz was honored with this name, which is given to a species of big black wader) because they knew that he is just an ordinary man. But he wanted to know if it was true that your blood would make barren the land where it fell and would dry up the rivers. I immediately replied that that was always the case. He asked me why and I told him, "These whites are sent by God, and if men kill them, God punishes them. He thought about this for a long time and then he went away. But I spent the whole night crouching at the door of your tent; I shall sleep well now."

Providence is kind to missionaries. Perhaps we really owe our safety to the unwise expedition the other day to the Machame uplands, which could have been fatal to us.

Then there was the four hours' march from the river Umbwe to the German station at Moshi. We found the sick porters whom we had left there. That evening, the weather was splendid. The sun gave the slopes of the great mountain a soft light and a friendly warmth; we gazed on the strange lands which we had just left and whose smoke we could see rising up on every side in long whitish columns into the clear sky. We could hear the distant voices of shepherds on the hilltops, mingling with the sound of their flutes. The soft mooing of the herds of cattle coming back from their pastures rose from the far-off valleys. And near us, the water of the irrigation channels gurgled as it went through the modest waterfalls, the birds sang in the neighboring glade, the cicadas answered them, flowers were scattered on the hedges, and everything had a festive air. Everything felt good. And what a comfortable lawn we have. How pleasant to rest peacefully on it, and how good life is, Sina!

Chapter 20: The Ascent

Excelsior (Higher)! Across the Upland Farmland, the Thickets, and the Virgin Forest. A Night on the Higher Plateau. A Mass for Africa Offered on an Altar at 6,000 Meters. Climbing the Mountain. Lost and Found.

We have now seen the most interesting and the most heavily populated districts of Chaggaland: Marangu, Kilema, Kirua, Moshi, Uru, Kibosho, Machame, Useri, and Rombo on the east. We did not go to Kibong'oto on the west, but got reliable information on it, but we have yet to complete all the items in our program. *Excelsior, excelsior* (higher).

Mgr. de Courmont himself wanted to go further up "as high as one can go." We were there at the foot of the largest altar which God has given to this continent; we were under an obligation to go and offer the holy sacrifice of the mass there and pray for the whole of Africa. *Introibo ad altare Dei, ad Deum qui laetificat juventutem meam* (I shall go into the altar of God, the God who brings joy to my youth).[1]

Everything was prepared for our journey to the summit. M. d'Eltz was going to come, and as usual would take responsibility for the supplies. Mandara had given us two guides, and we ourselves would take those of our men who seemed to have sturdy legs and youthful enthusiasm. Finally, the Anglican missionary Dr. Baxter arrived just as we were about to start, with his servant and his dog. On his head, he had a big hat, intended to serve as an umbrella in sudden showers, and as a parasol in hot weather. His hand gripped an enormous stick, shaped like a Swiss alpenstock, and on his feet he wore hob-nailed boots. He wore a jersey against the cold, a raincoat to protect from rain, a jacket with a thick wadding against sudden falls in temperature and trousers padded against, well, I have forgotten against what, though the doctor carefully explained it; finally, a gun like those old-fashioned arquebusses, to deal with the elephants, buffaloes, panthers, and the other dangerous mountain animals. With all these loads, our good friend had scarcely

---

1. The Tridentine Latin Mass so began.

taken ten steps before things began to fall. But he held fast to his principles and his belongings, and so we got started.

Fairly quickly, we crossed the ridge of the hills which serve as pastures, and walked along the little path which runs alongside an irrigation channel where the water plays merrily beneath the bracken. We passed close by the beautiful Nanga waterfall, which is the boundary of Moshi and Uru. We went under arches of clematis with marvelous flowers, and so, bit by bit, we got to a sort of plateau which was being cleared for farming at that time, with the ferns, the *pteris aquilina* of the moors of Brittany, replaced by bean seedlings.

The farmers and their helpers ran toward us and asked, "Where are you going to get lost today?"

We answered, "Up there on the mountain."

"As far as the forest?" they asked.

"Right up to the sky."

They looked at us pityingly, but also with a certain respect, and seemed to be thinking: "These poor strangers do not know about the spirit that guards our summit. Do they have to come so far to look for death?" On this side, on the other side, and all round the last stretches of farmed land—1,400 to 1,500 meters up—the forest is really a set of thickets exploited by the Chagga in the same way as our French peasants use our woodlands. To our right and to our left, there are wooded hills, but also deep valleys and swift-running streams which rush into unseen ravines, whose far-off sound makes us halt.

> *Listen to the resonant waterfall, murmuring in the shadow of great trees!*

Excelsior! (Higher). Little by little, we enter the gloomy forest. The straight path becomes wet and slippery, at times covered by thick plants which have sprung up suddenly, blocked by creepers, kept down by the huge trunks of trees which have been growing for some centuries, only to be blown down by the most recent storm. The little stream whose course we are following and which we find again further up even when we have lost it for a while, runs down quickly, with water up to the top of its banks. As it flows, it brings into being a fantastic quantity of flowering plants, among which are begonias, balsam trees, and two kinds of banana trees, with large green leaves marked by black patterns.

But how can I describe the forest itself to give some idea of it?

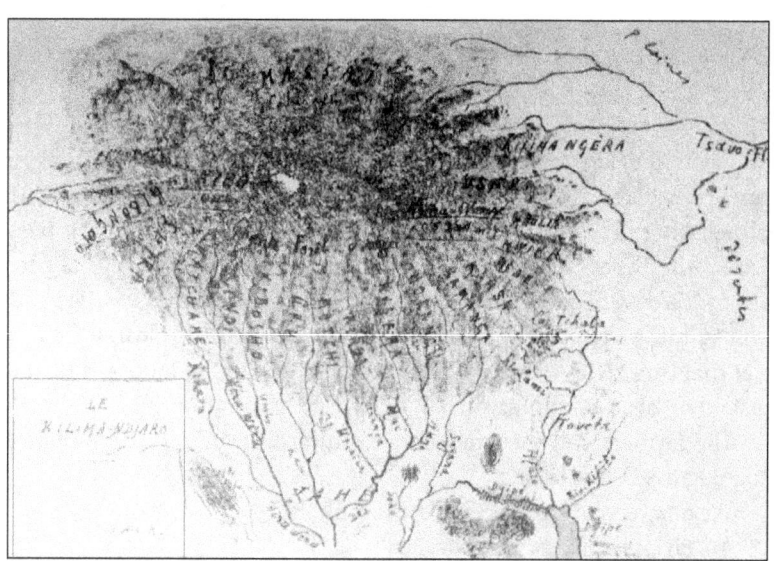

CHAPTER 20: THE ASCENT

The sun disappeared. We could not even see the sky. Everything was green, but a greenness of varying shades, depending on the species, the distance, and the exposure to the atmosphere. Sometimes, there was no visible horizon; at other times, we had views down steep precipices whose sheer depth frightened us from looking. On one side we could see the elegant and picturesque forms taken by the tree ferns; on the opposite side, the tangled maze of the big creepers, which, coming from some hidden source, seem to be looking for the sunlight, spreading their leaves and often their flowers upon the branches of the trees. There were everywhere frail shrubs which had, over a period of years, failed to push themselves alongside the older shrubs, and which vegetated gloomily, having given up hope of ever seeing the sun.

But what really astonished us was these enormous tree trunks, elder statesmen of the forest, fantastically massive, as old as the mountain on which they grew, covered with bumps, scarred by cracks. They were weighed down with creepers, with orchids, with ferns, with moss, with shrubs, even trees, in fact a whole layer of parasitic vegetation growing on them as if these great trees were intended for that purpose. Often branches, worn out by carrying such a weight for so long, fell noisily on the surrounding trees and gave these an unexpected opportunity to grow higher. Much the same thing happens with us human beings!

Sometimes even the old, worm-eaten giant falls on a day when there is a big storm. On such a day, the forest having shivered like a victim of malaria, the thunder rumbles in the distant summits, lightning flashes repeatedly, then when night comes rain falls like an avalanche, the wind howls as though it blew from hell, and the earth shudders as though it were going to open. Then the great tree falls, dragging with it all that grew on its trunk and branches, crushing with its weight all that it had sheltered in a frightening collapse. Apart from such a happening, the vast forest is noiseless, save sometimes when an elephant walks through it, trampling on the undergrowth, and tumbling into some gully. No song of a bird, no noise of an insect.

But this strange scenery has a character of its own, caused by the penetrating cold of the atmosphere which even seems to touch your bones, which surrounds you all round, and which leaves silvery drops on your body. Above, beside you, all over, it creates a whitish, touchable atmosphere, quite uncanny, in which the trees, the ferns, and the creepers, some distance away, seem to be fantastic shadows. Without wanting to, you become, as you push forward, obsessed by the feeling that you are at the gates of hell, in some corner of that forest which Dante has described at the beginning of his immortal poem: "In the middle of the journey of our life, I found in a dark wood . . ."[2]

However, the higher we got, the rarer big trees became, and there is a change in the vegetation. We had first of all come across heather at the edge of the virgin forest in an impressive clearing where, as from an open window, we could see the vast plain spread out, with the rivers and streams that flowed through it. But as we went higher, the heather plants increased in number and in size, looking very like trees. There were no more begonias or balsam trees, but there were plenty of ferns of different varieties, of lycopods, a charmingly delicate little violet, quite without any scent, strange results of cross-breeding, extraordinary plants, all making a new world.

Excelsior! (Higher). We took a rest, which had become necessary, and a very welcome meal, and then a rapid scramble upwards which led us to a sort of meadow, where, in places, the moss-covered soil holds water like a sponge; elsewhere, however, we could explore without worrying, and it was really enjoyable, as we ran along, to pick superb gladioli or a scabious or buttercups. A few grey-colored butterflies were flying around, and we could sometimes hear rather weak bird calls.

There was still a ridge covered with stunted trees which seemed twisted and rather gloomy. When we had gone through them, we had reached the end of this very unusual forest which surrounds the higher slopes of Kilimanjaro like a gigantic belt, 3,000 meters up.

Before us, at that point, we could see a kind of plateau spread out, like a park, but with some ups and downs, covered with graceful-looking grass, and given beauty by some clusters of trees. But all of them are covered by greyish, damp lichens, hanging like the long beards of old men, occasionally shaken by a mild wind. Looking at these sad countenances, you might have thought that they belonged to old patriarchs, who had lost the power of movement and been turned into trees. On the lawnlike grass, we could see evergreens, some varieties of geranium, some clumps of absinthe, and little clusters of flowering heather. And there also we had that strange mist, thicker than the forest, and also whiter, damper, and colder, oozing continually its dampness on us. We had no sunshine: there was a feeble light, a total silence, a muddled gloom, which weighed upon us—it seemed to be a landscape for restless souls, in some corner of Limbo.

I kept on gazing at the scenery, my thoughts wandering without any definite object, when suddenly behind me there was an explosion: what could it be? Was it a mine going off, or the sound of a cannon firing? I jumped round. Good God! Dr. Baxter is lying on the ground, his legs waving

---

2. *Nel mezzo del cammin' di nostra vita, mi ritrovai per una selva oscura . . .*

in the air, holding his arquebus with his hands, and beating the ground with his bald head. Having got to the place where we would camp, he wanted to test his gun without delay by taking a tree as his target, and then he had fallen suddenly backwards. But he quickly got up, without any injury, and, magnificently calm, simply said, "That was an experiment!"

At the limits of the great forest

Very near there, in a hollow, there was a spring of icy water, which we enjoyed, and, very quickly, three tents were set up: one for the porters, one for Mgr. de Courmont and Father Auguste, and one for M. d'Eltz, the doctor, and me. It was four o'clock. Our men were busy looking for firewood and settling down, while M. d'Eltz's cook, an extremely resourceful Seychellese, quickly made us a meal with the available foodstuffs and we found it enormously enjoyable. After the meal, we took a few short walks around the camp; we then sat down beside the fires, and finally, as the song puts it, "Everyone went to bed."

Mgr. de Courmont slept with calm and dignity, as is fitting. The porters, for their part, did their best to stoke up the fires which they had lit. They found their tent cold, so they made a circle round the flickering flames, telling each other what they thought of things, bit their fingertips, and, when the mist turned watery, accepted passively the water which ran down their spine. Really, this was extraordinary. Everybody knows that Africans can stand great heat, but they can also put up with occasional cold weather much better than we can. If we were wearing the clothes which they have, we could not stay out of doors on such a night. This capacity for endurance is the result partly of their being less sensitive to climatic extremes than we are, and partly to the fatty layer of black pigment which underlies their skin.

We—that is, M. d'Eltz and I—were already in bed, lying on our camp beds in the thick woolen blankets which Mandara himself had lent us, when, by the modest light of the lamp hanging at the door of the tent, Dr. Baxter came in.

"Jombo," he cried in a loud voice. "Jombo!"

His servant ran up, puffing like a grampus, carrying an enormous parcel well tied up in a big sack. "Do not miss this! It is sure to be good fun."

Jombo straightaway set about taking off his master's shoes, a difficult business, but one crowned by success, the boy falling down on one side, the man on the other, with a slipper between the two.

Then the parcel was opened. Oh! What a parcel! It contained absolutely everything: woolen blankets, big overcoats, long breeches, very long flannel belts, waistcoats, mittens, thick jackets, pillows, cushions, a washbowl, an umbrella, a scarf, a water pot, and another pot. I looked on all this, increasingly excited by my sinful curiosity; but there was M. d'Eltz's camp bed, which seemed to be shaking from some sudden explosion. Then from under the blanket, there came a stifled laugh, which soon, losing all control, exploded in tremendous roars of amusement. Indeed! We simply could not maintain our calm, and he and I were soon echoing each other's laughter without, however, upsetting in any way the source of our amusement.

But things got still funnier as the doctor prepared to go to bed. He put on all these new items of wear, carefully explaining to us how dangerous draughts and cold spells are for the health. Finally, looking huge in his night clothes, and as comic as he was huge, with an impressive nightcap, he took the big sack, breathed with dignity in its depths, sighed, and then pulled it over his skull.

M. d'Eltz cried out, "Steady!" to Jombo, who obeyed instinctively and without thinking. The parcel rolled on the ground, like an enormous sausage, taking with it Jombo, the bed, the washbowl, and various pots. No theatrical show, no carefully prepared comedy could come close to scenes like these. We were infected with laughter as by a disease, and it was nearly the case that we spent all night seeing that this excellent doctor was safely in bed.

By morning, however, everything was calm. While my tentmates slept more peacefully than one could have expected from the night's adventures, I got up quietly and poked my nose out of the door. It was extremely cold, only 3 degrees centigrade, when we were accustomed to at least 30 centigrade. The mist seemed to be dissolving into an icy drizzle. Some of the porters who were crouching at the foot of a tree before a fire that was going out, looked like mummified corpses pictured in Indian sculpture.

I walked slowly toward Mgr. de Courmont's tent. When I got there, I said, "*Benedicamus Domino* (Let us bless the Lord), following the rather pleasant custom of our seminary days. He answered courteously, "*Deo gratias*" (Thanks be to God). But his way of saying it told me immediately that the night in his tent had been less entertaining than it had been in ours.

Life is like that—some people are laughing while others are suffering. Human beings do not receive the same blessings at the same times. Monsignor had fever all night. He now felt much shaken up, but absolutely nothing would make him give up the mass which he has promised to himself and to Africa. The portable altar was set up and he began the prayers, and so the sacrifice of the mass was completed. Wherever in the world a priest offers mass, it has everywhere the same value. Yet here, a bishop sent by the vicar of Christ (the pope) to the most neglected of all the races of the earth was offering mass for them on the highest mountain of the continent in which they live. Surely the prayer of Christ, present in the Eucharist, to his Father to grant mercy and salvation, had a special force and power. Just as mountain springs give birth to rivers, so may such a mass send forth on all the missions of Africa the rivers of grace on whose banks the flowers and fruits of Christian morality can grow.

And so the bishop said a memorable mass at 3,000 meters above sea level, and Fr. Gommenginger and I received communion. We too offered a sacrifice, wholly inadequate in comparison with the sacrifice of the mass, but which it is not in our power to enrich. We offered our strength and our lives, and we gave them forever. Dear God, it is not much, but it is offered to you and for Africa, with willing hearts.

The time was six o' clock. After a hurried and rather sad breakfast, Mgr. de Courmont, much to his regret, stated that he had to go back to the German station for fear that he would suffer another and more severe attack of fever, and he would need to be carried, which, in the forest, would be nearly impossible. Fr. Auguste Gommenginger would accompany him with a certain number of our porters. But I felt that the journey down would be difficult through the mist and along these slippery and ill-marked paths.

We were still determined to try and complete the climb, and without wasting time we pushed forward on the path which goes round the mountain slopes linking the upper reaches of the districts of Machame and Kibosho to that of Useri. With us three (Le Roy, d'Eltz, and Baxter), there marched the two guides given by Mandara who were very reluctant to continue, saying that they were completely ignorant of this part of the mountain and that if we continued, it might bring death. Behind them came two soldiers under the authority of M. d'Eltz, Dr. Baxter's famous Jombo, Dr. Baxter's dog, and last of all, my faithful friend, Nderingo, to whom I had willingly lent a pair of tattered trousers and a pair of well-worn slippers.

The mist was extremely thick. We could see nothing on the left, nothing on the right, nothing in front, nothing behind. There was nothing by which we could orient ourselves. We could only see our feet, and occasionally some dark shape, which seemed to rise in the distance, as if it were a supernatural apparition, a spirit which had been commanded to keep the uninitiated from going up the mysterious mountain. With compass in hand, we bore due north, whatever the risks may be, until we met a long flow of dried lava. We all agreed that if we follow the course of the rocks we shall reach the place from which they started, that is to say the craters near the summit. So we continued our journey upwards, which was sometimes rather difficult but more often rather easy, generally on a smooth surface without valleys or plateaux. With things being like this, our efforts were rewarded, and we climbed Kilimanjaro as though it were an enormous staircase.

The plants and shrubs became more and more wizened, and it was fascinating to see disappearing behind us the different forms of vegetation as we pushed on. There were no more trees, and scarcely any shrubs, and those that grew there became steadily shorter and rarer. The dwarf heather followed us for a long while but eventually disappeared. There were still evergreens which had lost their color, curious cross-bred plants, and little Cape shrubs. We were very careful to break off branches on our route, we made heaps of stones, used our sticks to knock down clumps of plants, and tried to memorize the shapes of out-of-the-ordinary rocks, all in order to have landmarks for our return journey.

Then, suddenly, M. d'Eltz, the strongest of the three of us, began to suffer from a very bad headache, which was most painful near the nape of his neck, with palpitations of the heart, and a feeling of tiredness all over his body. It is mountain sickness, which is known to result from rarefication of oxygen and the acceleration of breathing. Dr. Baxter advised him to turn back—the doctor himself felt very thirsty, but M. d'Eltz was determined to carry on to the end, even if this would mean that he would fall down and we would have to pick him up. Happily, this did not happen, for soon after his determination was rewarded by an almost complete cure. Near a rock we found a flask full of water, and we felt it appropriate to take a short rest. But where were our men? What had become of them? Quite some time earlier, Jombo and Dr. Baxter's dog had disappeared, and so had our two guides. Nderingo was dragging himself on, and told us that he was overcome by sleep. The two soldiers did their best to keep up with us, but their faces showed their lack of enthusiasm. We were then 4,000 meters above sea level.

CHAPTER 20: THE ASCENT

A gigantic groundsel, *senecio vulgaris*

Soon we set off again, still marking our way with a series of signs, but almost giving up hope of seeing anything. Then all of a sudden the mist lifted as though it had been cut by a knife, and we could look at one of the most beautiful views one could imagine. There before us was the summit of Mawenzi, with rocks worn out by the passage of time and split into long blackish needle shapes, with awe inspiring precipices, sheets of snow scattered here and there on the summit's sides, and long streaks of what had been red cinders and solidified lava. On the left, we saw the glittering dome of Kibo and the sheer wall of ice, which seemed to block any approach. A plateau of twelve kilometers in length links these two giants, and provides their base. We were able to see all that, and it seemed, so to say, to be within the reach of our arms, since with such clear air everything seemed to be near. The sky was marvelously beautiful; if there were clouds, we were above them, and, up in the sky, there was the sun, which we believed we had lost, so delightful to see, and whose warmth was so pleasant.

Then we seemed to experience a new burst of energy. We marched on, we went up higher. Oh Kilimanjaro! What wonder of the African world of nature drew us on as a lover draws his beloved; there we were, on the plateau at 4,800 meters above sea level.

Now the soil—covered by innumerable fragments of volcanic glass, of spongy scoria, and reddish volcanic ash—was very hard. Up there, short, dry kinds of grass eke out a wretched existence; but here was something very curious. There were rocks which looked as though a giant had piled them on top of each other, and in whose crevices could be found the dried remains of a very tall plant with an impressive appearance. It is Johnston's giant groundsel, reported some four years ago by the explorer of that name. Helped by Nderingo, and without too much difficulty, I cut off part of the roots, to take the seeds.

Animal life is very poorly represented at this height. However, we could see a small grey butterfly floating gently over the blades of grass, a little lizard, also grey, was warming itself in what heat the sun gave; then nearby a few grasshoppers were jumping around; finally, footprints of a big antelope, the Pofou (*boselaphe canna*) showed that lowland animals sometimes come up the mountain. Moreover, there was no animal or bird sound, except for the cry of a little bird, which, at a moment in time, came to surprise us, greeted us, passed, and went its way.

We started the return journey, but we could see nothing of the panorama that lay behind us, nothing of the great forest, nothing of the enormous foothills of the mountain, nothing of the seemingly limitless plain, or of the rivers that flow there, between them and us. A silvery mist was spreading like a frosted mirror or a sea without a horizon, cutting us off from the inhabited world. We were not in heaven, but we seemed to be no longer on the earth.

While my companions rested and gazed, I felt myself again wanting to go off on my own to a big hill, which dominated the whole plateau, and so I went up it. Now I was alone, with nobody near. I was, so to say, in a beautiful private chapel, thinking how great God is, how little we human beings are. I seemed ready to stay there for days, for weeks, even for months, at such a distance from the lower depths where human beings in their wretchedness struggle along. Suddenly, I was seized by an indescribable but piercing feeling of overwhelming solitude and of a total and universal silence. Fear gripped me. I turned, and there below me, in a hole, I saw snow, the spotless snow of Kilimanjaro. Then, remembering that I had the honor to arrive there, I planted among the stones a little cross of heather, and said a little prayer to my God, and in my thoughts I sent a greeting to my far-off country, over lands and seas.

CHAPTER 20: THE ASCENT

It was three o'clock. As we prepared to leave this marvelous place in the mountains, we were all a little sad that we did not have a tent or water or firewood or anything to eat, which would have enabled us to spend the night there and, the following day, to try to climb Kibo. But we had to accept things as they were, and having emptied our flasks and our bags, we set quickly off on the return journey. On our way we found, one after another, those of our men who had dropped off from sleep and exhaustion. We found ourselves once again in the mist, and we thought ourselves very fortunate to find again the marks which we had left when going up, in order to guide us on the way down.

Unfortunately, little by little, the mist grew stronger, the day was coming to an end, we began to miss our marks, we were extremely tired, and we felt that things had got difficult and even worrying. We were particularly unfortunate in seeing all the time a kind of mirage; before us, we saw dimly through the heavy mist, hills and trees which we did not recognize and which seemed to be blocking our way. Where were we? Despite the dangers we kept going in a rather crazy hurry, trusting in providence. The night, cold and foggy, seemed to get darker; we were tired out and tortured by hunger, and I must admit we seemed completely lost.

What would become of us? Where could we sleep? We could not light a fire; we could not eat or drink. Feeling near to despair, M. d'Eltz fired a rifle shot, then a second one, then a third. We could scarcely hear the echo, for the noise vanished in the darkness. A little further on, another shot, which again failed to get a response, and so it went on, till he had finished his cartridges. We still kept on going, stumbling over rocks, slipping into gullies, blocked by the tufts of heather.

"Halt!"

Nderingo claimed to have heard down below us something like a rifle shot; would that it was true. No, we stopped a little, then, despairingly, plodded on.

"Halt again!"

This time, everybody had heard it. People were calling to us, and we answered. These were soldiers from the German station, who, seeing the night come down, had started searching for us, and fired shots to let us know that they were there. We soon found them, and we could, under the tent, have a well-deserved night's rest.

The next morning, we came quietly down the mountain. At the German station, we found Mgr. de Courmont, almost fully recovered, Fr. A. Gommenginger, sprightly as a young goat, and old Selemani, snoozing among the ashes of his kitchen, with his black, seemingly dried-up skin entirely silent, just like, truth to tell, those Peruvian mummies which are to be seen in museums, and which, like him, move from time to time.

We had climbed Kilimanjaro; we had even seen that there was snow beneath our feet.

Mount Kibo, view from Kibosho

Chapter 21: The Kilimanjaro Mountain Range

GENERAL VIEW. THE CLIMATE. THE GEOLOGICAL FORMATION. THE FLORA (BOTANY). THE FAUNA (ZOOLOGY)

The reader, having followed these missionary wanderings on the slopes of Kilimanjaro, will perhaps enjoy finding gathered together here, in an abridged form, various items of information gathered on the famous mountain, about its climate, its geological formation, its flora, its fauna, and its human population.

As we said at the beginning of this book, this astonishing massif placed at three degrees of latitude south of the Equator and rising to a height of a little over 6,000 meters above sea level, has all possible climatic variations. Below, at 700 meters above sea level, the plain is halfway to being a desert, and is dry, scorched, and hot, covered with light grasses which receive a very moderate degree of shade from the loose leaves of the acacia or the twisted boughs of some stunted trees. The same tropical heat is to be found in the forests which grow alongside rivers or which indicate the presence of water in the subsoil, but it is both tempered and deepened by the green foliage and the humid atmosphere. As one goes up, the climate changes, and one can compare the attractions of the tropics with those of the arctic regions. From 800 to 1,200 meters, the climate is temperate.

Further up, the weather is already damp and increasingly cold as one goes toward the 1,800-meter level, and, approaching this level, dwelling houses gradually disappear and, above all, in particular localities, there are more rainy days than dry ones. Going further up, there are still some signs of farming among the thickets. Further still, up till 2,300 meters above sea level, there is the great untouched forest, always humid and with a piercing cold, with a first line of plateaus, or, if you prefer, high meadows, where the mist may disappear on one day only to return the next. After this, there is the lower level of the mountain, strictly speaking, and then the upper plateau, and finally, the region of eternal snow. In Iceland, one finds this at 610 meters above sea level; here it is 4,400 meters above sea level. To sum things up, according to Dr. Hans Meyer, there is a normal temperature from 35 to 40 degrees centigrade on the plain around the mountain, and on Kibo itself, 16 degrees of cold.

The massif has a circumference of about 270 kilometers. "It is thus twice the size of Etna, whose lower slopes are all vast enough to support a population of over three hundred and twenty thousand inhabitants."[1] It is entirely volcanic in origin, as is moreover the greater part of Maasai country, to which it provides the entry, from the granite mountains of Nguru to those of Ethiopia. The forces of nature are still active in more than one place. But at Kilimanjaro, apart from a few light shocks which have been felt occasionally, everything has been calm for a long while. The Kibo (the white) and the Mawenzi (the friendly mountain?) are two craters; but, according to Thomson, the Mawenzi, which today measures about 700 meters less than the other, is the older of the two. As we have already seen, its summit is much more jagged. If it is much less white than its younger brother, this is because its needle-shaped rocks are too worn and too sharp for the snow to stay there a long time.

The German, Dr. Hans Meyer, accompanied only by the Austrian Putsheller, was able to climb up the Kibo by cutting steps into the wall of ice which blocks access to it, and these gentlemen used the techniques employed by experienced mountaineers. According to Dr. Meyer, the crater is 2,000 meters in breadth, with a large rift which can be seen from Machame; on it, there is a thick coat of ice, sixty to eighty meters thick, which surrounds the Kibo. There is always plenty of snow there, even more than we would have expected. When after a long stay in Africa I found myself looking at the ice and snow, I found it really fascinating, really beautiful, and like the Protestant missionary Rebmann, I automatically recalled the canticle of Daniel: *Benedicite, montes et colles, ignis et aestus, glacies et nives Domino* (Bless the Lord, mountains and hills, fire and heat, ice and snow, Dan 3:65–69).

However, a layer of white does not always remain at the same size. Apart from the fact that in October it goes down as far as 4,300 meters above sea level and below, only to go up much higher in July and August, sometimes in the evening it is possible to see big black patches which the next morning are again covered as it has snowed during the night. Well, this seems very simple to us, but it is something which the local Africans and travelers from the coast have found very puzzling. None of them knows what snow is. Therefore, to explain the change of color, it must be that the

---

1. Reclus, *Earth and its Inhabitants*, 431.

mountain is the home of a powerful spirit who, every morning at sunrise, to amuse himself, makes the white layer and the black patches appear, not to mention the red, the violet, and the orange. Another surprising feature of the mountain scenery is that one often sees at the top of the crater a point of light, dazzling in its brightness, as if it were an enormous diamond. People refer to it as the star of Kibo. According to an Arab legend, Kilimanjaro contains a vast quantity of precious stones with, as well, gold and silver. But up to now the only substances which have been found are lava, obsidian, and, it would seem, some agates.

Looking at the Kilimanjaro massif as a whole, the difference between the northern side and the southern side is striking. On the north there is little in the way of rivers or streams and the land is rather dry; there is a succession of foothills covered with thin grass and some groves of virgin forest. On the south, there is an enormous quantity of streamlets, waterfalls, and rivers which completely justify the name which the Taveta people give to this region—Water Mountain (from *Mlima*: mountain; and *Ngare* or *Ngaro*: water, which becomes, using the coastal pronunciation, *Ndaro* or *Njaro*).

Giant seneçons and the dome of Koto

These rivers and rivulets take three different directions. On the western side there are various streams which flow into the Tsavo, which in turn joins the Azi of Kamba country to become the Sabahi, which flows into the ocean a little north of Malindi. On the southern side, there are several watercourses which come together to form the Ruvu (the great river) which reaches the ocean at Pangani. Finally, on the western side again, there is another river with the Maasai name of Ngare n'eirob (cold water) which loses itself in the desert. The most impressive of all these rivers are, first of all, the Lumi or Mfuro, whose water fertilizes the oasis of Taveta and pours itself away in Lake Jipe to emerge again in turning round the northern point of Gweno: then there is the Soko, discovered by M. d'Eltz, which flows out of a hillock in the plain, which is full of iron ore; finally the Weru-Weru (Black River), so called from the black stones over which it flows.

I must also mention a lake, the Chala or Chara, which is to be found on the eastern side of Kilimanjaro at the bottom of the crater of an extinct volcano. The lake is circular in shape, very deep and completely protected from the winds. This extremely calm sheet of water has something awesome and mysterious about it, which has not failed to impress the Chagga. There are plenty of crocodiles there, but no fish. Recently, a British lady, Miss French Sheldon, has thoroughly explored it, guided by our friend, Dr. Baxter. Her journey received considerable publicity, and I was rather amused to read a newspaper account of her travels in which the readers were told of her courage "in going from Lake Chala to Lake Tanganyika by boat, carefully exploring the great rivers of Africa, which have their source there." If one can accept what the local people say, there is a similar but smaller lake, at or near the source of the River Kilema. But strangers are forbidden to go there, and the path leading to it is kept secret. A sacrifice is offered there every year.

With such climatic variety, it is easy to guess how rich botanically Kilimanjaro is. This mountain is really a kind of vast amphitheater where there is an exhibition of a very wide variety of the plants which the Creator has sown on earth. Down below, we have the lotus and the banana tree; up above, we have the snowdrop and the everlasting flowers. Perhaps, one day, on a line starting from the plain and going up to the summit, representatives of all known botanical species will be planted, and this will be the finest botanical garden in the world.

I should like to mention that I collected 500 or 600 plants, of which only about 300 got safely to the coast; the others were lost in the course of the journey. My confrere and good friend, Fr. Charles Sacleux, at Zanzibar, had wished to classify them. A list of his classifications has in fact been published. Were I to reproduce it here, my readers would feel that the names, in Latin, are rather bizarre. However, even someone totally uninitiated to

CHAPTER 21: THE KILIMANJARO MOUNTAIN RANGE

the mysteries of botany cannot walk upon these plants, which grow in the center of the African continent and under the equatorial sun, without being astonished—an astonishment which blends with a very personal emotional thrill. Here are some of the plant names.

There are the bowers of *clematis*, which are to be seen on the edges of paths, these superb buttercups, these long clusters of wild reseda (*caylusa abyssinica*) which cover the hills of Kilema; the lowly violet which fits itself onto the worm-eaten trunks of the great untouched forest; these geraniums which, having taken a refuge there, grow on the high plateaus. Then there are the six varieties of delicate balsam trees which grow on the banks of streams like a double barrier of varied flowers. Then there are these little clovers (*trifolium polystachium, fresen; trifolium Johnsoni, oliv; trifolium subrotundum, stend; trifolium kilimanjaricium, taub*) lost in the thick grass where the goats and the sheep run up and down; these blackberry bushes, whose berries, as they grow red and then turn black, are watched impatiently by the children, just as they do with us.

There are also these begonias with iced flowers, the *umbelliferae*, the scabious, the gladiolas, the clumps of wormwood, these varieties of groundsel, and the lettuces (*lactuca abyssinia, fresen*). We must mention these speedwells, these plantains, the heather, the lycopodes, these ferns, lichens, and mosses. All this range of flora was for me already well known and well loved, and I was reminded of my dear homeland. But they are in the company of palm trees, dracoenas, banana trees—both cultivated and wild—enormous baobabs, astonishing sterculias, strange orchids, and milkweeds, all of which stay there to remind us that, even when we come back to Europe, we have not entirely left Africa behind. On the lower slopes of the mountain, we find a thick, fleshy, unusual plant, which belongs to the sarcophyte species. And something else equally surprising: from what one knows of Ethiopia, of the Cape of Good Hope, of Ruwenzori, and of the Cameroon, the flora of Kilimanjaro is clearly related to that of these other mountain areas, and it can now be said that the higher slopes of the African mountains have most of their plants in common.

Compared to the flora, the fauna is not all that varied and holds far fewer surprises. However, I collected shells at various levels of the mountain and received the following letter from M. Alfred Grandidier, member of *l' Institut de France*. What he says is far too kind, but still very interesting for anybody interested in conchology.[2] I am only quoting the passage which refers to Kilimanjaro and the shells which I collected there:

---

2. The scientific study or collection of mollusk shells [Editor].

M. Bourguignat, the recognized authority whom you know, has studied systematically the collection of shells which you have fortunately made during your magnificently successful journey.

Here are their names: species from the lower slopes of Kilimanjaro: *planorbis courmonti* (an air-breathing fresh water snail), *vivipara unicolor* (a freshwater snail), *Cleopatra kinganica* (a freshwater snail), *Cleopatra Letourneuxi* (a mollusc), *Cleopatra Le Royi* (a new species of mollusc), *Melania tuberculata* (a freshwater snail), *Melania Courmonti* (a new species of freshwater snail).

Species from 2,000 meters above sea level and above: *Helix Le Royi* (a new species of snail), *Helix Courmonti* (a new species of snail).

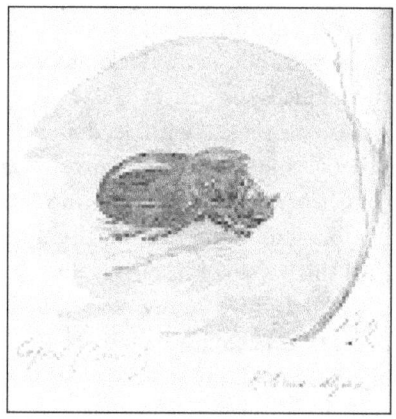

A beetle: *Copris dracunculus*

Total: five new forms, which is already very interesting. But what delighted M. Bourguignat most of all, is that these forms fully confirm his theories. That is, the forms gathered on the lower slopes of the mountain are Central African forms, whereas the two other forms collected at the level of two thousand meters above sea-level or above are not African, but European; they resemble so closely two kinds of shells from the Alps and Transylvania as to make a confusion between them possible, and they have acquired this European style because of the climatological influence of the high ground where they lived. M. Bourguignat had already observed the same effect in the case of species from the Ethiopian mountains.

CHAPTER 21: THE KILIMANJARO MOUNTAIN RANGE

I have nothing to add to these helpful details sent me by my learned friend, except to express my gratitude for the original way in which my humble name has been given a chance of immortality, in placing it on the shell of a living snail. Well, we have quite a future before us, provided that the little creature does not stop existing.

With regard to the insects—arachnids, dipterans, hemipterians, butterflies, hymenoptera, and orthopteran—they appear less varied than one might have thought. The majority of specimens collected up till now belong to species found over a large area of Africa, both in the plains and, above all, in the mountains. With regard to this point, it is possible that the granite massif of Nguru to the south, where the missionaries have collected so many new items, is richer than Kilimanjaro itself. I must however mention various carabs, scarabs, and buprestes (all beetles), which are always interesting to look at.

Crows with white necks

From the beginning of our stay, we have made a welcome discovery: the terrible termites, with their capacity to destroy everything, are not to be found on the mountain. Nor does one see anything of the wood-eating coleopterons which elsewhere have reduced the wooden frameworks of houses into a fine dust. A species of crab with a flat back is common in the rivers; it is also found further south at Morogoro and elsewhere. Johnston says that there are no fish; but this is because he did not go to the western side of the mountain where they are very abundant because the local people do not eat them. There is little variety of species among the fish who belong to the cyprinoides, a family of fish which includes carps. There are five or six species of snakes, some of which are very dangerous; but in general, they are only found at the foot of the mountain. I found and sketched a remarkable chameleon, of a kind I had never before seen. Among the saurians, I shall only mention the crocodiles of Lake Chala and two or three species of monitor lizards.

Turning to the world of birds, Johnston found six new species, and Fisher found other ones. It is possible to see honeysuckers, sparrows, and a special kind of African sparrow, a fat crow with a white neck, three hornbills, and a splendid turaco also to be found at Nguru, francolins, whose number rather bothers farmers who grow millet, guinea fowls, quails, turtledoves, pigeons, vultures, eagles and so on. As for domesticated birds, there is poultry, but people are only interested in cocks. The local Chagga do not eat fish and equally refuse to eat poultry, finding such food beneath them just as the Maasai do. However, they love to hear a cock, this prince of the farmyard, crow in the mornings.

If we look for the mountain mammals, we can note some gazelles, two or three species of big antelopes, particularly the one classified as *boselaphus canna*, whose footprints we recognized at over 4,000 meters above sea level; the two-horned rhinoceros, the wild boar who likes to visit plantations, the elephant whose footprints are more easily seen than his body, and the unstoppable buffalo. But one does not see zebras or giraffes or the hippopotamus, nor various kinds of antelopes; they are all inhabitants of the plains. In the large-scale forest, the hyrax (*hyrax d'Abyssinie*), a tiny rodent, is very common, but is also very much hunted. Its local name is *mbelele*. Its skin makes very fine furs with which the local people cover their shoulders. We can note also the *graphivrus capensis*, a small animal, of the size of a field-mouse with a long sweeping tail, which is found in people's houses, as is the ordinary rat. Hyenas prowl round the villages, small wild cats find a hiding place in the bush, and the roars of lions are sometimes to be heard; but leopards are so bold that they are an absolute torment to the shepherds.

CHAPTER 21: THE KILIMANJARO MOUNTAIN RANGE

Then there are bats and lemurs. There are also plenty of monkeys, dog-faced baboons, *cercopithecines,* and colobus monkeys. A colobus monkey can be really splendid, with its black and white fur, and its big, plumelike tail; but we shall meet them again in the forests of Kahe.

A view of Kilimanjaro.

Chapter 22: The Population of Kilimanjaro

The Chagga and Their Physical Type. Chagga Customs. Their Political System. Religious Ideas. The Language.

Let us give human beings our attention now. After all, human beings are the most interesting creatures in the world, despite the opinion of Socrates, who "having known a great many people, preferred his dog to all of them." The Kilimanjaro massif is inhabited by two very different ethnic groups: the Maasai in the north, the Chagga in the south.

The word Chagga is little used by those to whom it is applied; they usually call themselves after the district where they live. There are Waseri, Wakilema, Wamoshi, that is, the people of Seri, the people of Kilema, the people of Moshi. However, Swahili travelers from the coast use it for the Bantu farming people who occupy the southern slopes of the mountain, between 800 and 1,800 meters above sea level. Estimates suggest that they number between 40,000 and 60,000, but these figures are guesswork rather than reliable statistics. The state of continual warfare which exists between the different districts has caused migrations to Meru, and Dr. Karl Peters found, on the route from Tana to Victoria Nyanza, a Chagga community which had migrated from Kilimanjaro. Chagga can also be found on the coast, at such places as Mombasa and Pemba, where they have been sold into slavery.

Physically, the Chagga tend to be largely of the same type, though there is a certain amount of variation. Generally, the Chagga are medium sized rather than tall, but also strong, wide awake, brave, and well built. Skin color varies a good deal. One gets individuals with very dark skin, round headed, and rather short, but also other people with remarkably light skin, bodies that seem to be thrusting upwards, and long heads; this leads one to believe that they are racially mixed.

As this narrative has perhaps already shown, the Chagga are, as a people, very interesting, being intelligent and forward-looking. Some of them, for instance in Machame and Seri, have developed to a lesser degree than the others. But nowhere in this land have the coastal Arabs been allowed to settle down and spread the shameful immorality which is associated with them in

East Africa. Of course, this does not prevent them—indeed, the contrary is the case—being regarded by raw travelers and distinguished periodical journalists, as a valuable civilizing influence. How much wickedness do they try to cover with this convenient and prestigious term?

The Chagga are essentially a farming people, and it must be accepted that among African farmers, they really have a position of their own. Their system of irrigation is really outstanding. Water is collected, even on the far side of the virgin forest, channeled along the slopes of hills and the edges of cliffs, then brought down slopes, which are not easily noticed, to the place where it is needed, kept in reservoirs, sent to run here or there, then divided into a thousand little channels, giving everyone a share. I would wonder whether a European engineer would be able to do better. He would not, in any case, have been content with their very simple technology. As well as irrigation, the Chagga practice manuring, crop rotation, hoeing, and weeding. Almost the only thing they lack are chemical fertilizers, which, so it is said, will renew the face of the earth by providing one jar-full, sufficient to keep a whole family fed.

However, their tools for opening the ground are very primitive in their simplicity. Often enough, we are told that human beings, as soon as they passed beyond the animal stage, began to scratch the earth and to make tools, starting always with stone ones, and moving to bronze and then iron. Meanwhile, human beings learned to wear clothes, and fear of natural phenomena created religion. Would it not be more correct, and therefore more scientific, to say that human beings have always and everywhere used what they had at hand, without fussing? In many cases—I am not saying in all cases—these stages through which mankind has had to pass are theories based on inadequate observations. There are, for example, Chagga who have not yet reached this famous stone age, they are still in the age of wood, the first age of human tool-using, which has been left out of these theories of successive stages.

Their pickaxes and all the implements for planting are made of wood, and among these, to my surprise, was a kind of big pike with which they turn over the earth and get very good results. Other tribes in the south also have these pikes, made of ebony; and, curiously enough, they use iron tools to make these wooden tools. As for ironwork, no "primitive people" are better craftsmen than the Chagga. They have primitive forges, with bellows made from goatskins, and with wood charcoal instead of coal. They make hatchets, two-edged knives, strong straight swords, and, above all, spears which have been so beautiful in their shape and workmanship that some Europeans living on the coast do not believe they were made by the Chagga. Formerly, they got iron from Pare country, but now they get it from traders in sticks whose thickness varies from that of a string to that of a pencil.

There is not much interest in pottery. Housewives prefer wooden bowls to ones made out of pottery. The wood used is a soft variety, which their men folk can shape very skillfully, particularly in the Uru district, and with which they make a wide variety of utensils, troughs, household vessels, bowls, plates, and even objects serving as spoons and forks. Finally, having seen European pipes, they make pipes. Dear readers, wooden pipes!

This people also shows its artistic sense in the way villages are laid out. As has been seen, there are normally no large conglomerations in Chagga country; everyone makes his home with his family. There are two or three houses for the head of the family, for his wife, for the children, for the slaves, if there are any, and the cattle. Then, at the side, there is another building, smaller but well looked after, resting on poles, round like the other houses, and always very clean, where millet, bananas, beans, honey, and beer are kept. It is surrounded by a sort of garden, enclosed by a living hedge of dracoenas or capers with thorns. Above the door of this enclosure, creepers form a joyful arch of flowers and greenery, and generally also a little stream, with water from the nearest irrigation channel, gives this family enclosure a charming air as something taken from a country poem.

The diet is predominantly composed of vegetables. They grow the kind of millet known as eleusine, banana trees, the eatable lily or Caribbean cabbage, a great variety of peas and beans, sweet potatoes, several kinds of yam, maize, a little cassava, a little guinea corn, and some sugar cane. There is no keeping of poultry or fishing. When we were with Fumba, and also with Ngameni, the question of schools was raised. The chiefs promised us as many boarders as we could take, but on one condition and only one: that we did not make the schoolchildren eat chicken. This we accepted. Tobacco is also grown, which is smoked and chewed. It is very strong.

A great deal of milk and butter is consumed. Unfortunately, the butter has a strong taste of aromatic mountain herbs which are not always liked by Europeans. They are very fond of meat. Warm blood is much enjoyed. The common people often lack the chance to satisfy their hunger for meat.

Clothing is rather scanty, indeed only the chiefs, the elders, and the married women can be said to be properly clothed. Following the Maasai fashion, young men who can serve as warriors express contempt for being fully clothed, until the time when, having become older or richer, they cover themselves from head to feet with big pieces of cloth. As to the poor people, the "small men," the inhabitants of impoverished outlying areas, they put over their shoulder or round their loins some *mbelele* fur, part of a cowhide, or some shreds of cloth.

I must hasten to add that long clothes are not a necessary proof of morality. These poor children are as God made them, without any evil intention. Many a picture painted by your artists, on sale in our towns and eagerly sought after by the young and the old of the civilized world would, gentlemen, scandalize these "savages."

This is a society in which the wish to look well is certainly present. Men keep their hair in good condition and devote even more attention to their ears. A hole is made in the lobe in childhood, and, every year, indeed every month, they try to enlarge the hole which they have made in putting a piece of wood into it, at first the size of a matchstick, then the size of a pencil, then a finger's size, then an arm's. With this treatment, the lobe often touches the shoulder with the little ornament which has been put into it. In some districts, they stick a long piece of carved wood on top of the cartilage; at a distance, this looks like two little horns. As for the women, they are extremely clever at making elegant ornaments hanging down from the ears, bracelets, necklaces, and girdles, iron, copper ornaments, and tin bracelets. Other very popular items are made of little pearls of various colors. Often, invited to choose between a piece of good cloth and glass pearls, poorly clad people prefer the pearls; the cloth is useful, but the pearls are attractive.

In some localities, there are regular markets every two or three days. At Moshi, the market is held under a clump of big trees, and there, the housewives come, from everywhere on the mountain, bringing what they have to sell. Trading is done by barter, unless one considers as currency the glass pearls, the cloth, and other items from the coast, which often enough are only used for making purchases. Salt, made from potash, which can be found at certain places in the Arusha Desert and which is used in cooking, is also an important item in these markets. Moreover, they are very lively occasions, with very serious discussions on the value of this or that, but astonishingly order seldom breaks down, and these gatherings, composed entirely of women, are not under any kind of police supervision.

From a political point of view, Chagga country, from the foot of the mountain to its summit, is divided into several districts, which generally have a river as their boundary. Starting from the east, we have Kilima-Nghera (called on maps Kiliimangelia); Useri, a dry but populated area; then the district called Rombo, which is really the name of a former chief and includes Mulia, Chero, and Chima; then come Mwika, Msae, Mamba, Samanga, Marangu, Kilema, Kirua, Moshi, Mbokomu, Uru, Kibosho, Kindi, Machame, and Shira or Kibong'oto.

Each district has its own chief, and its own way of doing things, but as a result of conquests, alliances, and political cooperation—none of which are the monopoly of European states—some of these districts have more or less ceased to be independent.

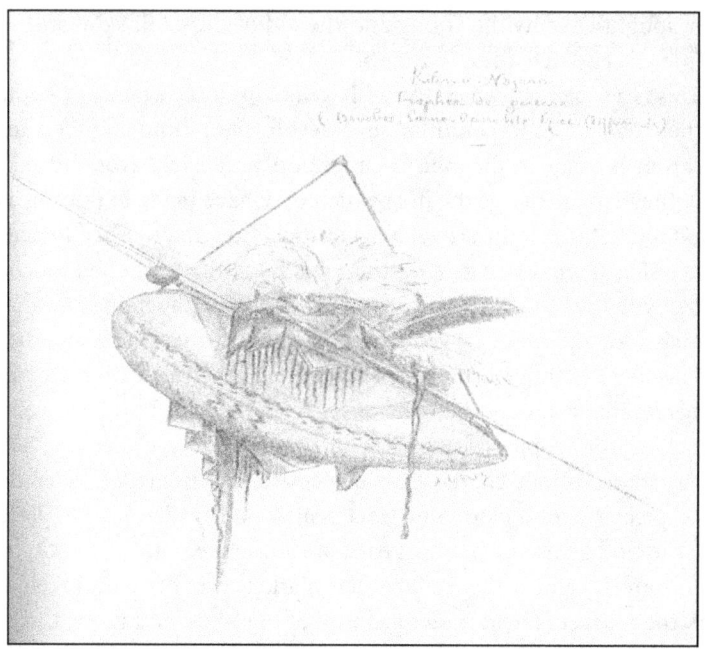

Trophies—shield, spear, headdress, dagger, feathers

The chiefs, who can also be called sultans or *mangi* are not autocrats. Their power is held in check by the advice of the elders and by what seem to be the feelings of the people; they are, however, very respected, and can rely on their people's obedience. The chiefdom passes from father to son, and, when a son is not old enough to rule, his mother acts as queen regent. A chief will always have three or four people who act as ministers. All the young men are ready to act as soldiers, and if danger arises, every man is ready to fight. Their loyalty is strengthened by hopes of having a good share of booty: slaves, cattle, and foodstuffs. All these chiefs are frequently at war, encouraged by traders from the coast who come here to buy slaves; because of this, Kindi, near Kibosho, has been entirely depopulated. At this present time, the presence of a German post will check the trade in slaves and perhaps warfare, because these two things are linked. One cannot say as yet that the Chagga enjoy peace and unity. The Chagga are certainly courageous. Their weapons include a really magnificent spear, bows and arrows, the *sime*, a kind of large cutlass, and clubs; they carry shields, as do the Maasai, whose style of warfare they enjoy imitating.

CHAPTER 22: THE POPULATION OF KILIMANJARO

We have already seen that the Chagga are disciplined, that they know how to make big trenches and solid barricades, not to mention an invention of their own: holes where they hide to ambush a passing enemy. Recently rifles have been introduced, including repeating rifles, with the necessary ammunition. In addition to these, Mandara has two small pieces of artillery. May God grant that these unwise presents from Europeans be not turned against their givers.[1] When the Chagga are fighting in a war, the different sides keep certain rules of conduct. When men are killed, women and children are taken prisoner, cattle carried off, banana plantations destroyed, houses burnt, and irrigation channels opened, that is all lawful; but it is wrong to kill or capture chiefs or blacksmiths.

The Chagga have, even in very fertile areas, a great deal of uncultivated ground; but nowadays with increasing European influence and slavery tending to come to an end, the population is increasing and all land will be taken up for farming. Perhaps German colonial rule will become a factor here; only the future will show what this will bring.

In Chagga country itself, there are few serious diseases; there are sores, rheumatism, and a lot of illness caused by worms (earthworms and toenias). But when the mountain dwellers stay for a while in lowland country—at Kahe, at Arusha, and particularly at Taveta—they very often come back suffering from fever and dysentery; because of this, the Chagga usually stay at home. Europeans, who by reason of a long stay have got used to the African sun, suffer on Kilimanjaro from the cold and the mist, sometimes also from malaria, but only when they have brought the germs from the coast or the surrounding plains.

With regard to religious beliefs and practices, Mr. H. H. Johnston states in his excellent report on his travels, that he has only been able to gather very little information. He does not however, unlike other travelers with the same experience, conclude that all religion is absent, and in this he is very wise, as we, who have been more fortunate in what we have seen and learned, can testify.

Let us start with a generalization which is relevant to what has been said already. Some theoreticians, following Lucretius, like to suppose that if mankind is everywhere religious, this is a result of fear. This question can easily be studied in Africa, where, as everybody agrees, the tribal societies are at the lowest rung of the social ladder. Now, I have been ten years travelling in African countries, making contact with very varied societies, and, to my great surprise, I have never found anybody who was frightened by natural

1. I had just written this when the newspapers reported that a German expedition commanded by Lieutenant von Bulow had been wiped out at Moshi by Medi, the eldest son and successor of Mandara.

phenomena. People are rather amused by thunder, they do not fear it; lightning does not bother people, and if sometimes they are afraid to go out at night, it is only through fear of wild animals. Now in certain cases, there is fear as to what God can do, what the ancestors can do, what the evil spirits can do. African religion consists precisely in protecting oneself against these powers, either by keeping them at a distance or by satisfying their demands, but it is not thought that their action, whether an act of vengeance or simply a cause of irritation, is linked to natural phenomena, such as hurricanes, lightning, and thunder. Theoreticians have thought that people in primitive societies share the same fears as they have, but they were mistaken.

Nor does one find any traces of the cult of the stars anywhere in east Africa, as formerly in Egypt and Arabia, India, Polynesia, and America among the brown or "Canaanean" race, which seems to have populated these countries. The sun is known as "He who is on high," commanded by God to bring the day when night ends; the moon is the heavenly body which measures times, seasons, and years; the Pleiades is the sign when it appears on the horizon that the agricultural year is beginning; as to the stars, they are lights, or "fires," whose beginning, end, and meaning are of no interest.

However, while the majority of the Bantu tribes of Central Africa and East Africa know God by the name of *Mulungu*, which seems to mean "The Great," here, on Kilimanjaro this same God, known to be the Master of all, is called *Ruwa*, which also means sun. But the Chagga unanimously protest when asked if the sun and God are one and the same being, and their use of the same word is similar to our use of the word "heaven" referring both to the visible sky and the invisible abode of the blessed.

Now, do we have to conclude that originally these Africans identified the sun with God, and that later, taking a step forward, they have separated them? As a great scholar, Max Muller, has clearly shown, the names of things have simply been epithets applied to them, or, if you will, adjectives qualifying them. Now the root of this word *Ruwa*, "sun," which elsewhere takes the forms of *Zua, Jua, Juve, Njuba*, or *Jua*, appears to be *Zu, Juu*, etc., which has the meaning "high, on high, above," so that the words referring to God and the sun really mean, each in their own context and without being applied to the same being, "That which is on high." With their limited vocabulary, these Africans would have thus given to God and to one of his creatures a term which suits each of them. It is the same with the Maasai word *Ngai*, which surprisingly means "God," "a superior being (a European for example)," "the sky," "rain," and so on. In fact, this word seems to come from an adjective which has the general meaning of "good," and these simple people apply it to everything that can be seen as such.

Despite this, there is a certain lack of clarity in these questions, and some scholars will surely be impressed by the similarity of sound between the *Ruwa* of Chagga country and the *Raa* or *Ra* of ancient Egypt, a word which applies to both God and the sun. In the same way, the Polynesians say *La*, *Laa*, or *Raa*, which is the same word. And what is equally curious in Oceania also, one finds the word *Rai* which means "heaven"; allowing for the permutation of the prefix, it is the Maasai word, *Ngai*.

Whatever the value of these hypotheses, which if examined in detail would take up a great deal of time, people who live among African tribal societies and study them as they are would regard as scientifically established the following: Africans, and for that matter the Europeans of the past, are not rising by their own efforts and without anyone teaching them from fetishism to more satisfactory ideas. On the contrary, they have come down and will continue to come down from good ideas to less good, and from less good to bad, unless their descent is checked. To put it differently, successive generations have passed on the soil of Africa, growing up, caught up in conflict, forgetting much, and learning little.

The Chagga, more than many other African peoples, had in their mountains a defense against invasion and therefore also against change and decadence. This is perhaps why they are superior to their neighbors of the same stock in farming, craftsmanship, and, I need to add now, in their religious ideas. The God whose existence they assert is, according to them, a personal being, the master of everything and the creator of everything. Plants, animals, and human beings belong to him. Also, every time a goat or a sheep or a cow is killed, it is done, we can say, with God's permission. The head of the family comes up to the animal, takes a handful of grass, spits over it, and also onto the animal's head saying, "*Nakupa Rua*" (I give you to God). After that, the animal, dedicated to God, can no longer go back to the flock or herd. There is a curious similarity between these words and "*Benedicite—Dominus*" (Bless us; let it be the Lord's). On both sides, there seems to be a reluctance to touch what has been created without the permission of the Creator.

But, better still, there is the real idea of sacrifice. One evening, at Machame, the day before Chief Ngameni was to accept an alliance with Mandara against Sina and hoist his flag over the village, five or six of his ministers and kinsmen came out, pulling a kid goat by one of its legs. I followed them. We reached a place where three paths met, and there, having spat on the animal, the formula already quoted was repeated, its throat was cut, and it was divided into three. One part was roasted and destroyed on the charcoal, it was God's share. A second part was eaten by Ngameni and his companions, it was a communion in the sacrifice. Finally, thin slices were cut from every part of the animal—heart, liver, head, skin, etc., then after two small heaps had been made, they were placed neatly on big banana leaves at the junction of the paths. I asked what the reason for this final ceremony was. They replied, "It is for the shades of our ancestors, for the birds, the insects, and every living creature, to give the world of nature a share in our sacrifice, and so that God may protect Ngameni."

The God whom the Chagga worship is not a local god, but the Master of all, so we were told, the Master of blacks and whites.

But there are also offerings to the *Mzimu* (souls freed from their bodies), the manes (shades) of the ancestors. Once a year people go from Kilema and Marangu to make an offering at a mysterious lake in the crater of an extinct volcano, where it is said the first chief of the country drowned himself. His soul is still there and every year he receives in sacrifice a little white lamb "spotless and innocent," whose remains are thrown into the deep waters.

People carry amulets to guard against all sorts of dangers, but it is only fair to say that they often include medically useful plants.

Here is something extraordinary. People have told me that they know nothing of the *pepo*, or devil, who elsewhere is very important in the lives of Africans and Europeans.

With regard to life after death, they have a very muddled idea of it, but there is such an idea, apart from the belief in the survival of the human soul, after the body has come to an end.

Everybody accepts the principles of family life, respects the moral obligations of society, knows the difference between right and wrong, and murder, adultery, theft and so on are universally condemned.

We regret, though, to have to say that there is no respect for the life of a child who has not yet seen the light of day, if there is any reason for not wanting him to live. At the moment of birth, a midwife decides whether the child should live or die; but at least among the Chagga the father can reject her decision. In any case, the child must remain in the house where he or she was born until he or she can walk and he or she is only named when he or she can answer to it. This occasion is not accompanied by any ceremonies, except a meal and rejoicing. Later on, the child is given something to do appropriate to their age; a little girl has to pound grain, a boy looks after a flock. Circumcision, which is performed around the age of fourteen, is an occasion for dancing and festivity but has no religious significance. We know that it has existed in Egypt and Ethiopia; it has even been found in Polynesia, in Central America, and the West Indies. While the Bible tells us how Abraham and his family adopted circumcision, it does not intend to say, as is often thought, that it was the first time it was practiced.

The Chagga are often monogamous but also have the opportunity to be polygamous; it all depends on how rich one is, for this is a country where marriage is expensive. However, in every case, and particularly with the chiefs, the first wife is regarded as the real wife, and the others must show her respect and obedience. They all take meals apart from, and after, their husband. Each one has her own house, where she and her children live.

When a girl has reached marriageable age, she has to receive pre-marital instruction for three or four or five months from an elderly aunt or friend of the family who has been chosen for this. After this, she comes out with bells on her legs—perhaps warning bells—until the wedding day. This wedding is, as we have seen, a kind of market deal which, when completed, allows the bridegroom to take the bride. She has to resist, or appear to; it is the make-believe kidnapping which is found among several African tribes as well as elsewhere.

When a death takes place, it is not attributed, as elsewhere, to the ill will of an enemy. It is a natural happening, which everybody has to experience. If the dead person is a child, an unmarried man, or someone who has died childless, their body is not buried. It is carried deep into the woods, covered with leaves, and left there. If he is married and a parent, he is buried in the house on the right of the door; a mother is buried on the left of the door. Here we have in this custom a parallel to the ideas found in ancient Egypt, in India and elsewhere, where the absence of descendants is regarded as the worst of misfortunes.

Now, do people hold firmly to all these different customs? When the people told us about them and asked our opinion on their value, we had to say that among all these Chagga customs, some were good, some were neither good nor bad, and some definitely bad. They replied, "It may very well be so. But have you not come precisely to tell us what is good and what is bad? We shall keep what is good and give up the rest." My poor dear Chagga friends, may things be just as you have said.

The Language

I have not yet said anything about the language. Yet it is one of the most interesting and most important aspects of the thought and the way of life of a people. Chagga belongs to the great family of different languages marked by their prefixes spoken by the Bantu peoples who, from the Atlantic to the Indian Ocean, occupy practically all Africa south of the Equator down to the Cape. Basically, they have the same grammatical principles. Their vocabularies can differ a good deal, sometimes because the words in one language depend on roots entirely different to those used in neighboring languages, sometimes because changes in either consonants or vowels make them appear different or finally because they have kept or adopted expressions which the other languages have lost or never adopted.

The analysis of all known languages places each in one or other of the three great divisions: *isolating* languages, *agglutinative* languages, and *inflected* languages. However, it is only fair to state that there is perhaps no language which belongs purely and totally to one of these three divisions. In all or almost all cases, there are words which indicate a transition from one to another division, and this may indicate that the language is moving from one division to another, or that it has in fact moved, but retains some elements from its former condition.

Having noted these possibilities of linguistic overlapping, we can say that we understand by *isolating languages* those languages whose words do not combine with each other and which only convey meaning by the way in which they are placed in relation to each other—according to the position which it has in a particular phrase, the same word can be a noun, an adjective, a verb, a participle, or an adverb. Thus, in Chinese, *Ngo-to-ni* can mean "I beat you," while *Ni-ta-ngo* means "You beat me." In conversation, the different levels of tones help to indicate the meaning and the relation of individual words.

In the *agglutinative languages*, the roots of words are joined together, one giving the primary meaning, the other or the others being joined to this one, to indicate its gender, its activity, its mood, its tense, etc. The elements which make up the word keep their own meaning and can more or less have their specific function indicated and analyzed. This is the case in Turkish and Swahili, and such is the case with Africa's Bantu languages which, interestingly and surprisingly, are more developed than Chinese. Thus, one says in Swahili, *Nina*, "I have"—*Ni*, "I" and *Na*, "with" (that is, I am with), which means "I have."

A Chagga shield

Finally, the inflected languages, such as Latin, Greek, Hebrew, Arabic, etc., have, like the agglutinative languages, the majority of their words formed from two or more roots; these are combined however in such a way that one does not recognize the original roots. Thus, we say in French, *J'aimerai* (I would love to) for *Je aimer aurai* (I-to love-would have).

But let us come back to our African languages and show more clearly how the roots of words agglutinate. In French, you need seven words to say *Le couteau que je lui ai donné* (the knife which I have given him), but Swahili speakers can manage with two words, "*Kisu nilichompa.*" To be absolutely fair, we have to admit that the first word is the equivalent of two words, and the second one is the equivalent of six: *Ki-su ni-li-ch-o-m-pa*. The personal pronouns, subjects, relative pronouns, complements, to say nothing of conjunctions, are inserted into the verb: they are agglutinated. Just as with a patchwork where one can see where the different parts have been stuck together, most of the words which have been agglutinated can be easily divided into their original roots.

In these languages—some of which lack and some of which possess the definite article— there are eight or nine classes of noun, singular, and plural forms, but there are no genders. When one wishes to distinguish a male person or animal from a female, or vice versa, one adds the marker for masculine or feminine identity. But instead of our male and female genders, we have categories which are linked to the classes of nouns, four or six or eight of these categories, or even ten or twelve. Fr. Sacleux of Zanzibar has been the first scholar to give them the name of *polygynous* languages, rather than Bantu. This word, Bantu, means "the people" and hence Bantu languages are human languages, an assertion which seems a bit hard on the speakers of other languages.

We have the personal or animal category, for persons or living creatures, the vegetative category which refers to varieties of plants and vegetables, the general category for objects which do not belong to other categories, the abstract category, the honorific or noble category, the category used for something small or imperfect, the locative category indicating where something is, etc. Each category has a specific prefix which, attached first to the subject noun, is then attached to the words dependent on the subject, the adjective, the pronoun, and the verb. The subject, we might say, marches in front and draws the whole phrase to follow it, wearing the same sort of clothes. In rather the same way, a guide would get a caravan to follow him along the narrow pathways of the hinterland.

In the spoken language, the verb is extremely important; in order to use it for all that one wants to say, one can use it with a very varied range of forms which always keep the basic root. From the same verb in its active mood can be derived such forms as the passive, the neuter, the intensifying, the reciprocal, the causative, the directive, the reversive, etc. An example will help us understand the marvelous richness and the equally marvelous simplicity of these "primitive" languages. The root *ung* has the general sense of "to unite, to tighten together." Hence, *Unga*, to unite, *Ungwa*, to be united, *Ungia*, to unite to, for, in order to, *Ungana*, to unite one item to another, *Unganya*, to make to unite, *Ungua*, to disunite, to burn, *Unguza*, to make to be disunited, to make to be burned.

We find the same richness in the tenses. In the past tense there is a variety of forms based on the same root, which indicates an action which has been made—a general past. Then there is a form which indicates something which has been done and whose result continues in existence. There is also a form which indicates that the act in question came after, or happened before, some other action. Again, it is possible to indicate that a particular action was made at the same time as some other action. Finally, we can note forms that indicate that the action has not yet been performed, or that it is being performed at this very time.

If, now, we go back to the nouns, we find specific expressions to indicate the successive stages through which, for instance, the same instrument, the same fruit, or the same animal have to pass. People who speak French, or for that matter German or English, or any other civilized language, think they have said all that needs to be said, when the word "coconut" is used for the fruit of the coconut palm. But this is just poverty of language. Instead of a single, not very clear word, Swahili has available: *Kidaka*, a coconut which has already taken shape; *Kitale*, a more developed coconut, filled with water; *Dafu*, a coconut which provides a good drink; *Koroma*, a coconut which is not yet completely ripe; *Nazi*, a ripe coconut, which is still green; *Kibata*, a dry, ripe coconut; *Zimi*, a barren coconut, without water and without a kernel.

That is the case for Swahili, but the languages spoken inland are almost as rich. People are nowhere in difficulties to find an appropriate name for everything known, visible or invisible. There, every part of the mountain and the plain, every river and every stream, everything to which reference can be made is named. And these names form sentences, which are subject to rules. These rules in turn depend on grammatical principles. These principles are so precise, so exact, even so philosophical, that one is almost forced to adopt the phrase of an eminent Orientalist, speaking about the Turkish language, that these languages "appear to be the result of the deliberations of an academy composed of distinguished scholars."

Some years ago, certain rather naive people were hoping to find in the interior of Africa satisfying specimens of the missing link between the apes and man. But this has proved another vain hope. No! "Beastly" is the last word to apply to our parishioners!

PART THREE

From Kilimanjaro to Zanzibar

Chapter 23: Kahe

The day was 7th September, a Sunday. While we kept the day special by prayer and rest, a messenger arrived with the news that King Sina of Kibosho had again invaded the territory of his neighbor, Ngameni, at Machame, cut down the banana plantations, taken a fortified camp, and carried off a lot of women and children. Such was the way he kept his promise of friendship. M. d'Eltz went straightaway to Mandara, and they decided that war was the only answer, a really big war, for which one would gather all the available forces from Chaggaland, from Pare, from Kahe, and from lower Arusha in order to deal finally with the menace of Sina.

But what could we do? After we had thought about it, talked about it, and prayed about it, Mgr. de Courmont decided what we had to do. M. d'Eltz insisted, with his habitual kindness, that Mgr. de Courmont should stay under his protection, and that Fr. Gommenginger would stay here, waiting to see what would happen. If the situation at Machame settled down, we would start our first mission at Machame, if not, we would settle at Kilema, where Fumba was still anxious to have us. In any case, Moshi was out of the question. Monsignor and I would take the way to the coast; en route, we explored Kahe, lower Arusha, Pare, and the area of Maasai country which includes the Ruvu basin, the Sambara, the Zigua, and the Doe. Then we would reach Bagamoyo which would lie to our south, passing through our mission at Mandera. As soon as possible, a new caravan would set out to reach Fr. Gommenginger with the necessary personnel: a Father, a Brother, twenty young Christians, and everything needed to set up a new mission.

In the meanwhile, we went down together to lower Arusha to stay with M. d'Eltz. Our good friend, Dr. Baxter, went with us, dreaming of wonderful hunting, which he expected to find around lower Arusha.

We took leave of Mandara, who handed over to M. d'Eltz the child of one of the Pare chiefs who had been taken prisoner in a previous war, so that he could be given back to his father. Then we went down the mountain slopes, and continued in a southeasterly direction, across the semi-desert plain. After a march of four hours, we reached the banks of the river Deu, which runs down from Kilema. The forest was magnificent; the trees, like columns with tall shafts, covered everything with their majestic foliage. The flowing water was quiet, resting from the twists and turns and falls which it would have undergone on the higher ground, and bringing coolness and life everywhere. In places, this strip of forest is literally cluttered up with raffia palms. This extraordinary tree has leaves six to ten meters long that grow across each other, get mixed together, and become intertwined in an impenetrable confusion. The fruit hangs down in long clusters, which is the delight of countless cheeky monkeys, and in the broad mud which spreads as far as the shadows of these age-old thickets, buffaloes, rhinoceroses, and elephants pass happy days.

It was there that we camped. There were no human habitations, our only neighbors were the wild animals, but these kept their distance and this first day's hunting drew a blank. The next morning, we were awakened at five o'clock by the monkeys, who hurled insults at us from the tops of the trees, and we set off. Having crossed the Deu, which we saw again later on, with the amount of its water increased by a channel coming out of the Rau River, we entered Kahe by two narrow gateways.

Kahe is the name of a little community, a kind of oasis similar to Taveta, formed by the rich alluvial deposits brought down from Kilimanjaro by the numerous rivers and streams which are to be found there. The population can scarcely be more than 2,000. They dress in the Maasai style, but in physical type, culture, and language they are close to the people of Taveta and lower Arusha. The men usually wear linen cloths, while the women wear tanned skins, pearls, and cowries. They are an essentially agricultural people, intelligent and courteous. There are a lot of banana groves, fields of sweet potatoes, yams, Congo peas, beans, and maize. Irrigation technology is well developed, and something that was new to us in Africa, spaces divided into vegetable beds and cultivated plots, all watered and weeded, just as one of our gardeners would do.

The people also rear cattle, which, just as at Taveta, are kept in cow sheds, or, to be strictly accurate, in the houses. Their religious and social ideas are those of the neighboring communities. However, they are not as strongly republican as the Taveta people: there are two chiefs, with more or less equal powers, surely proof of a harmonious temperament.

We had only just settled into our camp when we began to receive a stream of visitors. A mission would also be welcomed there; but what can we do? So many fields to be cultivated, and so few workmen!

Here we are in the heart of the virgin forest, in a clean, cool clearing. Above us, the tall trees, straight as a ship's masts, provide a wonderful green dome.

The whole setting is so charming that we really had to let ourselves feel at home in this wonderful maze where everything is so big and beautiful. Surely in this silent world of tropical nature, God speaks to the soul ready to listen in a language so gentle and yet so penetrating. Each one of us sets off on a stroll, following a pathway which seems to attract his imagination, or which is suggested by a passing whim. One man chooses to sit down under a forest giant, another follows the little paths which run through the woods, a third sets off, a little recklessly, into the depths of the forest. The nature that we encounter here is not the gloomy, cold, misty, and yet awe-inspiring nature that we found on the mountain. As we walked, we felt the delightful coolness given by the green leaves above us, but we knew also that the sun was in turn above them, Africa's sun, with its intense light, its life-giving heat, and its power of making the earth fertile.

A little beyond the zone of human habitation, as you go up the rivers that flow from Machame, the Weru-Weru for instance, you soon come across big game, particularly buffaloes, but taking that direction can be dangerous. The Kamba hunters have literally riddled the ground with elephant holes. Falling into one of these could be a very serious mishap for a human being. These are ditches, a little more than two meters wide and three to four meters long, and are divided into two by a wall inside them. The whole ditch is carefully covered with grass and branches, among which the hunters often include those which the elephants find particularly enjoyable.

At night, at the time for wanderings here and there, to which an elephant has grown accustomed, he strolls forward, following the route that he has carefully marked out for himself, seizing with his trunk a branch on his right or his left for his amusement. Suddenly, the soil gives way under his front feet: he has fallen into the death trap. But seeing that the path before him seems safe, he instinctively pulls himself together, and moves forward. This proves a tragic error, for while his hind-quarters are trapped in the first ditch, his head is swaying from side to side in the second ditch, and his stomach rubs against the wall dividing the two ditches. The colossus has lost all his strength and can do nothing except wait for the hunter to fire a poisoned arrow.

The wild life of Kahe has a special character which is given to it by the presence of a particularly remarkable monkey, the colobus (its zoological name being the *colobus guereza*, or *colobus caudatus*). There are three varieties of colobus. One variety has a long, straight tail and is found in the forests of southern Africa; the second, found in Ethiopia, has a tail which ends in a thick tuft; then the third variety has a broad, white, silky tail and it is only in this region that it can be seen. Supposing you are in the heart of the big forest, you take a walk and gaze around you admiringly, you lift your head to hear the birds calling to each other among the greenery of the trees, sometimes you follow the groups of very ordinary little grey monkeys, who scatter as you approach, running away like a gang of rascals caught pilfering.

But then, from very high up, in the intricate interweaving of branches and creepers, a gentle sound, softened by the distance, reaches you; it seems that some creature is trying to slip away. Then you take a hard look, you try and locate the sound, you move forward, then backward, very gently, your body leaning forward, your neck pushed up, your eye fixed in its gaze, your finger on the rifle trigger, and there it is! Up above, behind a branch, a little black head ringed round with white, motionless, anguished, with its body hunched back and its tail hidden, its hands clutching the tree as if it were a clamp, is watching you.

Colobus monkeys of the Kahe Forest

Then, if you do not think that you are committing a crime against a member of what was once your family, fire! You must fire a bullet; lead-shot will not do the job. The poor creature shudders for a moment, loses hold of the branch, and falls, falls, falls, slowly and heavily, coming down in a way that could make you weep, with a thin line of red blood staining his marvelous coat of shimmering silk, black or white, but never touched by a grain of dust. But, at the sound of the rifle shot, other members of the band have left their home on the edge of the sky, see them running along the branches, jumping, almost flying, spreading behind them their magnificent white tail as though it were a plume.

When, by evening, we had got back to the camp, we found that the two of us had killed six of these poor things, shooting them for their skin. But even after this, we kept on hearing something like the sound of a fierce and furious battle in the depth of the forest: it was Dr. Baxter who had fired off many bullets at a colobus monkey which had stuck firmly to a branch, refusing to come down. When night fell, our valiant hunter had come back to the camp, bringing two other monkeys which he had killed in the daytime. He told us he would collect the third the next day, while going past the tree from which it must have fallen.

At the same time as he arrived, one of the local chiefs came to see us. The poor man had tears in his eyes, and his voice trembled, as he asked for pardon and pity. "Pardon and pity for our monkeys," he said, "which have never harmed anybody, which never steal anything, and which eat only the fruit of their trees. If they came down from their trees, it is only to drink at the river. Then they come by families, and, so that they do not dirty themselves on the way, the mother follows immediately after the father, and the children follow their mother, and each of them lifts up the tail of whoever is just in front . . . And, finally, our elders state that our ancestors like to be present in these creatures so that they can still roam round the Kahe forests, and from there watch their children working. And so," this very sincere man concluded, "if you kill them all, where will our souls go?"

We set off next morning to avoid killing them all. As was only right, our caravan stopped as promised at the foot of the tree which the doctor had indicated. He looked round the foot of the tree, he gazed up above. Lord, have mercy! He found now that he had fired sixteen rifle shots—but at what target? At an old piece of white wood which, in the evening shadows, he had taken for a monkey's tail.

Chapter 24: Lower Arusha

On the Plain. Hunting in the Wilderness. The Government Post at Lower Arusha. The Time for Saying Farewell. A Rhinoceros at the Mouth of My Rifle

It took just an hour to pass through the forest which here, as at Taveta, came to a sudden end, giving way to a real desert which had its own particularity. The grasses, mainly of the graminaceous family, are short and thin. There are occasional acacias, but also wide areas absolutely without any kind of vegetation, then there are some rather exceptional bushes, such as salsolas, which one hardly sees except in coastal lagoons. Only in occasional places, where the soil is raised up a bit, forming a more fertile layer, are there trees, grouped together, linked by various kinds of creepers, forming attractive clumps. You are constantly being reminded by smooth pebbles, by alluvial lime, and by nitrite salt, spread out in whitish lines, that all this territory was formerly occupied by an inland sea, whose last remains are to be found in two salt lakes: the Mangora, to the east of Kilimanjaro, and the Ndyiri to its north.

The landscape, such as it is, however, is not without charm, taking its setting into account; to the north, Kilimanjaro, massive and superb, which from here, can be seen in all its grandeur. To the east, there is the blue wall of the Pare Mountains; to the west, the enormous cone of Mt. Meru, a former volcano whose crater is sometimes covered by a white layer of snow.

Further to the left is Upper Arusha, occupied by people related to the Taveta people, but more aggressive and culturally close to the Maasai. How isolated we felt! And what marvelous open spaces! And such impressive scenery! Having travelled together for some time, we decided to split up so that we could cover more ground and try to find in this wilderness something really meaty for our next meal. Mgr. de Courmont, Fr. Auguste, and the porters were to follow a track which would lead them to the German post at Lower Arusha; M. d'Eltz took off to the right, I went to the left, and Dr. Baxter, whose enthusiasm was undiminished, took a zigzag way through the wilderness, from where frequent shots from his rifle kept informing us of how he was getting on.

We had been moving ahead in this fashion when suddenly we heard M. d'Eltz's big rifle fired once, then again. We ran in that direction and found him facing a mortally wounded buffalo which had sprung at him. Happily, he had time enough to bring his rifle onto his shoulder, and a third shot brought the buffalo down on the ground. The porters immediately laid down their loads, pulled out knives, and, sitting on the buffalo, they dedicated themselves, with tremendous enthusiasm, to sharing its meat.

Kibo and Mawenzi

Further on, I saw a herd of zebras. I crouched down as best I could behind the wretched clumps of bushes. I soon found myself in open ground where I could not stand up without causing them all to run away. Whatever the risk, I chose to send them a greeting. What happened was really worth seeing; when the rifle shot rang out, these forty or fifty zebras all together gave the ground a magnificent kick, so that from it sprang up whirlwinds of dust, then they started to gallop, but stopped suddenly, grouped themselves in a line, and lifted their heads in an attitude of defiance. It reminded me of a cavalry squadron, obedient to every command, and acting as a single body. And how beautiful it was, in that vast African wilderness, to see these elegant animals, with their yellow skins, with, in contrast, long black stripes, gleaming in the equatorial sunshine.

I moved forward. A numerous herd of antelopes passed close to me. They were unafraid and trotted forward at a moderate pace. But there is a proverb that you should not chase two hares at the same time, and it still holds if you say "zebras" instead of "hares." As I came nearer to them, they began to scatter again, and I was delighted to see one who had difficulty in moving, stepped aside and stood still for a little while; my shot must have hit him. Running as though I was crazy, I managed to cut him off from the herd, and then I had to walk after him. For nearly an hour, I tried unsuccessfully to get up close to him, until the animal reached a part of the wilderness where the trees grew fairly close together. I managed to hide behind one of these trees, and, tired of the struggle, I fired my last bullet at the zebra who was standing up there. He galloped off at great speed, kept going for perhaps two hundred meters, and suddenly disappeared. What had become of him? Slowly, sadly, regretting that I had run so far without achieving anything, I set off in the direction the zebra had taken, when suddenly I saw him lying at my feet! My first shot had hit him in the hock, the second had reached his heart.

But what could I do, all alone and having lost my way? I cut the zebra's tail with a knife, and tried, going to a large clump of bushes, which we had agreed on as a landmark, to get back to the caravan. It was extremely hot. After about an hour's walk, I finally heard two rifle shots. Dr. Baxter and his men were coming back from their hunt. They had spotted a great deal of game and had fired repeatedly, but their enthusiasm was not rewarded with success. They explained that these animals managed to escape, even after having been hit by a shot that should have been fatal. As we went on together we saw, nearby, very recent elephant footprints, but we were too tired and too far from the government post to try any new searches. We crossed three strongly-flowing rivers on rickety bridges, and then caught up with, one by one, the stragglers from the caravan, and reached the German post of Lower Arusha toward evening.

There I showed the tail of my zebra, irrefutable evidence that I had at least come close to it. Meat! Meat! Straightaway some brave hearts set off to search for the fine meat meal, guided by the brief instructions I gave them, and, somewhat later, by the presence of numerous birds of prey, circling round in the sky. But when they got to the spot they found they had to fight over the zebra's remains with crowds of kites, marabouts, and vultures who, in less than three hours, had eaten practically everything.

The staff of the German post consisted of M. d'Eltz, an NCO called Kaiser, and some twenty African soldiers, Swahilis and Sudanese. On one side, the Europeans occupied a large, cool house; opposite it were the soldiers' quarters. A formidable double fence made of tree trunks formed a square around the buildings. Everything is very clean and very well kept. In one corner, there is an enormous heap of animal heads (elegant gazelles, various kinds of antelopes, wild boars, giraffes, zebras, hippopotamuses, buffaloes, rhinoceroses) which demonstrate both the varied animal population of the surrounding wilderness, and the success in big-game hunting of the master of the post.

It is a low-lying, well-watered country. It is another oasis formed by three rivers which come down from Kilimanjaro, and farmed by a small population, similar to the people of Kahe and Taveta, like them living by farming and livestock keeping, settled in autonomous family groups. Both agriculture and pastoral farming are very productive. Life there is quite pleasant at this time of year, but in the rainy season, the whole country suffers from flooding, and there are uncountable mosquitoes. To the east rise the uninhabited Litema Mountains, where the rain falls very rarely.

The importance of the Lower Arusha post is that it is at the point where most of the Pangani caravans are organized and buy provisions before going into Maasai land or returning to the coast. But what makes it an attractive place is the enormous amount of game in the surrounding countryside. A small detail is sufficient to make my point. We stayed four days there—sixty people in all, counting Africans and Europeans—and all our food came from two men's hunting expeditions.

However, we had to think about moving on. On the morning of the 13th September, we reorganized the caravan, and while continuing to hunt as we crossed the wilderness, we took a southwesterly route toward the Ruvu, which in this area had been already enlarged by most of the rivers coming down from the mountains. There were many herds of antelopes; occasionally, we saw a hare moving through the undergrowth; some ostriches could be seen in the distance, looking similar in the long grass to a clump of grey-green bushes. Then, among the animals whose droppings are its nourishment, a crested crane walked proudly, holding itself straight up, with its splendid plumage, and its beautiful golden crest of feathers. We managed to kill a very young buffalo whose meat was immediately shared out.

Then we came to a river. A small island made it flow in two streams, both very broad, and therefore rather shallow. At that time, we were able to ford the two streams, with water coming up to our waists.

The time for saying farewell had come. Goodbye to the valiant Dr. Baxter, who was going to stay for some days to hunt game in the wilderness. Goodbye to the admirable M. d'Eltz, who was for us and who will be for the new mission a protector and a friend, exceptional in his kindness, generosity, and unselfishness. Finally, goodbye to our dear Fr. Auguste Gommenginger, whom we left there with two Catholic children. For him there is the honor of being the planter of a church, the herald of salvation, the founder of a civilization, the benefactor of a people.

Nderingo stayed with him. This poor lad took me aside, behind some brushwood, and said, "We shall not see each other again!" His large dark eyes filled with tears, and he took off from his neck a copper necklace and asked me to take it. "Carry it as something to remember me by, for you have been dear to me." The poor man—so likeable. I advised him to be always really loyal to my brother (Fr. Gommenginger), to listen attentively to his teaching, and to receive baptism as soon as possible. I then left him, very quickly because I was really moved, and, as today I write these lines, just on the point of taking up a new posting, I feel obliged to send him my affectionate greetings. You were right, Nderingo, we shall not see each other again on African soil.

We crossed the river. The last farewells were shouted from one bank to the other, and while those who had travelled with us went back to the post, we pitched our tents on the edge of the desert which we would have to cross. The river banks are astonishingly barren and dry. There was a line of tall evergreen trees which provided shade along the river's course, but, apart from them, the way from Kahe to Sambara offers only parched soil and loneliness. That was how we were, lonely and rather sad. That afternoon, Mgr. de Courmont asked me to explore the neighborhood, to take our minds off the sadness of our goodbyes and, if possible, to get for the caravan a supply of fresh meat for the next few days.

I set off with two of our men. Soon enough, a herd of zebras appeared in the distance; I fired. The herd scattered, as was usual; but it seemed to me that it was the most striking of them all who had been hit, and so we set off to track down this impressive squadron of zebras. We tramped over hill after hill, all with bushes on them, and prickly with thorns. The zebras would bob up for a few moments, then run away again and finally raced out of sight. The sun was setting, I had lost sight of my animals and even my men. I felt that my duty was to return to our camp.

I strolled on alone, my rifle by my side, my imagination roaming all round, when suddenly I heard a muffled sound; the ground shook, and in the shadows I saw something like a skidding omnibus or a steam train getting up to speed.

Before I could take up a fighting position, the monster was right before me: an enormous rhinoceros which, no doubt disturbed while resting and suspecting me of ill-will, was ready to throw himself with his head down at my harmless self. I had indeed a rifle in my hand, but not only was the rifle not ready, but in my case, a bullet would only tickle his skin; however, I remembered hearing that this animal was too stupid to chase his enemy, and I found the courage to move to one side. I was very happy to see him go straight forward, breathing and sniffling, trampling on the bushes in his path, and sending up behind him the pebbles and the dust.

An hour later, following the river and watching the smoke from our fires, I made a not very triumphant entry into our camp.

They asked, "What about the meat?"

I answered, "It is still running."

Chapter 25: In Maasai Land

The Caravan. At the Foot of the Pare Mountains. These Two Ladies. The Wilderness. Among the Maasai. Meeting Mwane-Mane. Among the Ndorobo. A People's Blessing.

Our caravan had undergone some changes. Before leaving Kilimanjaro, we said goodbye to the Muslims recruited at Mombasa, and this was a relief for us. We had handed over to Fr. Auguste Gommenginger the two young Christians who travelled with us. Finally, at Lower Arusha we found some Pangani men who, after a journey to the interior to buy ivory, wanted to go back to the coast. They were too few and too lacking in weapons to travel by themselves and so asked to come with us. We accepted this very readily, since among them we could find guides for this journey into the unknown and even an interpreter for dealing with the Maasai. This was a man called Salim who had the devil's own daring and an extraordinary glibness in speech.

On 14th September, at six o'clock in the morning, we started off, taking a straight eastern direction. By eleven o'clock, having crossed a wilderness with an abundance of prickly thorns, we got to the foot of the Pare Mountains. When we were going to Kilimanjaro, we had followed this mountain chain from Gonja to Jipe. We were now keeping close to its western side from where we were that day, to the wall which marks its end on the south side. But we lacked detailed information on this route, and the map of this little corner of Africa has yet to be made.

This was Mabua. Down below the mountains, there is a stream which runs north to Lake Jipe. The foothills of the mountains are covered with treelike euphorbias whose stems stand up as though in some strange plantation. We fired a rifle shot, at which the local people came down, only a few at first, and these distrustful, gazing at us from a distance. Then they became gradually bolder and brought us flour, sugar cane, beans, and maize. This was an unimpressive countryside if you were looking at it from the plain.

But if you go up into the mountains, there are flat stretches of land which are cool and well cultivated, with splendid herds and quite a large population, even though it has suffered in warfare. They are timid and live in isolated groups. They hide their houses behind rocks, and do their best to prevent the streams running down into the plain, so as to prevent the Maasai and the caravans from quenching their thirst.

Ndorobo woman

The men arrived despite all this and we met some twenty of them going hunting with big bows. Near there, on the path, they had set up a long barrier of stakes and tree branches with, at various points, narrow openings where deep ditches were hidden. On an agreed date, a great number of hunters come down onto the plain to track down game by driving it gradually toward the barrier. The animals see the opening and rush through, falling into the ditches which have been covered with grass, and then the hunters finish them off.

When we got to Mabua, we found two Maasai women and a boy. They were loading three or four donkeys with sacks of maize which they had come to get for the elders. When Salim questioned them, they told him that many Sogonoi Maasai had crossed the river, and that there was a large Maasai camp in the neighborhood, adding, "these are days of misfortune, and the cattle are dying from illness. Look, like that."

And the old woman took a fistful of dust which she threw into the wind. She was talking about a dreadful cattle epidemic which had spread death among the beasts, from the mountains of Ethiopia to as far as Mozambique. By then it had reached Senegal, having spread across the Sudan. In East Africa, when it had run its course with the cattle, it attacked the buffaloes, and even, it is said, the antelopes.

But what a strange thing! These two women did not seem at all worried by the arrival of our caravan. They were alone and without weapons or anything that could protect them, except perhaps their faces, which would have matched women who were full-time sorceresses. Other women in such a situation, would have rushed into the brushwood from fear; these two went on calmly with what they were doing, and when the donkeys were duly laden, they said goodbye and set off, telling us that we could use the place where they had encamped. They were ladies whom nothing could worry.

We took five and a half days to go round the Pare Mountains, with daily marches of from five to eight hours. There were no more paths, except toward the south. The Maasai are the only people who travel in this lonely land and they do not bother about paths. Wearing tough sandals made of cattle skin, and carrying a big spear in their hands, they travel like a romantic poet, without money or even a pocket. The only thing that they might fear would be what worried the people of ancient Gaul: the possibility that the sky might fall on the earth.

We civilized people cannot be like that. One whole morning we had to struggle with a seemingly impenetrable forest, full of thorny undergrowth, in which we had found ourselves ambushed. Even those who did not tear their clothes must have left a bit of their skin.

Generally, we camped in some picturesque mountain gorge where we could look for water, and where, in the evening, a cool wind blew. As a poet put it, "The wind which blows across the mountain."

On our right, in the far distance, beyond the Ruvu, was the rosy line of the Sogonoi Mountains, home of a branch of the Maasai. Then, to their side, we saw the uninhabited Masimani and Lassiti hills stand out against the sky. On our left, there were the iron-ore-containing Pare hilltops. Behind us, there was the massif of Kilimanjaro, which every day became less clear to our sight. And in front of us, behind the thorn bushes, the acacias, and the euphorbias, a surly natural world to which, little by little, one grew accustomed and which ended by becoming almost attractive, because of its air of liberty and solitude. It is really remarkable to see how we human beings adapt to everything!

Moreover, every day we met something interesting. At one place, we were travelling on when we were approached by three young people who said they had lost their way and were looking for their encampment. Elsewhere, herds of goats, guarded by some children, looked like uncountable white spots on the slopes of the mountain. Further on, we had to ask a large family of wild boars to give us space to camp. Elsewhere again, we tried to find our dinner among the herds of antelopes. In the distance we saw long black lines moving on the plain, they were cattle returning from their pastures.

Finally, at Same, in a mountain gorge on the banks of a little river, shaded by tall acacias, we found ourselves in the real Maasai country. These cattle-keeping nomads were attracted by the water, just as it attracts many herds of animals, antelopes, zebras, buffaloes, and even elephants whose footprints could be seen everywhere. In addition, pigeons, turtledoves, quails, and francolins enliven the landscape, and we had some pleasant days there. Before this, in our journey we had already met some rather elderly Maasai who showed themselves to be very courteous and, in their thoughtfulness, thorough gentlemen. At our camp, other Maasai came to greet us and hear our news—where we were going, from where we came, and who we were. I do not know what Salim told them of our capacities and powers, but hardly had he finished speaking when an old cowherd asked, in the most natural and the sincerest way possible, that we should be so good as to send them some rain as water was getting scarce and the grass was drying up everywhere. It would have been useless to argue. Our saying "No" would have been seen as a sign of ill-will. So we got them to stand in line and took photographs of them; the only thing our hardworking Salim had to do was to explain that when the rain came it would make the plain green again.

Toward midday, the cattle arrived; they certainly must have numbered at least 2,000 and it was really rather astonishing to see them come up in line to the drinking troughs prepared for them, then move away to make room for others, and finally go away to join other cattle in a specified place with the exactness of children trained to do this kind of exercise. Once there, they stayed standing up during the heat of the day, leaning upon each other and so forming a perfect circle, ruminating, keeping flies off with their long tails, and gazing into space with their large melancholy eyes. The calves were separated and placed under the care of some children. These youngsters were perfect cowherds: thin, energetic, and agile, they seemed to guess whatever the animals wanted to do, and if there was any thought of disobedience they hit the recalcitrant ones with their long sticks as a warning, an act which made the calves toe the line. The donkeys—big grey creatures with a black cross on their shoulders—seemed less obedient; they are at the disposal of women for whom they carry water, provisions, and tents.

The day after our meeting with the Maasai, we turned to our left, entering the gorges of the Pare Mountains which hitherto we had passed on our left. After a tiring march, we reached a big Zigua village whose chief, Mwana-Mata, received us royally. We were given a bull for supper, to say nothing of the flour, beans, pumpkins, and other delicacies. Mwana-Mata was rich, but his wealth brought him problems. The Maasai, he told us, harassed him, taking anything they wanted. So he had decided to move to the other side of the mountain, to get away from such troublesome neighbors.

The Maasai have in fact settled this area, which was covered with their encampments and herds; really, coming to the village, they were the only people we saw. But that is not all. Our arrival at Mwana-Mata's village fell on a market day and the open space in front of his village was covered with people from different ethnic groups, with a startling variety of dress and extraordinary objects. There were Pare, Zigua, Maasai, Ndorobo; old men, warriors, young men, women and children, donkeys, cattle, goats, chunks of meat which had turned horribly high, baskets of maize, heaps of pumpkins, and every kind of vegetable.

When the trading was over and Mgr. de Courmont was busy teaching Selemani a new way of cooking steaks carved out of the bull which we were given by the generous chief, I went for a walk, accompanied by the indispensable Salim, in the company of some Ndorobo who took us to their village.

The Ndorobo village was a collection of twenty or so straw huts, small and wretched looking, thrown among the rocks unsystematically, surrounded by an unimpressive fence of tree trunks. This unusual ethnic group does not belong to the Bantu family; physically, they are different, in shape slim and tall, with lean limbs, and a long, well-shaped head. Their skin is dark and their hair Negroid. They put red coloring on their face, rub themselves with grease, and dress in animal skins. They are dependent on the Maasai whose language they speak, just as the Boni are linked to the Galla. The Maasai do not allow them to keep cattle or to carry spears. They are armed with long bows and poisoned arrows and live by hunting, and they are the people who provide most of the ivory from Maasai land. The southern Ndorobo live scattered in small groups. Further north, on the Mao escarpment, beyond Lake Baringo and toward the foot of Mount Kenya, they are more numerous and have a stronger position in relation to the Maasai.

They received us very well, and struck us as gentle, rather sad, but resigned to their lot. They asked questions and made requests which showed a rather touching simplicity. But what was unpleasant were the smells that hung round the village. There was the grease which they had spread on their bodies, this meat which they were smoking, these bones lying about, and these bits of animal intestines, over which two little red dogs were quarrelling. Come here, scholars of Europe, you will see a living, exact, and free image of a Stone Age settlement. Poor people, when will it be their turn to see the light of redemption shine in their souls?

The next part of our journey took us to Makuyouni (at the sycamores), a name justified by the great number of wild fig trees which overshadowed a dried-up stream. From them, an army of monkeys bombarded us with deafening cries. Then, the next day, we got to Maboga, a Sambara village near which two large Maasai camps had been established. The whole day was taken up by visits from the Maasai who came in a steady stream. A tall, grisly old man, the leader of the group, had a long discussion with Mgr. de Courmont. It ended with their being very happy with each other, and the old Maasai gave his lordship the long stick which he had used for years in guiding his herd, a real pastoral staff from the far-distant past. Happily, his lordship did not have his crozier with him; overwhelmed by such charming politeness, he would perhaps have given it in return to this enthusiastic fan who would surely have asked for it. All the same, this old child of the wilderness, with his blend of dignity and exoticism, received us in a way that could give a lesson on the way to receive a bishop to more than one French mayor.

As evening began to fall, guided by the chief of the Sambara village and our interpreter Salim, I went to repay these visits. We soon recognized the outskirts of the camp by the vultures perched on the acacia trees and the marabout storks which moved with philosophical calm along the big paths trodden out by the cattle. Both groups, quite unalarmed by our presence, waited for their share in the coming meal. Under the trees, a few elders played at bao, a kind of backgammon widespread in Africa, with very beautiful marbles made of ivory. The camp itself was round in shape and surrounded by thorny branches which protected it from wild animals. Behind this fence cattle skins are for sale, placed on bent and pliable tree branches. There is no doormat, nor bedside rug, nor wardrobe with a mirror. You might say it is the cave of Cacus,[1] but, all the same, it is beautiful. The grand old man of whom I have already spoken announced his arrival, introduced me, and straightaway I am surrounded, weighed up, and admired—I think—as something rare and wonderful. For my part, I look around filled with admiration for them. Here are authentic Africans of the wilderness, not the "savages" you see paraded in fairs, genuine representatives of that people whom the British explorer Thomson rightly called the most handsome and the most extraordinary of all African peoples. Certainly, they are the terror of all the neighboring tribes; but when you see their impressive physique, their bearing, worthy of an academic, their self-respect, their dignity, and the delicacy of their manners, you cannot help remembering what St. Gregory the Great said of other pagans, "What a pity these men are not Christians."

Little by little, their shyness wore off. They shook my hand, everyone wanted to touch my white skin and a big mama was bold enough to show me her last-born. She was carrying him on her back in a goatskin bag and, a little shyly, asked me to be kind enough to spit on his head. Salim explained to me that it was a form of blessing, and that, for this remarkable people, my

---

1. In Roman mythology, Cacus, son of Vulcan, was a giant who lived in a cave on Mount Aventine.

saliva has something of the sacred. I spat generously while the baby looked at me with eyes like carbuncle stones, and I finished, according to my habit, by making the sign of the cross on his forehead. Straightaway, all the mothers, all the children, all the elders came forward for a blessing. Everyone wanted a blessing with my saliva and I was extremely obliging.

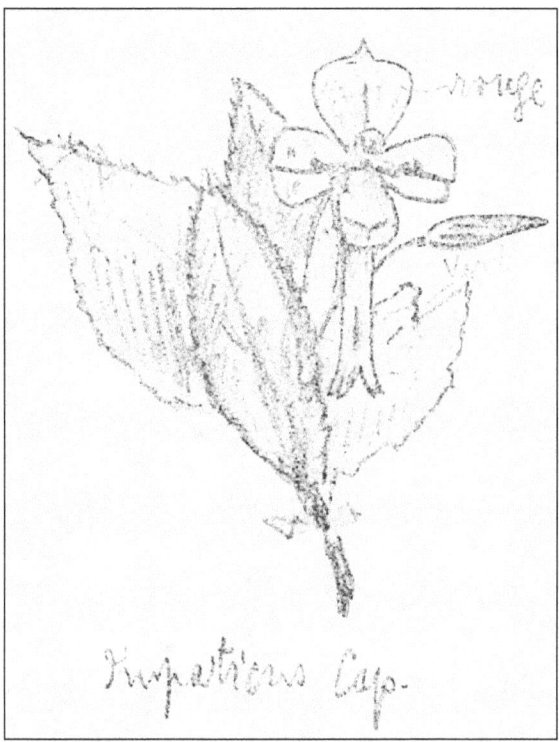

But, with such a crowd, my tongue ran dry. A lady noticed this, ran to her tent and brought back a big calabash, full of milk, which she handed to me. I refreshed myself with great gulps while Salim roared with laughter. Revived, I managed to be generous with my saliva, to everybody's pleasure. But I had not realized what would be the result of my politeness. While I was at work, people took hold of my arms, rolled back my sleeves, and all these smiling pairs of lips appealed to the white-skinned man with a request for rain.

"Ah, sir, just give us some rain, just rain."

Later, going back to our camp, Salim kept on laughing.

I said, "What is so funny?"

Salim replied, "Well, er, because. . ."

"Is it because of my blessing?"

"It is because of the milk. Was the milk good?"

"It had a bit of flavor, as they say. Why?"

"We all eat our meat with salt, to give it more taste. Well, to make the milk tastier, these dear Maasai put, so we are told, cows' urine into it."

Chapter 26: The Maasai

Maasai Land. Brothers and Enemies. Political System and Way of Life. Physical Type and Personal Presentation. Tools and Weapons. The Maasai Life Cycle. Maasai Religious Beliefs.

It would be regrettable to give only passing references to this extraordinary people, little known as they are and with whom no Frenchman, apart from missionaries, has yet made contact.

In East Africa, the territory occupied by the Maasai covers from north to south six degrees of latitude, from one degree north to five degrees south, being the equivalent of 150 leagues, and from east to west two or three degrees of longitude (from 35 degrees east of Greenwich to 36 or 37 degrees). But it can be said that their raiding and their significant influence reaches from the rivers which flow into the Indian Ocean to the shores of Lake Victoria Nyanza, and from the south of Ethiopia down to Gogo country.

This Maasai homeland is geographically very variable. In the south, it is a dry, desertlike, and low-lying territory, where other ethnic groups occupy the magnificent mountains, such as the Nguru, the Pare, Kilimanjaro, and the Meru Mountains. Further north, however, there is a plateau, 1,800 meters above sea level, where junipers, heather, and other plants give the vegetation a European look. The climate is cool and the soil is watered by quite a number of rivers and streams.

The people referred to as Maasai can be divided into two ethnic groups: the Maasai strictly speaking, and the Kwavi. These latter have, after a long series of wars with their "elder brothers," finally seen their political power broken up, and today they are grouped in a number of settlements of varying strength, at Lekipya (northwest of Mount Kenya), at Ndyensi near Baringo, at upper Arusha, at Taveta, and Nguru, and so on. Many Kwavi have become agriculturalists while keeping some of the ways of doing things that they had when they were strictly nomadic. Their physical type is undergoing some changes, partly through their adoption of a new way of life, but above all, through frequent intermarriages with other ethnic groups. All the same, they are everywhere welcoming, honest, and easy and pleasant to deal with.

The Maasai, strictly so called, are divided into different clans, each linked to a particular area. There are the Maasai of Kilimanjaro, which they call *Donyo Ebor* (White Mountain) and sometimes *Engadyi Engai* (House of God). Then there are the Maasai of Sogonoi and those of Matumbato, of Kaptei etc. All are cattle-keepers and there is no question of craftsmanship or trade or any kind of farming. You can get ivory in their country, but they get it from the Ndorobo. All their attention is given to their herds. If they are, as is well known, fierce warriors, it is only because they are, first and foremost, herdsmen, for they raid the neighboring tribes for cattle, not to take slaves or build up an empire.

We were told that all the Maasai recognize a great chief, Mbatian, who today is very old, very rich, and famous for his magical powers. He has no need to have herders look after his cattle; we were told that if his stick were carried in front of his herds, they would follow it. He lives on the northern slopes of Kilimanjaro and he has friendly contacts with Mandara, who told us about him. Besides this, his name is repeated thousands of times a day from one end to another of Maasai country in the songs and choruses of the warriors. "We are praying to God; we are praying to Mbatian."

In each clan, the government is patriarchal. What brings a chief to power is not his ancestry but his wealth, his courage, his intelligence, or, rather perhaps, his priestly functions, his skill as an herbalist, and his capacity to predict what the weather will be.

Within the borders of a particular clan, people are scattered in various encampments according to the state of the pasture land and the availability of water. Moreover, even where there has been war between different Maasai clans, when peace has been made, they develop a mutual respect and understanding and frequent visits take place. The Maasai then are seminomads by temperament and because it is the kind of life they like. But it is really necessary for them to live in this way. Indeed, one can say that in at least the south of Maasai country, where all potential farming land has been occupied by agricultural tribes, the earth gives them what is really essential: an area in which they can wander.

This way of living certainly does not favor laziness, and if one keeps a keen eye on a little Maasai shepherd and his ups and downs, one has to admit that by evening he has merited his rest. In the same way, the women have to walk what are sometimes very considerable distances to get water and provisions, to milk the cows, to prepare the meals. When an encampment has to move, it is again the women who have to fold tents, collect the poles, and carry everything on their donkeys. As to the young men, they can hardly find war just an amusement. The elders and men who have reached maturity have more free time, and they use it for conversation and discussion, for creating a peaceful atmosphere around them, and for visiting their neighbors and looking for new pastures.

The physical type of the Maasai links them to certain Nilotic ethnic groups, such as the Latuka and the Bari, as does their language; but the very particular upbringing to which they have been subjected over several centuries has made them into an absolutely unique people. The women and children are often dirty, grimy, and sticky-eyed; swarms of flies chase after them. The elders, with dried-up limbs and faded features, are no longer what they were in their best years.

But the young men, say those between seventeen and thirty, surely represent the ideal of the African warrior. They are often six feet tall, sometimes more; their admirably proportioned bodies, their limbs with the strength of steel and their general attitude, characterized by a distinctive dignity, gives them a bearing which has no equal. Add to that an astonishing gift of speaking, with the voice made to rise and fall, with movements of the hands, and a stance which could arouse the jealousy of our best public speakers.

The skin color of the Maasai is chocolate brownish, their hair is long and curly, but their features clearly distinguish them from the normal Negroid type. Their heads are round or oval, their noses straight and rather prominent, the chin fits into the head without being too long. The cheekbones are high, and the eyes have something of the slit look found in the Mongolian race. The teeth, which are strikingly white, often look as though they had been pushed forward, due perhaps to the habit contracted when young of biting bits of meat which are much underdone.

Ordinary clothing consists of cattle skins carefully tanned, yellowish in color, and almost as easily handled as would be more elaborate clothing; when there is need for it, they know how to sew them and decorate them with glass pearls. But the children and young people are not very interested in clothing. However, if they find a piece of skin, they will be happy to use it to cover their left shoulder. The elders, however, like to cover the parts of their bodies which can get chilly, with long cloths arranged with great dignity. As for the women, they have a modest but rather unusual style of dress, which covers them from head to foot. In addition, their arms and legs are normally surrounded by metal rings from the wrist to the shoulder and from the ankle to the knee. Round the neck, long rings of metal provide Maasai ladies with a kind of armor plating, and, finally, they hang heavy rings from their ears that need to be supported by a strip of leather going over their heads. In all, the metal ornamentation must weigh at least a dozen kilograms, to say nothing of the pearls and the pieces of leather. Evidently, in every country, one must learn to suffer if one wants to keep up with fashion.

For the Maasai, the ears have a special part to play in making oneself presentable. From childhood upward, a hole is made in the ear lobe, and then the hole is maintained and enlarged by a small piece of wood or ivory or metal which one puts there and which makes the hole bigger and bigger. Finally, the ear lobe under such pressure becomes enormous, you can put your arm through, it hangs on your shoulder, and men put through it artistically designed little chains, which have quite a graceful effect. Everybody wears sandals which are tastefully made and which are held together by leather thongs whose end is rolled round to make a button. Beards are not fashionable. Maasai are careful to shave and to remove body hair. Red ochre, together with a white clay, butter, and animal fat, is important in giving a Maasai a good appearance; it is the equivalent of make-up, skin cream, and the other perfumes of the tribes of Europe. Everyone who wants to look handsome uses what is at hand.

The household utensils are calabashes and various bowls in which one keeps fresh milk, curdled milk, butter, grease, and meat. Animal skins can be sewn into bags, they have water skins, and tents are made with animal skins pressed flat and fitted on to curved branches. One uses shields to make a sort of packsaddle for donkeys, which make them look rather odd.

In contrast to the neighboring tribes, Maasai women carry their loads in bags tied to their shoulders by straps, just as do our [French] soldiers. Maasai men never carry anything. If they must bring something, for instance the skin of a bull which they killed, they drag it behind them. Is this lack of experience or pride? They always regard carrying a load as fit only for donkeys, and that is the nickname they give to the Muslim porters in the caravans that pass through their country. The elders have, hanging from their necks, snuff-boxes made of bamboo, sometimes quite artistically designed.

With regard to weapons of war, there are head-smashing clubs, long cutlasses, and a magnificent spear made of shining solid iron, bright as silver, which the warriors use with such skill. The shields, made of buffalo or cattle skin, are large, and carry on their outside, in black, red, and white, the totemic signs of the clan to which the owner belongs. But their weapons are not made by the Maasai; they are the work either of the Chagga of Kilimanjaro or of the El-Konono, a tribe of blacksmiths similar to the Ndorobo and, like them, forming an ethnic group which provides services to the much larger Maasai family.

Let us go on to consider morals, the way the Maasai relate to each other, and their beliefs. There is no special ceremony at the birth of a child. It must be said that baby boys are preferred, as they can steal cows, whereas the girls can only milk them.

But it seems that the killing of babies, found in a number of Bantu tribes, is unknown, except when they are very seriously deformed. The newborn baby is straightaway put into a leather bag which the mother carries on her back, and so he or she passes the beginning of his or her life in this veil of tears. As soon as the child can move about on its own, whether walking or crawling, it is left to its own options, and is not bothered with being washed or with any other tedious attentions. Later a boy will make himself a bow and arrows, he will begin work as a shepherd, and for everything else, he, like everyone else, lives at his father's or mother's kraal.[1]

---

1. Kraal: a traditional African village of huts, typically enclosed by a fence.

As he grows up, he begins to show off. He postures before a herd of goats, standing up with one leg on the knee of the other; now and again, he has to work as a cook, calabash cleaner, and server for the young warriors who live as a group on their own.

Circumcision, which is performed when boys are approaching adolescence, and which has no religious significance, admits him to the ranks of the junior warriors. His father will give him a shield and a spear. He will then live in a kraal for junior warriors, among both boys and girls; this is a period of initiation and training. All these young people live together, keeping strictly to a diet of blood, meat, and milk, not taking any alcoholic drinks, avoiding the use of tobacco, abstaining from any kind of vegetable food. They have sentry duty at the camp and have a variety of forms of military training, mock attacks, seizure of villages, cattle raiding, warrior dances, foot races, forced marches, etc. They also acquire a moral permissiveness which will perhaps be the major obstacle to the spread of Christianity among them.

The young Maasai then begin with a milk diet and keep it up as long as they can, for say a week, then, when they feel a need for meat, they take a stiff dose of some purgative. Then, five or six of them go and kill a bull or cow in an out-of-the-way spot. After that, the group of friends enjoy riotous banquets of beef steaks with blood in them, so long as there is meat available. That is the Maasai idea of a picnic. On such occasions one can drink water—honey beer is not permitted—but what one really prefers is the warm blood of the animal one has just killed or another one of which one has taken hold. One of its veins is then cut open, and the youths drink from the opened vein. Afterwards, the skin is sewn back and the animal is free to run off, having willingly cooperated, since the cattle are used to this way of doing things.

The *Morani* (warriors) elect at their kraal a military leader and a spokesman. Then, having decided on the expedition's objective, they set out, not without appropriate exercises, jumping, exceptional feasts, and prayers. Warriors on active service have a special uniform; round the head one wears a strip of leather, the ends tied together under the chin and with long ostrich feathers as decoration, forming an impressive fan around the warrior's head. On his back, he has a loose-hanging coat of white cloth, crossed by a red strip. On his shoulders he carries a thick cape, with feathers from vultures and kites. In front, he has a goat skin, cut into straps, or, better still, a monkey's skin, with the hair still on it. He keeps his cutlass and club on his right side. He holds his shield in one hand and, in the other, a magnificent spear which he holds with pride. The final touch is given by a fine coating of oil, mingled with ochre, on his skin. And skin with ochre mixed in is fascinating. It is strangely impressive to see a battalion of these young Apollolike warriors, dressed in this fashion, setting out to capture the herds of the neighboring peoples. The shock of seeing just one Maasai has often been enough to put hundreds of other Africans to flight, as they are much less fierce, or put on less of a show.

The Maasai are silent when they are fighting. Moreover, they display a high degree of discipline, of self-control, of cunning, of tactical sense, of energy, and of audacity. When there is a need for it, they are capable of outstanding bravery. But fortunately they have a wise fear of rifles, and when a volley strikes their ranks, there is a really funny situation. They throw everything away, shields, spears, head-coverings, in order to run away as quickly as possible. They only keep their sandals.

A Maasai youth

If the neighboring tribes united against the Maasai, they could resist them. But very often it is one of these tribes that calls the Maasai in against a common enemy from motives of jealousy or revenge, just as has often happened in the history of Europe. Moreover, a Maasai does not believe that, in acting as the bandit whom everyone must fear, he is behaving unjustly. Tradition tells him that the God who rules the world gave their ancestors some cattle to look after, but as it was a very large herd he left some with the neighboring tribes, and nowadays his descendants come to claim their property. . .

It is during this period of his life that the Maasai is the boastful, grasping, rowdy, wind-bag, with a taste for smashing heads, with whom so many caravans have clashed. The Maasai regard the life of a man from the coast as being of the same value as a worm. But as the years pass, the body grows heavier, the stomach is less demanding, and the young man becomes a sensible human being. The warrior marries one wife, two wives, three wives according to the number of cattle he has for getting partners. From then on his diet changes and so do his habits. Occasionally, he will still cut into the veins of a bull or cow to drink its blood, he will still accompany some raiding parties and give them advice. But, instead of a purely meat diet, he will also take flour, bananas, and honey, which he will beg or buy from the neighboring farming tribes. He will take tobacco to chew it, he will drink mead, and in general will have the same enthusiasm for peace as he once showed for war. In these conditions, he is delightful to meet. This old son of the wilderness develops a striking graciousness in whatever he does.

The Maasai has an attitude of contempt for other Africans, including the Muslims, who are often of mixed race and who dress more or less in coastal style, but this is balanced by an equally strong attitude of respect for Europeans. When they meet us going along the paths of their country, they give us a bunch of various grasses as a symbol of religious respect and of peace. And I am telling you the plain unvarnished truth when I quote the question posed about us missionaries by a Maasai in their encampment:

"Are not these people the sons of God?"

"Oh, no!" we said immediately, "God is much greater than we are; we are scarcely even the least of his slaves."

The Maasai shook his head with an air of naive incredulity and said, "Then they are slaves who have a great resemblance to their master."

But what then does this remarkable people think about God? God in Maasai is *Ngai*, and this is a word that springs readily to a Maasai's lips, be he a young warrior or a wise elder. Moreover, his existence, or rather his activity, is closely linked to the sky, to rainfall, and to major natural phenomena. I was told that he is prayed to in public at the gate of the kraal every morning—the Maasai ask him for rain, for green grass, for many children, for the end of a drought or epidemic, and for victory in war.

There are few nations which pray as much as the Maasai, but their prayer has a very wide range of requests.

It must be admitted that the Maasai lack a developed theology. They put great trust in certain of their fellow Maasai whom they regard as having a priestly authority and to whom they attribute exceptional powers. There are things that frighten them in the form of superstitions; for instance, cows must be milked only at night and on no account should milk be boiled.

They have an idea of the soul, for once anyone has died, his name must never be pronounced, in case his spirit, hearing it, comes back to wander among the living; and, it might be mentioned, this is something very unfavorable to keeping oral traditions alive. Finally, there are sacrifices offered to request something or to expiate a fault; thus, when one wants to ask God for something a sheep is killed, its body is divided into pieces, and the pieces brought together in the sheep's skin are taken up a mountain or left where two paths cross each other.

If a small child dies, he or she is buried in the camp or even in a tent. But if it is an older person who has died, a bull is killed to provide the partially digested contents of its stomach with which to purify the kraal, and the body is carried out of the kraal and placed under a tree in a shallow grave, which one of them covers with green grass and stones, after having put a calabash of milk beside him. When night comes, the hyenas finish the ceremony.

Moreover, the Maasai do not have any amulets, nor are they afraid of ghosts, nor do they have fetish shrines. When I asked a Maasai what he thought of the devil, he replied simply, "There are no devils among us."

Young people have a great respect for the elders. Having said that, I must also state that quarrels are frequent and people often come to blows. When, in a quarrel of this kind, a man gets killed, people ignore the accident; but if someone has been killed in secret, say by an ambush, the killer is severely punished. We Europeans—who have a great deal more of the savage in us than we realize—have the same idea. If you run a knife into someone, you will make yourself very unpopular. But if you fight a duel with swords, people will admire you—particularly the ladies, just as in Maasai land.

To sum it all up, these nomadic people understand the existence of good and evil; they have a sense of morality, which evidently they understand in their own way. There is belief in a God who not only exists but looks after us, in the soul, in life after death. They have the idea of sacrifice, of atonement for sin, and of prayer. These are the basic elements of all religion.

Furthermore, it is fortunate, both from the point of view of European colonization and from that of the peaceful coexistence of the neighboring tribes, that the Maasai are not Muslims. If militant Islam were blended with their natural instincts, it would not be possible to make contact with them. Will it be possible one day—one would like to say soon—to build on this surprising foundation the Christian structure of faith and worship which God has revealed to us? To bridge the gaps in their understanding of religion? To baptize this exceptional people who have been little studied by Europeans and among whom no mission has been planted? Why not? It would be necessary indeed to have much energy, patience, tact, and prudence, floods of sweat, perhaps even some sacrificial blood. The missionaries would have to share their nomadic life, and adapt to an entirely strange culture. But none of this would be out of the question for a missionary sent by the Catholic Church and who relies on divine grace. I mean, real apostles! Can they still be found in Christian countries? Apostles ready for everything and content with anything, for these marvelous raiders of Maasai land!

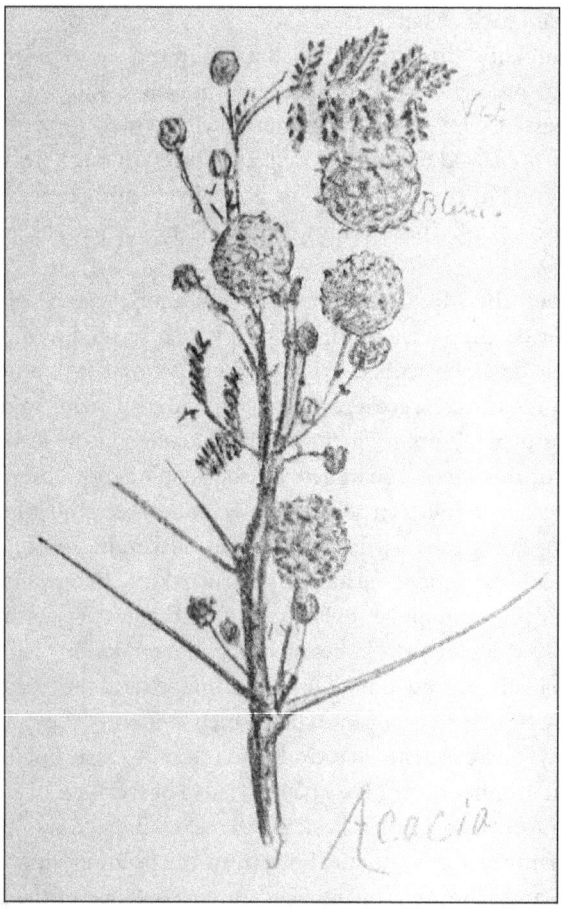

Chapter 27: The Sambara

THE END OF THE PARE MOUNTAINS. IN USAMBARA.
MEETING SULTAN SEMBOJA. AN IMPERTINENT BIRD.
A MAN, A GOAT, AND A CROCODILE.

Maboga is practically the end of the chain of the Pare Mountains. The chain comes to a sudden end with the Mwala cliff, whitish and formed of granite which rises sharply over the plain where the Ruvu flows. This river, which we have met previously, is everywhere overshadowed by tall trees, but, as if it were in a hurry to pour itself into the Indian Ocean, it flows down rapidly across some clusters of rocks and some charming little islands.

From that point, after a demanding march of eight hours, we camped on the banks of the Mkomazi, that river of clear water, whose source we had seen in going up to Kilimanjaro, near Gonja. The maps, very inaccurate for this unexplored area, fail to state that the Mkomazi runs parallel to the Ruvu, only joining it near Maurwi, where we were going to cross.

We were now in a country where we had not been before: the Usambara. When we had gone round the end of the Pare Mountains, we immediately saw another chain of mountains in front of us, but a little to the left; there was an enormous wall rising to 1,000, 1,200, and even 1,800 meters, culminating in an austerely impressive peak. Up there, one would find forests and land for grazing, on which the Mbugu, a rather exceptional tribe said to be related to the Kwavi and the Pare, keep large herds of cattle. Down below is the plain, at some points dry and without farms, elsewhere occupied by some villages. In the distance the Mkomazi and the Ruvu flowed toward the sea, and beyond them were the wooded savannahs of Zigua country.

On our way, we met fine herds of cattle guarded by Maasai, and then a group of their young warriors driving some cows before them. This had not been, it seems, a very successful raid. The Mbugu had defended themselves well and more than one of these young brigands was going home with his war uniform in tatters.

Then we reached Mazinde. It was the home of the famous Semboja, one of the more important chiefs of the country. In the past, having come under the influence of the Sultan of Zanzibar, he flew his red flag and adopted for himself and his people the basic elements of "Islamic culture." When war broke out at the coast between the Swahili and the Germans, he decided to support the Swahili, and chose to be, from the beginning, an ally of Bushiri, the rebel leader. As a result of this, a large caravan which Dr. Hans Meyer was leading to Kilimanjaro, accompanied by some Germans, was trapped on this road after fighting had started. Semboja arrested Dr. Meyer, the porters scattered, and the Europeans were made prisoners and taken to Pangani. Hans Meyer himself, with very scanty clothing, was forced into the service fetching water for some African Muslims.

This episode made Semboja a very interesting personality. We encamped near his village, on the banks of a stream with shade given by tall evergreen trees laden with creepers and clean water, which seemed to sing as it came down from the mountain. Soon, we were approached by someone with an unprepossessing face, wearing a white robe.

He had a Muslim way of presenting himself, a way which inexperienced travelers take as courteous, but which we, with rather more African experience, see rather differently. After the formal greeting, which seemed to lack both sincerity and warmth, the messenger invited us to call on His Majesty, Semboja, with our respectful good wishes. To this we replied that if His Majesty wished to welcome us in person, as he does with all Europeans, we were ready to receive him. Half an hour passed. Then we saw a group of Africans coming toward us who wore the white cotton clothes customary on the coast. Among them was a fat fellow, thick-set and not too young, wearing hat, jacket, and trousers. He was like an old colonial planter, with a sunburnt face, and a cynical air about him, whose best days were definitely in the past: it was Semboja.

Recently the wind had changed. His friend Bushiri had been captured and hanged at Pangani. At Zanzibar, the Sultan himself had been obliged to accept the terms offered him by the British, and Semboja, who was most definitely an opportunist, had pulled down from his flagpole the Zanzibar colors, replacing them with those of His Majesty, the Emperor of Germany. Toward us, the crafty old man showed exquisite politeness. We refused an ox, but had to accept a sheep with honey, flour, and salt, and he made very generous offers.

Later, I went to Semboja's village, built on a marvelously picturesque site at the foot of the great grey rock barrier of the Usambara Mountains. From there, it looks out on the fertile plain and the two rivers which keep it well-watered. His invitation to come was very pressing, but he explained that it was not for a formal reception—this would come later, with Mgr. de Courmont present. It was to have a friendly chat with me, to show me his private residence, and to ask me to treat one of his children who had an obstruction in his throat. So there I was with him in his private room. This, Sultan Semboja's hideaway, was really an old curiosity shop. There were plates, linen, money, writing cases, chairs, all making a chaotic state of things, totally lacking in any kind of artistic effect. But what was most surprising was the presence in a basket of several numbers of the *Mitteilungen de Petermann from Gotha*. Was Semboja a subscriber to this excellent geographical periodical? I asked him about it.

"Ah," said he in a rather relaxed way, "that is a souvenir of Hans Meyer's visit."

Then a woman slave came in, holding in one hand a dish with a big glass, evidently recently washed, for it had five very clear finger marks on it; with the other hand she carried an old bottle. Semboja took the bottle, filled the glass to the brim, and offered it to me, saying, with a crafty smile, "Just a little drop." The smell of the drink and the label on the bottle made me absolutely certain that it was a cordial strong enough to knock three sappers over, one on top of the other. I respectfully begged His Majesty to excuse me, as I was unused to anything so strong.

"That is all right by me," he replied, and taking the glass with both hands, he drank it all.

There was another interview, this time the official one. Mgr. de Courmont explained our Kilimanjaro project to the old chief and asked that our caravans which would have to pass that way would have his protection. Semboja promised to do everything that he was asked, and in his turn he asked for a mission station in his own district. Perhaps he was sincere; but the balance of probabilities is that he would have preferred a rum distillery.

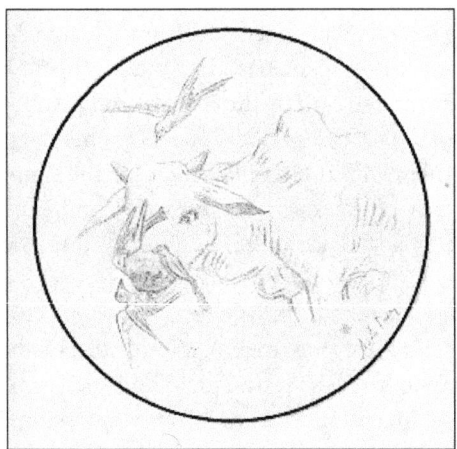

Birds picking ticks off cattle

The next day, we went down to the plain, passing in front of the Vuga Mountain, where Kimweri, Semboja's eldest son, was in charge of a big village. We crossed the Mombo River, then a large, rather shallow pond, and, after seven hours on the way, we got to Tarawanda.

This village is built on a small hill which overlooks the plain. It was noon, with a burning sun. The cattle returning from grazing settled down, unworried, close to us, while numerous birds with red beaks and bodies the color of ash fluttered about and with startling boldness took the ticks which swarmed on the cattle. They ran on their backs and hung from their dewlaps and got into their muzzles. They even got into their most private parts, without any feeling of shame. These honest bovines constantly showed their irritation by shaking their heads and waving their tails; but the greedy birds immediately resumed their hunt, their stroking, their apparent rashness, and their meal.

The next day, we were at Maurwi where a sizable village occupies an island in the Ruvu, and we pitched camp there for a day. When we were crossing the footbridge in that village, we saw something rather astonishing. Some goats, with their habitual lack of caution, were grazing on the river bank without the least worry when a crocodile came up, seized one of them, and vanished with it. But suddenly, a young man, who happened to be there, took off his clothes and, knife in hand, jumped into the river. There was a sudden whirling of the water, which we guessed marked a swift, fierce struggle. Soon, the young man surfaced with the goat, and was loudly applauded by the bystanders. He had torn the goat from the crocodile's throat. The poor creature was dead but at least the crocodile had been rightly punished and his conqueror had earned his dinner.

At Maurwi, at Korogwe, and elsewhere along the lower reaches of the river there is a distinct ethnic group, called the people of the Ruvu. They are of Zigua origin, and are farmers, livestock keepers, and fisher folk. The Usambara country is very interesting. Some of the mountains are almost 2,000 meters high and form a cool and fertile plateau. This is the home of the Mbugu mentioned already, while the mountain slopes are home to Usambara farmers who live in villages of varying sizes.

Opposite Tanga, a small ethnic group, the Bondei, similar to the Mbugu, lives by farming. With the possible exception of the Mbugu, all these peoples speak Bantu languages. It is not too far from the coast. Blessed with a fertile soil and opportunities for selling their crops, the farmers live in relative prosperity and commonly wear linen clothing. Everyone understands money and is ready to accept it, and Swahili is known everywhere.

To take another aspect, some people have become Muslim, at least superficially. If Arab political power had not collapsed, Islam would probably have made many converts in a short time. But the population remains basically attached to their own religious tradition and missionary work could prove very successful. But, alas, where are the laborers for the harvest? And where are the funds to support them?

Chapter 28: Zigua

How to Get Provisions. We Meet Selemani's Brother. A Tribe Which is Committing Suicide. At Mandera. In the Doe. Back Home.

At Maurwi, we had the option of two routes: one to Pangani, the other to Zigua. We did not take the road to Pangani, which was followed by our guide Salim and his friends who were going back home; while the route to Zigua is much longer, it permitted us to learn about a region still little known, even though it is not far from the coast. Moreover, we would have the pleasure of meeting en route Selemani's brother, one of the big men of the region, and further on to visit our mission at Mandera.

We had scarcely left the Ruvu Valley, enriched as it is by the presence of coconut and mango trees, when we noticed a change in the soil. It became reddish and, in the savannah, covered by long grass which had begun to dry up, the trees scattered here and there took on the appearance of the *pori*, uncultivated and uninhabited land, which is found everywhere on the way from Bagamoyo to the Great Lakes.

We had reached Zigua country. It is an arid country with a scattered population with, in places, a horribly thorny kind of acacia peculiar to this district. The first village we reached was Kinamo. We camped at the foot of the little hill where it is built, and straightaway two or three of our porters ran to tell the chief of our presence. Within a quarter of an hour, the whole population came, trembling with fear, to present their very respectful greetings. They apologized for not being able to offer us a cow, but perhaps we would be kind enough to accept a sheep for ourselves, while there would be a half-dozen baskets of flour for our men. We need not bother about water. It was in short supply, but already all the women had gone to get it for us.

Such attentiveness in this country astonished us. It seemed to come from fear, rather than from good will, and so I put some questions. The truth came out. Those rogues, our porters, had told them that this was a German army unit, and we were absolutely terrible. I had ordered them to put all the villagers to the sword—not that we had any sword to which to put them—if they did not bring within an hour all the provisions that were demanded. The porters added that they were very upset by this order but they absolutely had to obey it.

We did our best to calm the poor villagers who seemed a very decent lot. Before the day was over, their new mood of cheerful friendliness showed that I had succeeded.

The next day, on the march, during a break, Selemani slipped away into the undergrowth. As usual, he was stooping, bent down, unwashed, greasy, clothed in horrible, tattered rags. Where had he gone? While everyone tried to guess where, lo and behold, our old cook reappeared, shining like the sun. A spotless cotton robe whitened him from head to feet. His loins were girded with a long belt, flaming red in color. On his head an enormous turban made him look like a Mogul emperor. With unusual dignity, he handed the cooking pots and saucepans to a child, keeping only his old arquebus, and then raised his nose, opened his eyes, and on he went!

The reason for all this was that we would soon be arriving at the village of his famous brother, and it was only reasonable that Selemani should appear before him and his people in all the splendor that he could summon up. So there we were. The village is called Kiwanda and is quite large. The chief, Mohammed Sowa, received his brother and ourselves with due politeness. However, this politeness, while correct, was entirely without any enthusiasm. Perhaps, in his state of health, Mohammed could not summon up any enthusiasm. He was an intelligent man, it seemed, and had been influential in the district, but was by this time so broken, so bent, so tottering, that one wondered if he was not approaching the end of his life. As a present, he gave us a half-empty bottle of Hamburg gin. I must say that he had the courtesy to warn me that he had already tasted some of it and had not liked it. I thanked him and, without touching it, returned it to him, telling him that drinks, unlike certain people, improve as they get older.

As the name indicates, Mohammed is a Muslim; he had even a small mosque near his house, and a preacher from Pangani sought to make converts in his village. Despite all this, it was he who, last year (1889), handed over his co-religionist, Bushiri, to the infidels, I mean the Germans. The rebel leader, after being defeated near Bagamoyo, came to hide himself in Zigua country, from which he hoped to be able to reach his former home on the outskirts of Pangani where he had some personal interests. Mohammed, having come to know about it, immediately sent a message to Major Wissman and gave him guides to track down Bushiri, who was arrested, tried, and hanged.

Devout Muslims might have regarded this as treason, but there is a story behind it. Sometime before the war, Bushiri and Mohammed had had a legal dispute about the ownership of a slave, which Bushiri had won. Mohammed had warned him, "I will get my own back." And when the chance came, Mohammed got his own back.

Our march from Kiwanda to Mandera took three days through a countryside marked by little hills (some of which were very picturesque), but where water is rather difficult to find and, when found, is often brackish, which makes life difficult. The people are farmers, but keep some cattle; the villages are not very numerous, and Islam, spreading from Pangani, has adherents scattered over an increasingly large area.

But the really sad thing to note is that, throughout this area, infanticide is a disastrous scourge. In one village of twenty households where we stopped, there was only one child aged ten. Such a place has a desolation difficult to imagine. No laughter, no playing, running, or jumping, no songs, no smiles; the faces of men and women wore a deathly sadness. Each one of them, influenced by a diabolical superstition, had a conscience weighed down by two, three, four, ten murders. And these are murders of children who could not defend themselves and had no one to plead their cause.

Bagamoyo, avenue of coconut trees

A much-respected missionary, the late Father Cado Picarda, threw himself into a struggle against this infanticide; other missionaries have followed his initiative. I myself, in travelling through this country, have offered warnings, advice, and even threats, in response to what they had told me. But what is happening and what will happen? It seems that this tribe is committing suicide. If the German administration, now accepted in this part of Zigua country, does not take drastic action, the suicide will be complete, before twenty years from now.

I must say that these poor people are steeped in superstition. After I had taken a very modest meal one day just before two o'clock, the chief of the aforementioned village came to see me. He wanted to explain that they lacked water, which was a hardship for them, and that they looked to me to provide them with it. Not the first time that I had such a request.

I said, "Do you want me to make rain fall from the sky?"

He replied, "No. We know you could easily make rain fall from the sky: but this would only last for a day or two, after which we would have the same difficulty."

"Well, what then?"

"It is this. Show us a place where we can find water; that is the only thing we ask you to do."

"Will you keep on killing your children?"

This produced a solemn assembly of villagers, great embarrassment, and a fierce debate. Putting on a slightly arrogant air, I said from time to time to anyone who wanted to listen, "What a stupid lot these people are! They have not yet understood that the blood of children dries up the soil. What will become of them when they have nothing more to drink?"

Finally, they took an oath to respect the life of the children who would be born in future; but I must show them somewhere they could get water.

Unfortunately, I did not have a complete knowledge of the underground currents of water which the Creator has put there for our use, provided that we take the trouble to look for them, so I said to the chief, "That is all right. I shall give you my reply two hours from now."

Straightaway, I began to explore the surrounding area. My aim was to find a valley whose shape and, more particularly, the plants growing there, suggested that there was water below the level of the soil. I soon found what I was looking for, and, better still, I discovered a partly dug well, surrounded by high green grass, at the bottom of which I could see a pool of muddy water. I went up to the village again and asked the people to follow me. Nobody had anything to say as we went toward the spot I had discovered, and, when we got there, I spoke to the crowd gathered around me. "Dig there and you will get water."

"It is extraordinary," said the chief. "We have done so already, and found water. These Europeans. . ."

"So what happened?"

"Then, when we had found the water we were afraid of the spirit who protects the place, because we made the discovery without asking his permission. And none of us dared draw water from there."

I made them sit down. I spoke of God, who has created everything for the wellbeing of humankind. I instructed them as best I could and got them to repeat their promise not to kill their children. The idea behind this killing of children is that if the child is not born a perfect human being, if the way it comes into the world is in some way abnormal, it is thought they will bring misfortune to the family and the village and has to be sacrificed. In this place, the conditions for recognizing a poor little one as a real human being are so strict that not two out of ten babies can pass the test. Moreover, the test as to whether a baby can live or must die is in the hands of some old women who, once they have strangled one baby, keep up the bad work with the other babies. Surely the coast could supply rope enough for the necks of these detestable witches?

However, the nearer we got to the Mandera mission, the happier people's faces; there was more life in the villages and there were more children—already the influence of the mission is being felt. We got to the mission; what a happy occasion! Father Superior was trying to settle a dispute which two villages had submitted to his arbitration. Father Felix Boule, who helps him in the more difficult cases (*Felix qui potuit rerum cognoscere causas*—"Happy the man who understands the causes of things")[1] was just that moment teaching catechism in the shade of an orange tree to those preparing for baptism. Really, he strikes a magnificent figure with his austere face, his carefully controlled gestures, and his long red beard, worthy of a biblical patriarch. Quite near there, Brother Alexandre Faure, a courageous veteran of missionary work, is assembling materials for his new church.

But, as soon as our porters had fired a few rifle shots to announce Mgr. de Courmont's arrival, everybody stopped his work, hastened to the bell which was pealing out with all its power, and in a few moments the whole Christian village which is beside the mission was there, to say nothing of other neighbors and passersby.

"And to think," Father Superior said, "that yesterday we had news of you from Bagamoyo and Zanzibar."

"What news?" I asked.

---

1. Bishop Le Roy is riffing on the word "Felix," which means "happy" in Latin, but which is also a man's name.

"That you had died on the way."

"Only dead?"

"Yes, but not entirely. We had heard from Pangani that two were coming back, Mgr. de Courmont and one priest; the third member of the party had died in Maasai country. Some of us said, 'It is Father Auguste Gommenginger, he is not as strong as the others.' Others said, 'No, it must be Father Le Roy. He takes risks.' But almost everyone added, 'Whatever has happened, it is a pity.'"

In fact, this tragic story had circulated around Zanzibar and I found out later that a newspaper reporter had got it into print. Some confreres in America and Sierra Leone had read the newspaper and had prayed that I might rest in peace. For this, I am glad to have the chance to thank them publicly. But I must say that I was equally touched, sometime later, when I got a letter from a close friend, who had read the same story and wrote to know if it were true.

After our stay at Mandera, we crossed the Doe, a land of hills and cannibalism, more populated and more intensively farmed than Zigua. At that time, everything was peaceful, but how could I travel in this area without recalling all the very difficult times that Fr. Charles Gommenginger (who has since died a heroic death at Tane) and I experienced, when we came here during the German campaign to occupy the country. That was the time when one of our porters was eaten in front of us with pepper and salt. Then we came to a river, which we crossed in a small but heavy boat; we had reached the countryside around Bagamoyo.

The sight of the coconut palms at the Catholic mission told us that the end of our journey was at hand. We formed into a long "Indian file," the rifles were loaded for a triumphant volley, and our porters put on an extraordinary collection of rig-outs, monkey skins, plumed helmets, pearl necklaces, and other more or less picturesque adornments which they had brought from the far interior.

We entered the mission majestically and slowly. Even Mgr. de Courmont had to participate. He was at the very end of the procession, holding his pastoral staff in his hands. I mean, of course, the pastoral staff which the chief of Same gave him. Then, at a given signal, these valiant porters, who had tried our patience during the three months of the journey, but to whom now everything is forgiven, broke into a Maasai song, with tremendous success, which gained them enormous admiration from the passersby. People ran up, rifle shots were fired, different bursts of cheering mingled, the bells were rung, the chapel was opened, and we gave our thanks to God. The journey was over.

Onlookers as we passed

Postscript: Twenty-Four Years Later (1890–1914)

If we count up the steps taken by a missionary in an un-evangelized land, some are fruitless, some are wasted, but this cannot be said of all of them. He will experience sufferings, sometimes from things, sometimes from beasts, sometimes from human beings, sometimes from all of these together. St. Paul made this point in his own time. But when, later on, he looks back on those unexplored roads which he watered with his sweat, he sees light breaking through the darkness which had reigned there. He forgets the miseries of the past and only remembers the delightful experiences, he has only smiles for his present situation, and he steps forward into the future, happy with his lot and profoundly grateful to God.[1]

This is what I thought twenty-four years ago at the end of our expedition to Kilimanjaro, and I have been justified by subsequent events. Somebody who reads a novel will be interested in what finally happens to the various fictional characters, and, in the same way, our friendly readers will surely be happy to know what has become of this real-life attempt to found a Catholic mission in this far distant region of East Africa, dominated as it is by the Kibo glacier, and which has become for them part of their horizon. It is this which allows us to go back through the time which has passed since our journey. First of all, I have to say something about the political changes which have affected Eastern Africa in recent times.

1

It is well known that Zanzibar, with the neighboring islands and the stretch of coast which faces it, was for a long time an Arab colony, belonging to the

---

1. This postscript differs from that of the later 1928 edition, titled "Forty Years Later (1890–1928)."

POSTSCRIPT: TWENTY-FOUR YEARS LATER (1890–1914)

Imam or ruler of Muscat in Arabia. In 1828, one of these Imams, Sayyid Said, moved to Zanzibar, and, at his death, Zanzibar was declared independent. Under one of his sons and successors, Sayyid Medjid, Father Favre, Vicar General of the Diocese of Saint Denis (Reunion) at that time, came to start the Catholic mission in 1862; soon after Father Horner replaced him.

The rulers of Zanzibar established control of the coast by getting themselves accepted by the indigenous chiefs who were already Muslims, to whom moreover they left sufficient prestige and profit for them not to feel too upset at the loss of their autonomy. They then extended their influence little by little into the hinterland, encouraged and sometimes supported by the British Government, which intended to take over, when convenient, the territory which had been established with its knowledge and its cooperation. It is also certainly true that there was an agreement, dating from 1862, between France and Great Britain, by which these two powers agreed to respect the Sultan's territory; but diplomacy could easily ignore this minor detail.

This was how things were going when Europe's attention became more closely focused on Africa following the expeditions of Livingstone, of Speke and Grant, of Burton, of von der Decken, of Cameron, and of Stanley, and the intervention of King Leopold II of Belgium (founder of the International African Association).

This was particularly the case in Germany where interest in "the colonial question" increased day by day. Soon, an organization was formed which chose Dr. Karl Peters, with Count Pfeil and Dr. Julke, to try to adopt the policy with which M. de Brazza had been so successful in western equatorial Africa, namely to look for some friendly chief, like de Brazza's Makoko, in the mountainous region of Usambara, and to take note of territory which could be placed under colonial rule. That was in 1884.

The little expedition came very close to disaster. One day, when I happened to be at Bagamoyo, I saw a small caravan arrive in the mission courtyard. Two Africans who were carrying a hammock, put it down in front of me. I saw in it, wrapped in blankets, a gaunt-faced white man, whose wide-open eyes stared fixedly, marked by a bilious yellow color; the sight recalled a dead fish lying in a net. The two Africans explained to me that he was a "Datchi" (German, from Deutsch) who had been travelling in the Usambara Mountains and who was on the point of death.

I immediately sent for our excellent Brother Oscar, a native of Dusseldorf and I asked him to look after Dr. Peters, for this was the man in the hammock. Next morning, he was much better, and with increasing confidence he told us his side of the story:

Believing that I was dying, I had myself brought here, after a lot of hesitation, for I understood it to be a French Jesuit mission and I wondered what sort of reception I would get. You seemed quite welcoming, but I was not entirely reassured. However, with hunger and thirst practically killing me, I finally accepted a bowl of milk. I longed to drink it, but I left it on the table for most of the night. I felt sure that they had put some poison in it. Ultimately, I took a decision, and, boldly risking my life, I swallowed it in one great gulp. What marvelous milk it was! I felt much better and got to sleep. When I woke up, I was happy to find that, although you were Jesuits, you had not tried to poison me.

Despite the Jesuits, or because of them, Dr. Peters recovered and returned to Europe.

The next year (1885), Mr. Gerhard Rohlfs arrived as German Consul-General. On the 3rd of March, he informed the Sultan that his Imperial Majesty wished to establish a protectorate over "all the territories to the west of the Sultan's possessions." As the astonished Sultan was digesting this statement, a squadron of five German warships, commanded by Admiral Knorr, arrived immediately to make the point clear.

The next question was to be sure about what territory was in fact owned by the Sultan. As it was possible that the Sultan's reply would not be absolutely accurate, the services of European diplomacy—for which nothing is ever too difficult—were called into play to help the Sultan, Sayyid Barghash. A commission of three members—a German, a Briton, and a Frenchman—was set up to study the question and then to tell the Sultan about the extent of his territory. The members of the commission decided that the Sultanate of Zanzibar consisted of the island of Zanzibar and a coastal strip ten miles broad, from Miningani (Mlingano?) in the south to Kipini in the north, plus the neighboring islands and the harbors along the Somali coast.

When this had been decided, there was no further French involvement. France was recognized as having the right to annex the Comoro Islands and Madagascar, a right which had already been made effective. Britain and Germany, having claimed their shares of East Africa, set about making them profitable. With the backing of these governments, commercial companies were formed which invited the Sultan to let them administer his mainland territories, always to his advantage. The Sultan had to agree, and these companies received effective political power for a period of fifty years. The boundary between the British and German spheres of influence followed a line drawn from Vanga, passing north of Kilimanjaro and terminating at Lake Victoria Nyanza.

The Imperial British East African Company established itself north of the boundary without too many troubles. The German company was less fortunate; it soon had to face a widespread uprising led by Bushiri, a Swahili of mixed African and Arab background. The uprising went on for several months and, at times, victory seemed uncertain. Major Wissman, however, emerged the winner, as Bushiri was betrayed and handed over to him at Pangani in December 1889. Soon after, the German government took over the administrative responsibilities of the German East African Company (*Deutsch ostafrikanische Gesellschaft*). As it was unthinkable that the German emperor should be a vassal of the Sultan of Zanzibar, the Sultan found himself obliged to give up his sovereignty over the area administered by the company in return for five million marks (1 January 1891). From Vanga to Mozambique and from the coast to Lakes Tanganyika and Nyanza, the country belongs to Germany: it is German East Africa (*Deutsch Ost Afrika*), with Dar-es-Salaam as its capital.

The implementation of colonial rule was rapid and it brought the usual benefits and difficulties to missionary work. Two railway lines have been created, one from Tanga to Kilimanjaro, the other from Dar es Salaam to Lake Tanganyika. There has been an increasing influx of settlers. The indigenous Africans have received the privilege of paying taxes. Adult men have come to know the joys of forced labor for the whites for one month in every four. In German territory, everybody must put their best foot forward.

For its part, the Imperial British East African Company received the same privileges for a period of fifty years as the German company (24 May 1887). Then, by successive agreements, the company took over control of the Sultan's coastal territory for an annual payment of £11,350 (equal to 283,750 French francs). Eventually, the British Government followed the German example in taking over the administrative responsibilities of the company. Zanzibar itself was made a British protectorate, responsibility for which was transferred from the Foreign Office to the Colonial Office (1913). Zanzibar is no more an independent sultanate.

2

After this brief sketch of the political history of the East African coast, it will be easier to understand the religious development of this area.

Once the Kilimanjaro expedition (10 July—10 October 1890) was over, our big preoccupation was to send Fr. Auguste Gommenginger—who was staying on at Moshi as the guest of Baron d'Eltz, the head of the German government station—the support necessary in personnel and materials for the proposed mission station. However, he could only establish himself at Kilema on the 9th February 1891. My blood brother, Fumba, welcomed the missionaries, as faithful to his promise as I had been to mine. We shall return to Kilema, but first, there were other problems.

When Mgr. de Courmont returned to Zanzibar, he immediately received some worrying news. Fr. Charles Gommenginger, Fr. Auguste's elder brother, whom we had accompanied the previous year along the river Tana, with a view to founding a mission, was dying. Fr. Charles was on his own, except for the valiant Brother Acheul and some young African Christians, who were to become the nucleus of the mission village. As the opportunity presented itself, Mgr. de Courmont sent me to help him, although I was myself ill with an attack of bronchitis which I had caught on the Kilimanjaro journey and which shook me up in a depressing way.

I found Fr. Charles at Lamu (a small coastal town and a former Arab colony) in a little Arab house which he had rented. He was suffering from a very serious attack of fever and was being looked after by Brother Acheul, also suffering from fever and anemia, despite which he was as valiant as ever. They told me their story.

They had settled down at Ndera on the right bank of the Tana (the Tana River is formed by streams which flow down from Mount Kenya and the neighboring mountains) on a beautiful site. It was just where we had left them in November of the previous year (1889), some ten days from the coast by canoe. They had got down to work and, helped by the young Christians with them, they had cut down trees from the forest to make a framework for their house. Then they had made beams, floors, doors, and windows, and had begun a garden and started planting vegetables. The local people looked on with astonishment and delight. Everything was splendid until one fine day, the river, which had gradually risen, left its bed and flooded into the wide plains through which it normally flowed calmly and quietly. The missionaries had asked themselves why the local village huts were built on posts, like those in the lake villages of Europe in prehistoric times; they then understood the reason. Just like the Nile, the Tana overflows every year, at particular times, and from the same causes. The Africans, who had no idea that anything could happen differently, were now going by canoe along the streets of their communities, just as happens in Venice.

But the mission house was now under the water. Fr. Charles climbed up a nearby tree, Brother Acheul climbed up another, and so they kept community life going. The mission cook, Pacome—a name which comes from the monks of the Egyptian desert—was close at hand in a canoe tied up to a post. He tried to provide meals appropriate for the situation. He brought what he had produced to the unfortunate missionaries, swimming to them, clutching a bowl in one hand, and moving through the water with the other, puffing like a grampus.

This way of life lasted for three weeks, during which the missionaries struggled to be patient, recalling the admirable examples of Noah and his ark, and St. Simeon Stylite on his pillar. But all the same, St. Simeon had less water, and Noah had more company.

When eventually there was some dry land to walk on, Father Charles and Brother Acheul decided to leave the banks of such a temperamental river and to try and find a place elsewhere. But a great deal of work had been done and it would have been a pity to lose it all. So they decided to make big rafts with the wood from the forest, and to load them with the furniture, the kitchen utensils, the planks, the doors, the windows, the tables, the chairs, the poultry, and the goats. Then, aided by the grace of God, they would go down the river to the coast and there sell off the loads.

The missionaries and the young Christians set to work, and the rafts started moving down the river, to the astonishment and regret of the local people.

Unfortunately, from time to time one or other of these rafts would smash against floating tree trunks and one had to fish out the bits. Other times they were caught by the strong currents in the river which made them turn round on themselves, as though they were playing a game, sometimes for hours on end. It was all very amusing and very discouraging. Every evening, they went ashore for the night. The rafts were tied up and the missionaries lay down in the mud under some abandoned hut and slept there with the young Africans who travelled with them, the poultry, the goats, the rats, the vermin, and the mosquitoes all close at hand. And sleepless nights followed days of frustrating toil, passed beneath the blazing sun.

Finally, after sixteen days of travel and upsets, they reached Kao, a little Arab village close to the coast, on the Ozi, one of the branches through which the Tana reaches the ocean. But poor Fr. Charles, whose superhuman toughness had hitherto kept him going, had an attack of fever which nearly carried him off. A gang of Somalis heard that he was dying. They felt they could cover their greed with a veneer of fanaticism—how splendid to kill some Christians and take their belongings.

Fortunately, Brother Acheul was warned and quickly hired a small sailing boat, brought the dying man there by night, and hoisted the sails. At that moment, the Somali gang arrived, running and shouting their war cries. The sailing boat slipped away. The bandits jumped into some small boats, and rowed energetically, firing arrows after their escaping prey, and a desperate struggle went on for a long time. Finally, the Somalis, who were more used to fighting on land than on water, lost heart, and two days later our missionaries reached Lamu.

So it was at Lamu that I met Fr. Charles and Brother Acheul. They were thin, yellowish, haggard, shivering with fever, stretched out on unsatisfactory camp beds, but both had kept an extraordinary liveliness and a good humor worthy of apostles. When I had anointed Fr. Charles and given him communion, we had something to discuss.

"Let us think about what comes next," the dying man said. "When I am dead, there will be a problem for you. What are you going to do with my body?"

Brother Acheul replied, "Do not worry, Father, we shall give you a decent burial."

"I do not want you to put me in the Muslim cemetery."

"Do you want to be buried beside it?"

"No, for such a burial would mark me as an unbeliever."

Brother Acheul offered another choice: "There is a very suitable place near here, under a big tamarind tree."

"But every day the cows come together there to sniff the fresh air. I do not want to sleep under cows' hooves."

I thought I could intervene in this rather unusual discussion. "Have you seen at the entry to the harbor that big dune of white sand, facing the sea?"

"The wind is always blowing there," said Brother Acheul.

"We shall plant a big cross there. It will be like a lighthouse, and it will be a sign that we are going to stay."

"Ah, that is it," said Fr. Charles, still cheerful. "That is a place that will just suit me."

But providence was to give the faithful missionary another place of rest. Some days after, a British ship stopped and agreed to take our dying confrere. He died on this ship, soon after leaving Mombasa, a death full of faith and trust in God. Next morning, the ship reached Zanzibar. There was a French cruiser in the harbor; with the help of the captain and crew, the body of our deceased confrere was brought ashore, wrapped in our national colors, and taken to the mission cemetery. Not long afterwards, Brother Acheul rejoined him there.

A new mission had been founded. For when our missionaries join the sacrifice of their lives to the sacrifice of the Redeemer, it is then that we can be confident of success.

As soon as I was free, I set off for Mombasa, where I had already made several visits to get an idea of the country, but this time I intended to stay there. The aim was to establish our ministry of evangelization on Kilimanjaro from there and, within the limits of our resources, to plant missions on the very promising Taita massif, the Kikuyu plateau, Mount Kenya, and Kamba country, and then to get a foothold, by way of the hinterland, on the River Tana, since approaching it by its delta had proved impracticable.

This plan has been carried out. Today, the old town of Mombasa still has memories of visits from the ancient Persians, of colonization by the Arabs of Muscat, of the Portuguese occupation in the time of Vasco da Gama and Albuquerque, when Francis Xavier stopped there on his way to India. But this brief Christian occupation had to yield to Islam. Mombasa has now become definitively part of the British Empire. Its beautiful harbor has been equipped for modern shipping. A railway links it to Lake Victoria Nyanza, Uganda, and the Nile. Finally, as part of the Apostolic Vicariate of Zanzibar, all that part of "British East Africa" is an area for evangelization easily approachable and with a very promising future.

Fr. Charles Gommenginger, dying at sea before Mombasa, has, on behalf of all the missionaries who will follow him, opened up this country to our mission, just as St. Francis Xavier, dying on the island of Sancian, opened the way to China.

3

We left Fr. Auguste at Kilema. Fumba had given a small plateau, some 1,646 meters high, and this was chosen for building the mission. The site is absolutely marvelous. To the north, the silvery dome of Kibo and the jagged summit of Mawenzi rise before you. To the south, one's glance can sweep down the great mountain's slopes, coming to rest on the sparkling sheet of water that makes Lake Jipe, and then, trying to see the distant outlines of the Pare Mountains, or getting lost in the distant horizon of the Maasai plains.

Work on the buildings was undertaken with enthusiasm, but foodstuffs were not forgotten. Soon, the mission had a magnificent garden where vegetables from Europe, planted among those native to the tropics, grew marvelously. Relations with the local people were excellent, and the chapel, like the schools, filled up immediately.

Everything was going well when Mandara, the powerful chief of Moshi, died. His son, Meli, an ambitious and fiery young man who wanted to achieve something outstanding, immediately set about making himself the ruler of all the people of Kilimanjaro and driving out the Europeans. M. d'Eltz had left. His successor, Lieutenant von Bulow, who had adopted a purely military style of administration, marched against Meli with 300

Sudanese soldiers. This was a disaster: the force was routed, and the officers and NCOs, including von Bulow, were killed.

Meli's victory went to his head. He made a demand on Fumba, as on the other mountain chiefs, to recognize him as the paramount chief and to send away immediately "his" white men, unless it was preferable to kill them, in which case Meli wanted a share of their property. Fumba, who lacked the manpower to resist Meli, accepted—provisionally—his paramountcy, but firmly refused to betray his "white brothers," who were of a different tribe to von Bulow and had only come among the Chagga to do them good.

Then Meli tried another move. He made an agreement with Fr. Auguste. The missionary said that he wished to withdraw, while fighting was going on. The crafty chief did not object, but he asked the Father to be very careful to tell him the exact time when he would leave so that he could provide protection for him and his companions on their journey. Fr. Auguste planned to start on Monday, the 7th August 1891. Now, on Saturday, the 5th August, suddenly, toward 10 a.m., Fr. Auguste felt such a strong premonition that he had to obey it. So he set off immediately with all who worked under him.

On the march, from time to time, in the distance, armed men took their heads out of the fur coverings that concealed them and seemed to be discussing what they should do. The journey was long and tiring. But when night fell, Fr. Auguste and his companions were safe at Taveta. They were extremely surprised to learn that they had been in danger of death. Meli had not wished to kill them on his territory. Instead, he had stationed groups of thugs outside the area he controlled, with orders to kill Fr. Auguste and his companions when the order was given. But the order was not given, so the thugs let the caravan pass and the lives of its members were saved.

Now, on that very day, Mgr. de Courmont, who had returned to France a little while before, had gone on pilgrimage to Notre Dame de la Délivrande (Calvados) and was saying mass at 8 o'clock at the shrine for the protection of the mission which he knew to be threatened. Now, 8 o'clock in France is 10 o'clock on Kilimanjaro: Fr. Auguste was warned in time and his life and the lives of his companions were spared. Surely this answer to prayer deserves to be known.

The Germans could not, evidently, take their defeat lying down. However, it was after a certain delay, in July 1893, that von Scheele, the governor-general, arrived with 500 Sudanese soldiers and 20 German officers and NCOs. All the Kilimanjaro chiefs submitted, and the colonial administration was established.

However, Sina, the formidable chief of Kibosho, who had wanted to send us into the next world rather earlier than was appropriate, had quickly realized his mistake. When he learned that Fumba had received us and thus gained prestige for himself, he sent message after message to Father Auguste, until, in September 1893, when the Chagga wars were over, the cross was planted at the exact spot where we had just escaped death. As with the other new missions, the missionaries brought with them twenty or so young Christians who were apprentices as joiners, carpenters, bricklayers, and horticulturists in our houses at Bagamoyo and Zanzibar. We started work with them in the virgin forest which surrounds the mountain like a huge belt, between 2,000 and 3,000 meters above sea level. Two months later, we had at our disposal over 600 beams and 400 planks. A letter written at this time gives us other details:

> While some of our young people sawed up wood, others, on the spot where we had chosen to work, took up stones which had come from the extinct volcanoes and tried to shape them. But the really hard work was done, two days' journey from here, in the Arusha plain. We found very hard limestone there, with exceptionally tough wood, which had to be chopped into small pieces—all this in a vast, uninhabited wilderness, under a burning sun.
>
> At the mission, a Brother, aided by a team of children, cultivates the soil, planting potatoes, cabbages, broad beans, beetroot, even wheat. Everything grows just as in Europe. Our livestock is certainly lively: we have already cattle, sheep, goats, hens, ducks, and we await the arrival of that blessed and indispensable friend of the civilized man—the pig.
>
> Apart from our eighteen Christian young men who will get married in the near future, we have twenty-five Chagga and Maasai children. They are very happy with us, as witnessed by the noisy joyfulness which always reigns in the house. Later on, we shall try and spread our missionary presence wider, but we have to start by establishing our base, and that is what we are doing.

Sometime later, Sina died, and the elders asked Fr. Rohmer, the mission superior, to choose a successor among the sons of the old tyrant. He wrote to tell us at that time, "I believed that the least intelligent of them would be the best, and everybody agreed with me." Since then, other missions have had to be founded in various chiefdoms of the great mountain in response to the request of this fine Chagga people—one at Rombo in 1898, one in Uru in 1911, one in Useri in 1912, and one at Mengwe in 1913. Each one of our mission stations has (apart from the church and the missionaries' house) catechists' houses, schools, dispensaries, and already a good number of Catholics and an even greater number of catechumens. To sum it up, one can say today that the whole population has been won for Christ.

Old Fumba was naturally among the first adherents and it has been agreed that he would be baptized when he could no longer take any alcohol, "For," said he," that will be the sign that my end is near." In the meantime, he has decided to retire and his successor is his son, Kirita, who has become a Christian.

A big church, built of hewn stone—indeed a cathedral—stands today in the place where we pitched our tents. The fact that there were 2,000 Easter communions last year (1913) shows that Christian life flourishes there, and is spreading, step by step, throughout this fascinating, charming, and intelligent tribe which welcomed us in 1890.

Now that we have established the Catholic mission on Kilimanjaro, we have been able to give attention, as far as our human and financial resources have permitted, to the other key points of this country. A mission was founded at the port of Tanga (1896), where the mail from Europe comes in and which has the starting point of a railway line, which, running along the Usambara and Pare Mountains, reaches the base of Mount Kilimanjaro.

Another mission was founded at Mlingano (1902), in Bonde country, on the north side of Usambara. The mission of Gare (1897) was established toward the south of Usambara, on a beautiful plateau in the same range of mountains. The mission of Kilomeni was founded in 1909 on the Pare Mountains. The Kisiwani mission was founded in 1913 at the foot of the Pare Mountains.

In 1907, after an attempt at Mount Meru, which was a failure because of an African uprising against the German occupation, the mission moved to Kondoa-Irangi in the far interior. The next year (1908) a mission was established at Ufiomi. Here, twelve schools with a total of 1,600 children are a crowning achievement which promises a very bright future.

Naturally, the Europeans are not slow in coming. A variety of plantations have been started and the colonial occupation is becoming more and more effective. This occupation provides opportunities both for the Protestant missions and Islam. There are a number of different, and sometimes contradictory Protestant missions, whereas Islam is always the same and always intrusive.

But these factors are not decisive. The Catholic Church, with its limited personnel, its uncertain financial resources, its unshakeable doctrine, its demanding morality, continues to advance as befits the truth, fearless and firm through all barbarity and all civilizations. Peace and salvation, then, to all people of good will, whether they be master or slaves, men or women, old people or children, warriors or workers, white men or black!

On 5th February 1911, one of our missionaries, a native of Alsace, was ordained bishop in the Zanzibar pro-cathedral and given the responsibility of carrying forward the evangelization of this region, with the title of Vicar Apostolic of Kilimanjaro. Meanwhile, to the south, the two other vicariates of Bagamoyo and Dar-es-Salaam share the rest of the eastern coast of German East Africa. Here's wishing a long life to Mgr. Munsch.

Perhaps I could say something about various people mentioned in the account of our journey?

Mgr. de Courmont, his health broken by the harsh conditions of his apostolate in which he merited the glory of having opened up hitherto-unknown lands, handed over the immense region for which he had been responsible to colleagues in the episcopate who divided it between themselves. In his retirement in Paris, he continues the pastoral ministry which he began on the east coast of Africa thirty years ago. Fr. Auguste Gommenginger is still at his mission, looking forward to baptizing my old brother Fumba when the time comes. Nderingo lives at the mission. And Selemani?

Ah, Selemani! Sometimes after we had gone through his home territory, his brother, the Sultan, died. He went to preside at the funeral rites, and did so well, that, straightaway, he was acclaimed as chief. As the saying has it: "The king is dead; long live the king!" After this sudden rise to power, for which, without realizing what we were doing, we had prepared him, we had no news for three months. We thought, "Power often goes to men's heads." Then, one evening at Zanzibar, as a fierce wind blew, a poor old man knocked at the mission door and asked to be allowed inside for the night. Lord, have mercy! It was our old Selemani, who appealed to us to accept him for the rest of his life. He repeated with touching sincerity and in dreadful French, "*Moi fini crevé d'embêtement. Trop vieux pour passer sultan: donne à moi mon marmite.*» (I am fed up with trouble. I am too old to be chief; give me my cooking pot).

How could we refuse him? Selemani had a very warm welcome, but his death was not long delayed. His death was at least worthy of his life. One day, in the new mission Mlingano, near Tanga, our old cook had dozed longer than usual and forgotten to clean his saucepan. He swallowed a hard lump of gruel which had remained at the bottom. He died two hours later, poisoned by his own cooking. May God receive your soul, my poor Selemani. For if you were never altogether clean, you treated yourself as you treated others. Beloved world of Zanzibar, God be with you.

250   POSTSCRIPT: TWENTY-FOUR YEARS LATER (1890–1914)

Selemani

Farewell, vast savannahs, populated by herds of wild animals, rivers and streams flowing silently past shady banks, lofty mountains, dear African children whose speech had such charm, missions the more beloved the more one had suffered there. I left you for another harvest-field of the apostolate, at the call of obedience. But I long felt nostalgia for you. But today, writing these lines, I remember you, and I feel happiness in thinking that the work of my brothers has borne fruit. A new church has arisen on the mysterious mountain which I found entirely non-Christian twenty-four years ago, and, like a lighthouse, the cross planted there has lit up the whole of the horizon.

Britain, Germany, and Italy have divided the East African coast. But there are other lands open to France and the French missionaries, vast countries where there are innumerable peoples to whom we are called, peoples who for twenty centuries have waited for news of the Redemption. This is our work: come, young men, replace the missionaries grown old, who, before they fall asleep, seek new hands to whom they can entrust their flag.

Glory to God! And peace to men of good will!

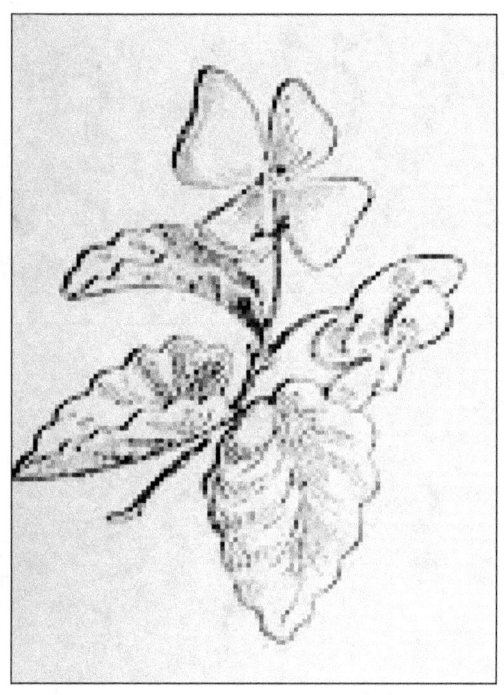

At Kilema, the beginning

POSTSCRIPT: TWENTY-FOUR YEARS LATER (1890–1914)

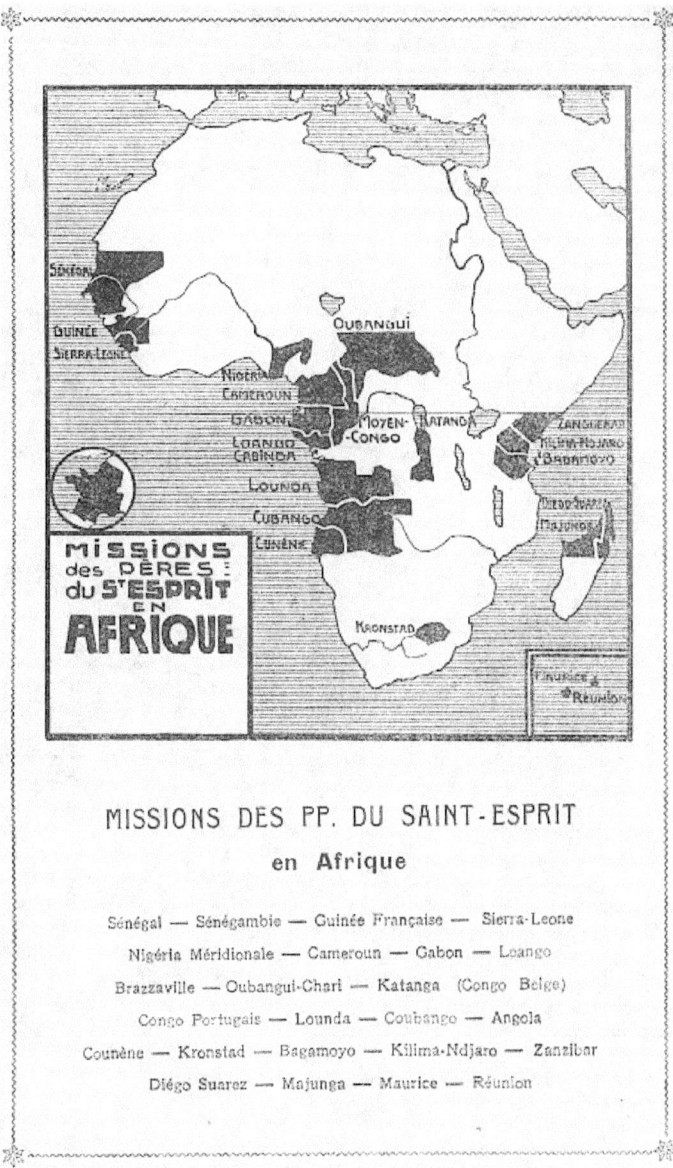

The Missions of the Holy Ghost Fathers in Africa

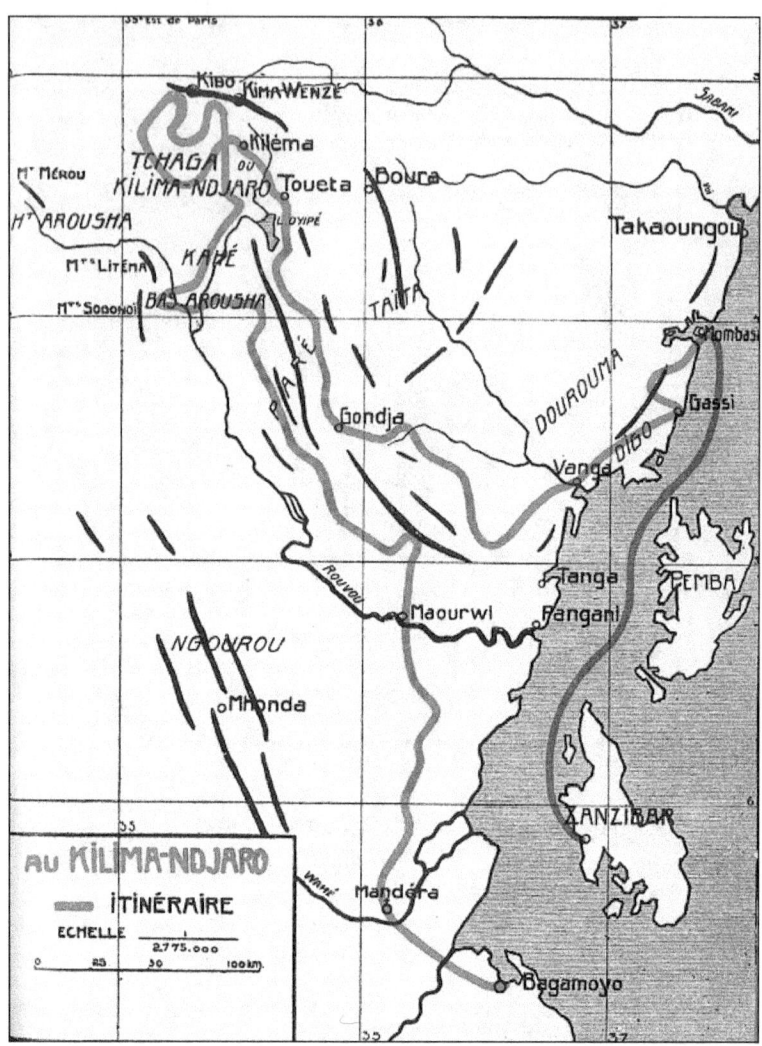

Mission to Kilimanjaro: the route taken

Fr. Adrian Edwards, CSSp.
1933 - 2017

Fr. Adrian Edwards was born in Norfolk, England, on July 13, 1933. Professed into the Congregation of the Holy Spirit (Spiritans) on October 28, 1960, he was ordained priest on July 1, 1965. He did undergraduate studies at Cambridge (1951–54), graduate studies also there (1954–58), partly as Research Fellow at the International African Institute (1955–57). It was while doing fieldwork among the Ovimbundu (central Angola) for his doctoral dissertation in anthropology that Adrian first came in contact with the Spiritans and decided to join.

Adrian's first mission was in the diocese of Makurdi, Nigeria, from 1967–70. There he continued anthropological research on the Tiv people and also did translation work. He returned to England to teach at the Missionary Institute, London, from 1970–73. Nineteen seventy-three found him back in Nigeria, working in the Federal Department of Antiquities, later the National Commission for Museums and Monuments. From 1977–1982 he worked among the Ogoni people in the diocese of Port Harcourt, Nigeria. From 1983–87 Fr. Adrian worked among the Chamba and Verre peoples in the Yola Diocese of Nigeria, moving to Maroua Diocese (northern Cameroon) in 1988, where he did pastoral work till 1996. From 1996–2002 he taught in the Grand Séminaire Brottier, Libreville (Gabon), and from 2003–2015 at the Spiritan Institute of Philosophy (now Spiritan University College) Ejisu, Ghana. He retired to Chester from there. It pleased God to call him home before his work could be published. All who read this book owe him a debt of gratitude and prayers.

Bibliography

Bender, Matthew V. "Holy Ghost in the Highlands: The Spiritans on Kilimanjaro 1892–1953." *Spiritan Horizons* 3 (Fall 2008) 69–89.

Johnston, Harry Hamilton. *The Kilima-Ndjaro Expedition: A Record of Scientific Exploration in Eastern Equatorial Africa.* London: K. Paul, Trench, 1886.

Reclus, Jacques Élisée. *La nouvelle géographie universelle, la terre et les hommes* 19 vols. Paris: Librairie Hachette, 1875–1894.

———. *The Earth and its Inhabitants* 19 vols. New York: D. Appleton, 1876–94.

www.ingramcontent.com/pod-product-compliance
Lightning Source LLC
Chambersburg PA
CBHW050345230426
43663CB00010B/1997